THE DIOCESAN PRIEST

THE DIOCESAN PRIEST

The Nature and Spirituality of the Diocesan Clergy

2-53.

BY GUSTAVE THILS

Translated by Albert J. La Mothe, Jr.

FIDES PUBLISHERS, INC.
NOTRE DAME, INDIANA

Published originally in French under the title *Nature et Spiritualité du Clergé Diocésain* by Desclée De Brouwer et Cie, Bruges, Belgium, 1948. This translation is from the Second Edition revised by the author in 1961.

PRINTED IN THE UNITED STATES OF AMERICA

FOREWORD

So many important persons have written in our time that posterity has almost nothing left to say, but only to consider, to learn, to imitate or admire; I will therefore say nothing new here, and about all that is mine are the needle and thread; for the rest I was only required to unravel and resew in my own way, with this advice from Vincent of Lérins: "Those things which you teach, so teach as to say nothing new, though you say it in a new way." These words of St. Francis de Sales at the beginning of his famous *Controverses*, are still current. Today there is no shortage of books dealing with the priestly apostolate, and these last few years have seen the appearance of some excellent ones. This book intends to bring together, in an overall view, the characteristic features of the diocesan clergy and the spirituality proper to it.

In order to proceed as surely as possible, avoiding the pitfalls of grandiose but fragile structures, we relied on some indisputable foundation stones: the Bible and the Roman Pontifical — Divine Revelation and the liturgy — traditional sources of all Christian thought, sources guaranteed by the high authority of the Church, sources extremely rich in clues regarding the nature, the *raison d'être* and the specific virtues of the diocesan priest.

It was our intention to present a seriously theological work, both doctrinally and historically. This accounts for the dryness of certain pages, the abstract and apparently less "practical" nature of others. It will certainly be less easy to read than books which have as their direct purpose the stimulation of pious sentiments, or the encouragement of the practice of virtue. But is it not equally mandatory now that the doctrinal and theoretical basis of asceticism be consolidated? Do we not want morality to be rooted in dogma, and action to seem to flow logically from being, in one luminous continuity? These pages are addressed directly to the believing intellect. They need reflection and sometimes demand study. Nevertheless, we hope that they will blossom in love, recalling the solemn words of St. Bernard spoken on the Feast of the Holy Precursor: "To shine too much is vain, to burn so much is little, to shine and to burn is perfect."

We say "diocesan" clergy rather than "secular" clergy. Of course, the term "secular" in itself has nothing pejorative about it, and its use in ecclesiastical documents even has certain advantages. But in the field of spirituality, it may at times have been the source of certain misunderstandings and errors. We are in the world, we must be there, and we want to remain there. But we are not of the world. We are not "worldly." The term "secular" seems at times to insinuate that we are. This regrettable comparison harms, first of all, the priests, whose apostolic mission radically separates them from the world, in life as well as in spirit. It also harms the faithful, who thereby acquire an imprecise idea of the ideals which animate our clergy.

But "diocesan" is not opposed to "Roman." This should be apparent from the spirit of universalism which runs through this book. Constant recourse to the Apostles naturally leads the reader to discover the keystone of the Catholic hierarchy — the papacy. Attachment to the diocese and fidelity to the Roman Church complement one another and summon one another forth.

Is it necessary, finally, to repeat that the apostolate

and the priesthood itself are not the exclusive property of the diocesan clergy? Accordingly, what is affirmed regarding the diocesan clergy is not thereby refused to the layman, or denied to the religious. Laymen and the religious clergy can lead a "mixed" or apostolic life as truly as we can. All priests, religious or otherwise, possess the same priesthood. Still, it was impossible to describe the nature and spirituality of the diocesan clergy without speaking of the apostolic life, without also emphasizing the requirements of the priesthood. In this regard we shall avoid unnecessary comparisons, which are at best liable to arouse useless polemics, whereas the Church only asks to be glorified in all her children. Thomas, as in so many other things, will be our guide here: "By means of Holy Orders some are commissioned for those most worthy ministries by which Christ is served in the sacrament of the altar, for which greater interior sanctity is required than is demanded even of the religious state.[1]

* * *

This new edition has been revised and corrected, in an effort to remove ambiguities and avoid misunderstandings.

---

[1] *Summa Theologica*, IIa IIae, q. 184, a. 8, c.

CONTENTS

PART ONE

RETURN TO THE SOURCES

CHAPTER ONE

APOSTOLIC ACTIVITIES

Is there in all the world a more interesting and fruitful occupation for us, priests of the ministry, than the study of the life of the Twelve? We are filled with enthusiasm when, at the age of thirty or sixty, rereading the Acts of the Apostles fervently, we follow St. Paul in his stirring and sometimes tragic travels. Theories on the apostolate are, of course, indispensable, nor can the dogmatic aspect of the priestly life be absent; they must be presented, especially to young clerics, whose work lies ahead of them. But the adult, soon tired of the principles and structures of the spirit — too soon tired, perhaps — turns by preference toward books which tell of the vicissitudes of existence, depict a man and reveal a soul. Here, as everywhere else, the best and the surest method is to return to facts. In order to gain a better knowledge of the nature of the diocesan apostolate, let us first look, with eyes wide open and attentive hearts, at our models, the Apostles of the early centuries, giants of external as well as interior labors in the service of their brethren, who struggled to transform the mentality, the concept of life, and the morals of a pagan world, without thereby losing any of their

3

own vitality, and by raising themselves even to the heroism of sanctity.

In describing briefly the activities of the Apostles and their successors, trying also to discover the inner spirit which animated them, searching their writings or their remarks, we will the more easily be able to describe what the diocesan clergy is.

The inspired books, it seems, should help us to know the Twelve and their apostolic ministry. Yet, the first effect of their perusal is to discourage the interested person, who finds himself at loose ends. The information we have about the Apostles is sparse; the sacred writers distributed it very parsimoniously. What precisely do we know about Philip, Bartholomew, Thomas, or Thaddeus? The few details we can occasionally glean about them or about their activities are so little compared to what we should like to have, what we *should* have, even, to know them well.

This relative lack of information has impressed all who have studied the apostolic era. "We are, as everyone knows, as poorly informed as we could be on the real activities of the twelve Apostles," M. G. Bardy[1] does not hesitate to write. Then he quotes L. de Lacger:

"The Acts of the Apostles really feature only Peter and Paul: Peter in the Jewish world, Paul in the pagan environment. They are completely silent on the Twelve, except for Peter and the two sons of Zebedee. Simple deacons such as Stephen and Philip are given a treatment which is not granted to Matthew, Thomas or Philip the Apostle, who nevertheless are mentioned in the Gospels. . . . This silence is surprising, and legend has attempted to make up for it. But it is a singular fact, worthy of note, that these legends do not situate the ministry of the Apostles of whom they speak in the Roman Empire, as if they were afraid to run up against accomplished and known facts, or to tread upon

---

[1] "Le sacerdoce et les missions à l'âge apostolique," *Vie spirituelle*, 50 (1937), pp. 86-87.

the proper domain of the Apostle of the Gentiles."[2]

Nevertheless, the little we do know is revealing. We learn that the Apostles were very different from one another in their spirit, their mentality, their natural talents. James, Bishop of Jerusalem, is the defender of the Jewish traditions, the preserver of the sacred usages received from the Patriarchs which assured salvation for generations of Israelites; Paul is the burning missionary, the Apostle of the Gentiles whom Israel held in profoundest disdain. There exist between them, from all indications, differences of character, and each preferred to stress certain doctrines. We know of the meeting between Peter and Paul in Antioch, of the famous "I withstood him to his face," about the disagreement which once existed, at least on the level of ideas, between Paul of Tarsus and James the Less. But we also know that all had chosen Christ as Master and Lord, and that all were engaged in prolonging His work of salvation in the world: for the moment, that is all that concerns us.

1. The "Disciples" of the Lord

THE APOSTLES

At the beginning of His public life, Jesus chose His disciples. He accustomed them progressively to His way of seeing things, confided to them gradually the interpretation of the parables, and initiated them without haste in the spirit which must animate the heralds of His religion. Then He sent them to "preach," and gave them "power . . . to cast out devils" (Mark 3:15) and "to cure every kind of disease and infirmity" (Matt. 10:1). The Gospels sometimes lift the veil which cloak those mysterious hours during which Jesus was molding His future Apostles.

Sometimes Jesus guided His disciples by His attitude alone; on other occasions, He became more explicit.

---

[2] *Le christianisme aux origines et à l'âge apostolique*, Rabat, 1936, p. 52.

Thus, not content with molding them by means of prolonged contact with His person (Mark 3:14), He gave them definite recommendations, which are very enlightening for those desirous of inquiring into the apostolic functions: "As you go," explains Jesus, "preach the message, 'The Kingdom of Heaven is at hand!' Cure the sick, raise the dead, cleanse the lepers, cast out devils. Freely you have received, freely give. Do not keep gold, or silver . . . for the laborer deserves his living. . . . Behold, I am sending you forth like sheep in the midst of wolves. Be therefore wise as serpents, and guileless as doves. But beware of men; for they will deliver you up to councils, and scourge you in their synagogues. . . . What I tell you in darkness, speak it in the light; and what you hear whispered, preach it on the housetops" (Matt. 10 ff.).

Later on, Jesus entrusted to the Twelve complete apostolic powers. During the Last Supper, they heard their Lord pronounce with great solemnity those words which were to rejoice the centuries to come: "Do this in remembrance of me" (Luke 22:19). After the Resurrection, responsibilities encumbered the fearful disciples: " 'Peace be to you! As the Father has sent me, I also send you.' When He had said this, he breathed upon them, and said to them: 'Receive the Holy Spirit; whose sins you shall forgive, they are forgiven them; and whose sins you shall retain, they are retained' " (John 20:19-23). At the moment of the Ascension: "Go, therefore, and make disciples of all nations, baptizing them in the name of the Father, and of the Son, and of the Holy Spirit. . . . Preach the Gospel to every creature: He who believes and is baptized shall be saved" (Matt. 28:19; Mark 16:16). Such are the Apostles, and, all things being equal, such are the parish priests whom we meet every day all around us.

From Pentecost, when the Holy Spirit descended on those who were at prayer in the Cenacle, Peter took command of the assembly of the Christians and of the council of the Apostles. He rose to address all the pilgrims who had come up to Jerusalem on the occasion of the festival, and declared to them that the Messiah, Jesus of Nazareth, whom the Elders and the Priests put to death, had risen and that He was the Savior of the world. It would seem that people too easily forget the key role which Peter played during the first ten years of Christianity, while Saul of Tarsus was still only a persecutor and a neophyte. The first chapters of the Acts of the Apostles give us an account of the apostolate of the Prince of the Apostles: his enormous prestige among the crowds which pressed forward as he passed, so that his shadow at least might fall upon the sick and heal them; his beautiful reply to the Sanhedrin which wanted to prevent him from continuing to speak of this Jesus, in whose name the most indisputable miracles were being wrought (4:1-22); his terrifying intervention when he had uncovered the sacrilegious lie of Ananias and Sapphira (5:1-11); his frequent disputes with the High Priest and the Sadducees; his sufferings and privations; his judicial persecutions and imprisonments in the name of Jesus Christ. The Acts also tell of the famous conversion of Cornelius, a turning-point in the history of the primitive Church. Breaking with the nationalistic traditions of the Jewish people, the founders of the Christian Church proclaimed the universality of salvation, and the call addressed to all to become part of the visible religion of the Lord Jesus (10 and 11).

Paul is better known. The account of his conversion on the road to Damascus is part of the cultural inheritance of the West. The history of his apostolic journeys nourishes the generous dreams of adolescents who wish to consecrate their lives to the work which was the preference of the Man-God Himself. Every year a new biography of the Apostle appears since his work is always contemporary and his spirit ever alive in our midst. Who can resist the spectacle of his life? We see him spend long months on retreat in desert regions before throwing himself into his apostolic career. We note his humble beginnings as the companion of Barnabas at Antioch, where he works in a minor capacity after having been called to the city. We follow him on

his long journeys in Asia Minor, Greece, and especially
in the city of Philippi, where around the year 52 he
founded the first Christian community in Europe and
where, according to all indications, he offered for the
first time on that continent the sacrifice of the New
Law; at that moment, the redemptive work took hold,
in a visible manner, in our midst.

Now what did Paul do in the course of his apostolic
wanderings? He appeared before certain believers, told
them what happened in Jerusalem, preached to them
about the Messiah announced by all the prophets and how
He was put to death by Israel. His first audience were
Jews. They could not bear the weight of his message; the
Apostle was threatened, persecuted, railed at, and often
scourged. And so he addressed himself to the Gentiles, to
"the Nations," in order to bring them the message of
ineffable hope which had remained until then hidden
in the depths of God, which neither Aristotle nor Plato
nor the sages of this world were able to discover in
their searchings, and which the Word Incarnate, then
His Apostles, were now teaching to every soul of good
will: that men, all the men under the sun, could share
the messianic riches, the revelation of salvation, the
gift of the Spirit, the pledge of eternal incorruptibility
and of untarnishable glory.

Each time Paul preached there were some who received the message of Jesus fruitfully — a Christian
community sprang up on the soil of Asia or of Europe.
Then the Apostle went on, planting new Christian roots,
or evangelizing another great city — Ephesus, Corinth
— to establish more solidly the doctrinal edifice of Christianity. Still, his desire was never assuaged. It was not
even enough for him to have sown the Gospel in Syria,
Asia Minor, Macedonia and Greece; he had to go to
Rome, the Rome of the Caesars; he had to go even further, into that mysterious country which bordered the
Mediterranean on the north: such at least were the
Apostle's hopes, hopes realized in part, signs of his generous spirit. We would have to refer here not only to
the chapters of the Acts of the Apostles pertaining to

his travels, but to his Epistles, all of them, and especially the Second Epistle to the Corinthians, which reveals the soul and the ardent, restless, loving and rough temperament of the Apostle of the Gentiles. About the other Apostles we do not know very much; but what reason is there to think that the grace of Pentecost did not act on them the way it transformed the heart of Peter and the spirit of Paul? The deacon Philip has left us a moving memory; but would not the Apostles all have left us a similar memory if the account of their lives, their activities and their apostolate had been preserved? The martyrdom of Stephen still moves the least well-disposed hearts; but would that not be true of all the other disciples? There is no need to list all the legends recorded by ecclesiastical writers, the historical truth of which we are unable to evaluate precisely. We can be sure without doing this of the apostolic holiness of the Twelve.

THE TWELVE AND OURSELVES

These giant precursors of the diocesan clergy led lives about which it would be easy to have exaggerated ideas. When we read in the Acts the account of the extraordinary events which immediately followed the descent of the Holy Spirit on the Cenacle — the three thousand men who were baptized by Peter; that "multitude of the believers [who] were of one heart and one soul . . . who had all things in common" (4:32); the "large number of . . . priests [who] accepted the faith" (6:7) — we may easily imagine that the Apostles preached every day, each time baptizing immense crowds, thanks to the vehemence of the salvific breath of the Spirit coming into the world. We forget, however, the long, dangerous voyages of Paul on the Mediterranean, also recorded in the Acts; we disregard the months and the years which he spent in prison or in exile, to remove himself from the wrath of those who pursued him; we also ignore the time which he devoted to manual labor, after the manner of the very men who were to receive the Christian message. This is an error, like that of young people who have an image of the missionary catechizing or baptizing the pagan masses without rest or respite, whereas these pioneers of the visible Church must often spend days getting to villages with only a few dozen inhabitants.

Moreover, there can be no question of applying to the diocesan clergy, without some distinctions, all that characterizes the Twelve. The latter were charged with a mission as "founders," and enjoyed a privileged situation. Sent to establish throughout the world the foundations of the universal Church, the true Church of Jesus Christ, they had received to this end special personal and inalienable powers. The Lord had given them unshakeable spiritual authority. He had promised them that they would always persevere in grace and virtue, and then He had assured them of the special protection of His Spirit of Truth. Thus, without fear of failing, all of them could be sure of representing on a permanent basis the power, the life, and the teaching of the Incarnate Word, all traits which may not be applied as such to any of their successors.[3]

Each of the Twelve, moreover, possessed the fullness of spiritual power. The diocesan priest receives a definite ministry which is part and parcel of the overall apostolate of the Church. Indeed, the work of redemption and of divine praise was entrusted by Christ to the universal Church, which includes the diocesan Churches; it is also conducted in religious societies. But a society is not a mass of elements juxtaposed chaotically and without order; it is a body with personal direction, whose multiple and differentiated organs are carefully arranged. Moreover, in a human body, different organs, distinct and specialized, collaborate for the overall goal; the same law prevails in ecclesiastical society. All priests do not share identically in the work of instruction, administration, or sacramental activities. Some are destined, for instance,

---

[3] On these nontransmittable privileges, cf. Ch. Journet, *L'Eglise du Verbe Incarné*, vol. I, Paris 1941, pp. 464-466.

for religious instruction in official institutions, others are charged with administrative or organizational functions, others, finally, are destined above all to transmit to the faithful, through the Eucharist, Penance, and the other sacraments, the sanctifying fruits of Christ's passion. Each priest actually is carrying out only one part of the work confided to the Churches by the Twelve. But because of this they are no less apostolic. The Apostles themselves did not necessarily exercise all the spiritual powers that were given them. Paul always declared himself to be the Apostle of the Word, the Gospel, the good news, salvation. To read what he wrote to the Corinthians, one may gather that he very seldom baptized. Is he any less an Apostle because of this? His example, or rather his case, is instructive for the nature of the apostolic life.

Finally, the action of the Apostles was demanded by the necessities and opportunities of the moment. There would be no point in requiring that the Christian Church of today be exteriorly similar in all things to the Church of the year 62, in order to be the true Church of the Lord; this would be requiring a very material identification. While the spirit of the Apostles is always the same, their works can, in the course of centuries, assume new forms; their intentions will of necessity cause the appearance of activities which were totally unforeseeable. In the first century, no one thought of building Catholic colleges, though today many of our best priests teach in such colleges. This is a new departure. In short, what was indispensable in Palestine or in Asia Minor in the years following the death of the Messiah did not acquire thereby an everlasting value. And it may be useful, even necessary, today to attach great importance to certain types of activities totally unknown in the first century. The work remains the same and the activities by which it is expressed change, just as an oak tree remains exactly the same whether hidden inside the acorn or majestically in blossom at the edge of the forest. The parable of the grain of mustard seed is always to the point. By renewing the

institutions in each age, we are respecting the intentions of the Apostles and conforming to the true tradition of the Church.

APOSTOLIC ACTIVITIES

With this said, it is clear that there are some *formally* apostolic activities, because of the fact that they pertain properly to those whom Christ chose to continue
His work here below.

First, *teaching* activities. "Go ye and teach." The first
disciples must have felt much more than we do the
primacy of teaching. We say primacy because the mission of the Church is not only liturgical, it is also and
primarily doctrinal. Of course it does involve the celebration of the Mass and the administration of the sacraments, but it consists first of all in teaching men and
forming them in a Christian manner. How could the
disciples have caused the Christian rites to be accepted
without interpreting their meaning to those they evangelized? How could they have required adherence to the
faith without specifying its object? The first Apostles
were somewhat in the position of visitors who ask us to
attend a public meeting of some kind: their first concern is to explain to us the meaning of this meeting, its
interest and importance. Always the primacy of doctrine. Perhaps we assume too readily today that the baptized, because they have duly learned their catechism
and have taken some courses in religion, really possess
this necessary fundamental doctrine. The disciples could
not make such an assumption. The Jews refused to
recognize this Messiah who had disputed with the Phari-
sees and the Sadducees, and who appeared to contradict the most solemn promises of the Patriarchs and
of Moses. The Gentiles openly ridiculed this obscure
Judean, the founder of a religion too simple for intel-
lectuals and too pure for those initiated into the pagan
mysteries. They therefore had to preach and continue
preaching. Not calmly, as if they were giving the customary Sunday instruction to the baptized, but with the

relentless drive of those who wish to persuade, convince and induce total adherence, yet with the clear knowledge that the very gift of divine life can only come from a superhuman source, the glorified Lord. Thus they were truly the "prophets" of the New Covenant, that is, the spokesmen for the Almighty, the heralds of the Christian religion.

Next came communication of *life*. The importance of faith for the believers stands out all the more from the fact that liturgical rites could not have been highly developed in the early days of the Church. While Baptism was surrounded with extensive and solemn preparations, and while the Eucharist was celebrated in memory and renewal of the Supper presided over by the Lord, the other sacraments did not have the settings which they have today. Besides, what were the first "places of prayer" of early Christianity? It is easy to imagine the fervor which must have united the faithful, especially during times of persecution. Our age, too, has known situations very similar to those in which the baptized had to exist during the early centuries; but we can be sure that the conditions under which the sacraments were administered then were very different from those in our own day.

It is nevertheless true that the sacramental rites are the sacred realities par excellence. These ritual activities, full of the presence of the Spirit, profoundly inspired the faithful, and increased to that extent the respect they showed to their ministers. Divine fear, however, is not what accomplishes the mystery of salvation in the sacraments, and converts feel that there is something more embodied in these rites than popular superstition or primitive dread. Thus, the disciples were recognized to be intermediaries between God and men.

Finally, these disciples were *good shepherds* in the image of their Master. When He sent them forth in pairs into the towns and villages to practice the apostle's mission, the Lord did not tell them merely to preach and baptize; He also ordered them to distribute freely along the way the goods of the soul and those of the

body, spiritual favors and temporal assistance. Sources
of good things and of life, they were acquiring thereby
an authentic paternity.

What is more, the leadership entrusted to them was
a true power. Strictly speaking, the *government* of the
Church is reserved to the hierarchy. But the direction
of the Christian people really implies a power which,
though it is not the *potestas regiminis*, the power of
governing, nevertheless involves obvious authority. When
the disciples spoke, cured, baptized or punished, it was
really in the name of the Lord, *in nomine Domini*. To
tend the Church of God, as Paul was to state it, consisted both of ruling her as well as assuring her subsistence. Because of the fact that the presbyters or
bishops were placed in charge of the common property
of the Christian communities founded by the Apostles,
they enjoyed real powers as those who must, by their
office and their function, insure unity and order, progress and prosperity in the infant communities. While
the pastor could sin because he "served himself" instead
of serving others, the believer, in turn, sinned if he
refused to subordinate himself willingly to his pastor.

2. THE EARLY HIERARCHY

ACCORDING TO THE SCRIPTURES

Before long, the Apostles had to have help in carrying out their mission. The blood of the deacon Stephen
was still flowing when the evangelical wave reached
Samaria, Syria and the island of Cyprus. It was incumbent on the Twelve to select in their turn men who
would thenceforth watch over the spiritual interests of
the young Churches. And so, from age to age, pontiffs
and priests succeeded one another in the communities
of believers created by the work of missionaries. From
age to age, the same redemptive life spread from country
to country with the same fervent ardor, in the same
spirit: the diocesan clergy remained essentially the
same, throughout the astonishing diversity of its redemptive activities.

There can be no question here of determining precisely the functions of the early hierarchy. Was there a charismatic hierarchy functioning alongside the apostolic one? Was there always some leeway in the various names which served to designate the collaborators of the Twelve? Was the "presbyter" identical with the "bishop"? There are special works which attempt to answer these questions. A few more modest examples will suffice to show that the nature of the diocesan clergy was always specified by contact with the history of the ancient Church.

Let us consider the Church of Antioch ten years after the death of the Lord. "There were found there," writes Luke, "prophets and teachers . . . Barnabas and Simon, called Niger, and Lucius of Cyrene, and Manahen the foster-brother of Herod the Tetrarch, and Saul. And as they were ministering to the Lord and fasting, the Holy Spirit said, 'Set apart for me Saul and Barnabas unto the work to which I have called them.' Then, having fasted and prayed and laid their hands upon them, they let them go" (Acts 13:1-2). These various activities did not remain long in the hands of the charismatic apostolate. Soon, they passed to the clergy. What were they, precisely? To preach, to direct the community, to pray, for all of this is "ministering to the Lord." The term λειτουργεῖν cannot be taken in the narrow sense of "liturgical or cultual" ministry; it designates early Christian worship, "including prayers, preaching by the prophets or teachers, chants, and the Eucharistic Supper."[4]

Thanks to the Pauline Epistles, our knowledge of the tasks to which the early clergy were assigned, is made somewhat more specific. Thessalonica, in the middle of the first century, has προϊστάμενοι, "placed in the Lord over the communities." These "spiritual superiors"[5] are

---

[4] L. Marchal, Art. "Evêques" in Dict. Bibl., Suppl., vol. II, 1932. The laying on of hands referred to in the text is apparently not the conferring of sacerdotal powers, but a solemn benediction: cf. G. Bardy, "Les origines du sacerdoce chrétien," Vie Spir., vol. 47, pp. 19-20.

[5] A. Michiels, De origine episcopatus, p. 169.

sent to reprove the undisciplined faithful, to encourage
the pusillanimous, to support the weak, and to invite
all the disciples of the Lord to render good for evil
(1 Thess. 5:12).

The Epistle to the Hebrews reveals to us the existence of ἡγούμενοι. These ἡγούμενοι are not merely
delegates of the community, but authentic spiritual
leaders. Their chief function is to preach the word of
God and to watch over the salvation of souls, for which
they will have to give an accounting when they appear
before the tribunal of the Supreme Pastor (1 Pet. 2:25;
5:4).

But above all it is the ἐπίσκοποι and the πρεσβύτεροι
who concern us here. The overseers and the ancients
are the rectors, the pastors, and the heads of communities whose life they cared for: "the ancients and
the overseers are the shepherds of God's flock" (Acts
20:17 ff.).[6] Bishops or presbyters, presidents or officers,
therefore have as their task to pursue in specific locations the work inaugurated by the Twelve. The latter
plant, the former must watch over the frail shoot blos-
soming in Christ, and tend it until it produces the fruits
of holiness. Their ideal is to work the Lord's field; also,
in every season, at every age, they will give to souls all
that suits them, like the farmer who goes out every
day to look over his lands and who gives them his attention, his care, and his labor at the required moment,
in tempore opportuno. Nothing can help us understand
better the variety, the multiplicity of the tasks assigned
to the clergy than the image of *agricultura Dei* already
developed by Paul in the first Epistle to the Corinthians.

There is this restriction, however: it is not the diocesan clergy who plow the field and turn it over for
the first time; this is the job of the Apostles. They
plant the new community and then pass by from time
to time, as a flying squad, to renew the enthusiasm
of the believers, to check on the work of their spiritual
leaders, and to sharpen their hope. By "apostles" this

---

[6] A. Michiels, *op. cit.*, pp. 216-217.

time, we do not mean only the Twelve, but also certain "brethren" endowed with the charism of the apostolate. From the beginning, in fact, the Holy Spirit inspired believers to abandon all things to go into distant lands and found new Christian communities; these are the "apostles" whose disinterestedness is the best criterion of authenticity (Ephes. 4:11; 1 Cor. 12:28). When the Twelve are dead and the charismatic apostolate has disappeared, zeal for the evangelization of non-Christians living within territory covered by the hierarchic Church will revert naturally to the presbyters and the bishops, the diocesan clergy. We shall see an example of this later.

THE EARLY CENTURIES

Let us now examine some of the features of the clergy in the early centuries.

Ignatius liked to emphasize that there had to be a perfect union between the bishop and his *presbyterium*: "there is but one flesh of our Lord, one altar only, just as there is but one bishop united to the *presbyterium* and to the deacons the companions of the ministry which has fallen to me."[7] The Bishop of Antioch is not speaking of the presbyters but of the *presbyterium;* for the presbyters, in his eyes, form a real community: "They constitute a senate, an assembly; they surround the bishop in the sanctuary; they form his spiritual crown; they collaborate with him in the celebration of the Eucharist, and the faithful must be subject to them as to their Bishop."[8]

The union of priests among themselves and the union of the *presbyterium* with the bishop are two themes dear to Ignatius. "You should be of one and the same mind as your bishop," he writes to the Ephesians (IV, 1) ; "that is, moreover, what you are doing. Your venerable *presbyterium*, truly worthy of God, is united

[7] *Epist. ad Philad.*, IV.
[8] G. Bardy, *op. cit.*, vol. 53, p. 19.

with the bishop as the strings to the lyre, and so, from
the perfect harmony of your sentiments and your charity,
a concert of praise rises toward Jesus Christ." For its
part, the "precious spiritual crown" (*Magnes.*, XIII, 1)
constituted by the *presbyterium* owes it to itself to encourage its bishop in all things, for "it is the duty of
every one of you, and especially of the presbyters, to
console the bishop for the glory of the Father, of Jesus
Christ, and of the Apostles" (*Tral.*, XII, 2). Thus,
throughout his literary work, Ignatius shows himself
to be the champion of diocesan unity and of the paternal
authority of the bishop over his priestly college. The
communitarian ideas which are in such high esteem
these days for apostolic reasons, find in him a doctrinal
and spiritual foundation which is solid, concrete, and
at times moving.

Clement of Alexandria insisted more upon the teaching role which has been confided to the *didascaloi*.
Living in an environment where philosophical culture
flourished, he retained a predilection for Hellenic intellectualism which the Christian revelation had not yet
entirely integrated into itself. Thus is explained the
great importance which he attaches to the doctrinal
function of the Church. The preacher must be alert and
perspicacious; he must be attentive to all that is happening around him, to the concrete, daily life of the
believers, in order to speak to them from a position of
knowledge. "He who speaks to an audience which is
present, feels with the times, judges with discernment,
distinguishes the one who is capable of hearing. He
observes the words, the manners and the morals, the
life and the movements, the attitudes, the voice and the
look, of every person; the square, the stone, the road
trodden underfoot, the fertile earth, the region covered
with forests, that which is rich, beautiful, cultivated,
that which can multiply the seed."[9] Also, before practicing his art, the teacher must review his innermost
dispositions and check the value of his activity: "it is

9 *Strom*, I, i, 18; G. Bardy, *art. cit.*, vol. 53, p. 152.

necessary that he who undertakes to preach to others examine himself to see if his goal is the utility of his neighbor, to see whether he is giving himself over to teaching in haste or in a spirit of jealousy, to see if his manner of spreading the word is inspired by vanity, if he is not pursuing wages other than the salvation of his listeners, if he is preaching in order to receive gifts, if he is avoiding calumny."[10]

But, above all, the priest with his bishop, is the *good shepherd*, attached to his flock, concerned with their lives, their faith, and their eternal salvation, attentive to their needs, eager to be of service to them whether in the temporal or the spiritual order, when earthly conditions are harmful to moral behavior. The priest is truly the "father" of his faithful. The whole spiritual life of the believers, including, later on, that of the pious virgins and the monks, was entrusted to the priest; all the redemptive tasks were taken on by him.

The clergy performed the work of religious formation, and also that of the *conversion* of strayed sheep. It is necessary, explains Clement of Rome to his young colleague, Polycarp of Smyrna, to assemble the faithful often, and to take care to call them together individually by name, so that they can have no excuse for not attending Mass.[11] In turn, Polycarp, describing for his priests their own mission, reminds them not to neglect the orphans, the widows, and the poor, to be merciful toward all and to come to their assistance; and, finally, to "convert the strayed."[12] In connection with this emphasis on caring for the "strays," on looking after those already within the hierarchic Church, G. Bardy notes: "We must not believe that the bishops were not interested in the conversion of the pagans. We are aware of the story of St. Gregory Thaumaturgus, a disciple and admirer of Origen. According to the legend, there were only seventeen believers on his arrival in his diocese of Neocaesarea, and at his death, there remained only

[10] *Ibid.*
[11] *Ad Polyc.*, IV, 2.
[12] *Ad Philipp.*, VI, 1-2; G. Bardy, *art. cit.*, vol. 53, p. 21.

seventeen nonbelievers. In any event, St. Gregory had
at heart the expansion of the Gospel and he certainly was
not the only one."

DIMENSIONS OF THE PRIESTHOOD

Better than any definition, the picture of our origins
has helped us, as diocesan priests, to know our task and
our function. It has especially become clear that the
scope of this apostolate, in those days, was equivalent
to the whole domain of the Church's mediating work,
from the long prayers which occupied the largest place
in the liturgical assemblies presided over by Clement
of Rome to the efficient administration of the new communities.

It would therefore be inexact, historically speaking,
to reduce the task of the diocesan priest to his *cultual
ministry*. Of course, the term "priest" can be taken in
its strict and limited signification: in that case, it designates him who has received the power of Orders and
has been "ordained for worship," especially, for the
Holy Sacrifice of the Mass. But in that event, one has
not exhausted the entire field of activity entrusted to
the diocesan priest. The English language has no term
which would permit a better distinction between the
priest who has received the power of Orders and the
one who is charged also with the teaching and administration of Christian communities.

In his study on the Christian priesthood according to
the Fathers, G. Bardy points out that the scope of
the apostolic work confided to the clergy conspicuously
exceeds the limits of the worship entrusted to the ἱερεῖς,
the "priests." Although the term ἱερεύς was very well
known to the pagans and Jews, the first Fathers scarcely
used it. Perhaps in that way they hoped to dissociate
more thoroughly the spiritual and universal Christian
apostolate from the Aaronic priesthood linked to the pre-
cincts of the Temple of Jerusalem. One cannot be sure
that Peter would have liked to be called "Summus
Pontifex"; someone else, an enemy of Jesus Christ, bore

this famous title. In short, "the Jewish people, and the
pagan peoples as well, had ἱερεῖς. The Christians were
led by bishops, whose mission was *unquestionably more
extensive,* since it included also doctrinal teaching, spiritual government, moral direction, but who counted
among the duties essential to their charge, the celebration
of the Eucharist, an eminently priestly function."[13]

In this sense, the mission of the bishop cannot be
compared with that of the Jewish high priest. The
Hebrews, a theocratic people, lived under the direction
of three groups of men with very diverse functions, and
moved within the framework of three perfectly distinct
and relatively autonomous institutions. First of all, the
priesthood, with its high priest, the priests and Levites,
reserved to itself exclusively, at least in the final centuries before our era, the worship of the Temple —
what today we would call the sacred ministry. With
them, the prophets, to whom would be added later on,
(gradually replacing them), the scribes and doctors of
the Law, represent the doctrinal mediation and the
teaching work of the Chosen People. Finally, the very
direction of Jewish life — both spiritual and temporal
— was entrusted to a Council of Elders, the Sanhedrin,
whose role was more or less effective; it is the moral
and religious aspect of this power which reappears in
the government of the Church.

But while the Jewish high priest represents only the
priesthood of the Temple, the bishop of the Christian
dioceses assumed the work of teaching as well as the
moral and religious direction of his flock. He is therefore charged with the responsibility which the ancient
economy had divided, schematically speaking, among
three distinct institutions. Just as Christ is the source
of life, truth and direction, so too the bishop, for his
subordinates, is the instrument of life, truth and
authority. And since the diocesan priests are, by definition and properly, the co-workers of the bishop, *co-
operatores ordinis nostri,* one may also believe that they,

[13] G. Bardy, *art. cit.,* vol. 53, pp. 22-23.

on the basis of their concrete mission, are called to this threefold apostolic mediation.

The diocesan priests are, therefore, primarily "envoys" *ἀπόστολοι*, not of men or in behalf of men, but of the Lord; they are sent into the world, there to be the salt of the earth, the leaven in the dough, the good odor of Christ.

They are all *"witnesses."* They bear in their eyes the splendor of the Word Incarnate — *et vidimus gloriam ejus;* they have received the unforgettable revelation of the Light par excellence — *quod vidimus et manus nostrae contrectaverunt de Verbo vitae;* they have seen on earth the glorious manifestation of the life that is in God — *apparuit humanitas et benignitas Salvatoris nostri;* at least some of them were able to admire the divine brilliance of the transfigured Lord. They will therefore tell the world something of their vivifying and illuminating experience.

They are in the *service* of the Master: *δοῦλοι*: service of the communication of the Good News, service of the Truth proclaimed to the world's face, service of the life transmitted to the generations to come, in order to make of the pagan masses an acceptable oblation, *ut fiat oblatio Gentium accepta, et sanctificata in Spiritu Sancto* (Rom. 15:16).

They are the *co-workers* of the Lord in the work of salvation *συνεργοί* (1 Cor. 3.9) ; they sow and they plant, but God gives the increase. They are the ministers of Christ and the dispensers of the divine truth; they are the aides, the workers, and the men of pain of the Lord: *ὑπηρέτης* (1 Cor. 4:1). They are the workmen who labor in the favorite vineyard of the Father, after His Son has been put to death by the unfaithful servants.

In short, they continue the work of their Master, this work which our theological treatises group under three headings: *ministerium, magisterium* and *regimen* (sanctifying, teaching, and governing). Christ was the truth, the life, and the way; the Apostles must be the same in their turn, like Him, with Him, and in Him.

3. EXTENSION OF THE FIELD OF THE APOSTOLATE

Let us examine more closely just where the frontiers of the domain of formally apostolic activities lie. "Formally" — that is to say, by their nature, without taking any intention into consideration, precisely because they are part of the mission confided expressly to the Apostles by the Lord. Among these activities, which are generally summed up under ministry, magisterium, and government, can we or must we count the prayer of praise and thanksgiving, as well as the technical efforts of organization or administration?

ADORATION AND PRAISE

The apostolate, it is said these days, involves occupations which are characterized by movement from on high down, from the Trinity or from Christ to mankind and the world. The Apostle goes out to the Christian people. He works for the edification of the Body of Christ: "Go, make disciples of all nations, baptizing them in the name of the Father, the Son and the Holy Spirit, teaching them to observe all that I have commanded you." He is charged with bringing the "good news," the Gospel of truth, to men. He is the "envoy" of God to his brethren, the channel of His grace, the witness of His thought, the representative of His benevolent Providence. The powers which Christ communicates to him: to transmit doctrine, to communicate life, to rule communities, imply this movement from high to low: *propter nos et propter nostram salutem descendit de coelis.* In short, the apostolate consists in sanctifying men by means of the Eucharistic sacrifice and the efficacious signs of Redemption, in diffusing the Christian conception of all things by the spoken or printed word, in directing individuals and groups toward the sources of divine life.

Is this interpretation commonly given of the life of the Twelve quite correct? Are we not unconsciously eliminating activities which are proper to them, certain tasks which certainly arise from the essential part of

their function and which, consequently, deserve the name
of apostolate on the same basis as preaching and the
administering of the sacraments? It is enough to return
to the principles which rule apostolic life to show that
the reply to this last question has to be affirmative.

Why are the communication of Christian truth and
the dispensation of the mysteries of salvation called
apostolic works by nature, if not because they are part
of the mission which was entrusted to the infant Church?
The object of the apostolate is thus identified with the
task entrusted by the Savior to the apostolic Body.
We find the object of this apostolate not by transcribing
the little we know about how much of the entire mission
of the apostolic Body each Apostle accomplished, but
by determining the totality of the activities confided to
the apostolic Body as such, to the ecclesiastical hierarchy.
But the essential function of the apostolic college is the
magisterium, the *ministerium,* and the *regimen in all
their fulness.* And the two activities of the priesthood
not included in the definition of the apostolate given
above — the prayer of adoration and of praise, as well
as the technical efforts expended in the organization of
the Church and of local churches — seem properly to
spring forth from the task entrusted by Christ to the
apostolic Body. In this case, they will have to be called
apostolic by nature. Here is the reason.

First of all, the *ministerium* transcends the simple
communication of divine life to the baptized and pagans.
It includes the religious texts and rites which proclaim
the adoration and the glorification of the Trinity. "Every
high priest, taken from among men, is established for
men in those things which pertain to the worship of
God, in order to offer oblations and sacrifices for sins."
The ministry of worship and prayer was essential to
the Levitical priesthood, the figure and preparation of
the Christian priesthood. The priests of all religions are
conscious of being intermediaries between men and God.
The Pontifical has the ordaining bishop say solemnly:
"Sacerdotem oportet offerre. . . ." The Holy Mass, the
apostolic ministry par excellence, is certainly an ex-

piatory sacrifice, but it is also one of glorification, of
adoration, of the Eucharist. The Divine Office, imposed
sub gravi, is the logical extension of this mediating offering. Finally, ecclesiology, in treating of the
ministerium, has in mind as much the movement of men
toward God as the communication of the life of the
Trinity to mankind. Therefore, by what right do we
exclude praise from the function to which the apostolic
College is committed, as spokesman of the Church? Still,
it is rarely said that the reading of the breviary and
the worship tendered the Trinity in the liturgy are, by
nature, apostolic works.

If this idea should seem slightly strange to us, might
it not be because our image of the apostolic life is but
an imperfect reproduction of the little we know of the
history of the Twelve and of the few principles they
have incidentally left us? St. Paul, the Apostle par
excellence, hardly ever baptized; are we to conclude
from this that baptizing is scarcely essential to the
apostolate? And can we refuse the designation of
"apostolic" to the fundamental acts of worship, because
the fortuitous nature of local difficulties and doctrinal
discussions did not permit the Apostles to make explicit
pronouncements on the matter and to say: "It is to us
that Jesus entrusted praise of the Holy Trinity; He
charged us with the prayer of petition and adoration in
the name of the Christian communities"? The "we will
attend to prayer and the ministry of the word" is a
theme which is already quite in line with the preceding.
And, since liturgical worship is essential to the Church,
how can we justify removing it from the domain of the
apostolate?

In his work on the dignity of the diocesan priesthood,
Masure comes to the same conclusion. He writes:

"The Apostles were assimilated to Christ the Priest
in all His ministerial duties. In order to be an intermediary between His Father and men, Jesus had prayed,
baptized, sanctified, forgiven sins, exhorted, consoled.
He had announced the good news and organized the
Church. The Apostles were delegated to all these func-

tions necessary for the extension and exploitation of redemptive grace. The first time St. Peter wanted to define himself as a priest, he as yet possessed no theological vocabulary and so he uttered words destined to resound through the centuries — words that are worth as much as all the theses in our manuals: *nos vero orationi et ministerio verbi instantes erimus*. *Orationi*, that was his priesthood oriented toward God, to adore Him, pray to Him, supplicate Him in the name of men; *ministerio verbi*, this was the preaching of the Gospel, evangelization, the priestly ministry as oriented toward men, to instruct, enlighten, convince, and sanctify them, to unite them to God. There is no isolated theocentrism or anthropocentrism about the priesthood, which is poised between the two, or rather exists for both, adoring God in the name of men, watching over men in order to give them to God, and giving God to humanity. Such was the apostolate in the days of the Apostle Peter, when the two words "apostle" and "apostolate" had not yet taken on the narrower meaning they have today, which designates preaching in all its forms, the evangelization of men. It then designated all the combined religious functions of Peter and of the Eleven, through which they prolonged all the religious functions of Jesus, the one and only Pontiff of the New Alliance."[14]

TECHNIQUE AND ORGANIZATION

Adoration, supplication, and thanksgiving having recovered their apostolic value, let us consider now whether it is legitimate to say the same for the technical efforts deployed in the organization and administration of the Church.

It will be readily seen that the first Apostles had, and claimed, the right of ruling the Church and the faithful in particular. St. James presided in Jerusalem; St. Peter, in Rome; St. Paul commanded at a distance. In short, the members of the apostolic body held the reins of Christian society. If at the outset they did not do so too visibly and did not immediately impose a

[14] *Parish Priest* (Chicago, 1955), pp. 26-27.

Curial pattern, it was because their communities were few and small.

To govern the Church is to enact her laws, to see to their full execution, to take measures against offenders, to administer. Ecclesiastical society has its Canon Law, its courts, its administrative offices. And when a diocesan priest carries out his governing function, he sometimes has the impression that he has gone outside the limits of the authentic apostolate. This impression returns each time that, in the area which has been assigned to him, he sees himself obliged to establish regulations, to judge certain cases, to restore order when it has broken down, to ensure the administration of enterprises. Why are these activities which are acknowledged to be apostolic when taken as a whole, no longer considered such when they are carried out in detail? To rule a diocese by means of diocesan statutes pertains to the function of the bishop as such; is it not the same thing to rule a parish properly by adapting the statutes thereto? When one discovers a method of organizing communities which assures the stability of the family, Christian education and the dignity of the Christian workman, is this not accomplishing in one place what the Apostles proposed for the whole world?

Let us not be too quick to deny technique and organization a place in the apostolate. One is not being a materialist in affirming that progress in techniques and methods can serve the cause of faith. How many times have apostolic efforts been ruined by a lack of organization and technical skill? Ecclesiastical society involves external, visible frameworks which are completely human and profoundly rooted in the multiple complexities of the present era. Research undertaken with a view to technical improvement and tests made in the application of new methods can therefore become part of the service of *administration,* and are deserving of the name of apostolate. And if the apostolate is not that all-embracing, then that which delimits it more strictly must be made known.

BETWEEN TWO EXTREMES

These theoretical considerations have definite practical implications. The diocesan priest who reduces the apostolate to the *service of mankind* is ill at ease when he has to open his breviary and pray in the name of the Church; he has the impression that he is devoting a tremendous amount of time to what is, to be sure, a pious and praiseworthy work, but not a particularly useful one, in view of the many people who have a claim on his time. If, on the other hand, he has an authentic notion of the apostolate, the Divine Office assumes, among all his duties, the place it should never have lost. Reciting the breviary is just as apostolic as preaching or hearing confession: all these acts are essential to the function of the ministry.

As to the priest who unconsciously reduces the diocesan priesthood to the *ministerium,* he feels ill at ease when the necessities of his apostolate summon him to such "material" formalities as organization and administration. He regrets losing so much precious time which he could, so he thinks, make so much more redemptive if he could devote it to fervent prayer before the tabernacle. Without being aware of it, this priest is identifying the apostolate with the *ministerium;* he is restricting the work of the diocesan priest to only those acts which pertain to the *ministerium,* whereas, concretely and historically, his apostolate includes the *ministerium,* the *magisterium* and the *regimen.* He thinks that he lives solely for the Mass and the sacraments, whereas he is also consecrated for the ministry of truth in all its forms, and for the direction of the faithful, like the Apostles. For those who think in this way, a clearer view of the apostolate would refocus their efforts and increase the sanctifying power of those efforts.

Another partially false attitude is that which reduces the apostolate to what benefits mankind. The Church, from her beginnings, seems to have accommodated herself readily to this mentality. The Twelve, whose task was to construct the Christian edifice, seemed more like ardent missionaries than well-trained liturgists. Later, the Credo affirmed its "propter nos et propter nostram salutem descendit de coelis et incarnatus est": Christ, and consequently the clergy, exist for men and for the salvation of mankind. Such is the motif of the Incarnation, repeated by many theologians subsequently; such is the raison d'être of the Incarnate Word. As for the twentieth century, it has brought the attention of men back to mankind itself, even to the point at times of making it into a kind of absolute whose extreme expression would be the "religion of humanity." Such theological ideas and philosophical currents are perfectly suited to the anthropocentric notion of the apostolate.

Others, perhaps in reaction, settle themselves in the *ministerium*, sometimes even with an affected enthusiasm for the cult of adoration and praise. It seems to them that they are going to sanctify themselves more surely at the foot of the altar than in human charitable concerns. Occasionally, the feeling of their own impotence causes them to take refuge in prayer, thanks to the ambiguity of the terms "abandonment," "serenity," "indifference," when applied to supernatural values. Again, wishing to protest against an altruistic anthropocentrism — the religion of humanity — some isolate themselves in another anthropocentrism, this time a selfish one. Some even try to justify themselves doctrinally: they explain that since salvation is in fact accessible to all men, thanks to the act of charity, what is "specific" to the Church, and therefore to the diocesan clergy, is the authentically Christian religion of worship, the liturgy. They are only partly correct. For in fact, both historically and concretely, the Church is not reducible to what is "specific" to her, any more than a man can be reduced to what is "specifically" human. She encompasses the worship which comes specifically through her, but also the communication of the divine life, even though this life can be acquired beyond her visible zone of influence. To profess affection only for that which is "specific" to the ecclesiastical society is characteristic of an intellectualism which has lost contact with reality.

The diocesan priest, following the example of the Twelve, can therefore in all serenity give himself over to liturgical praise and concern himself also with the technical organization of his parish; these activities by their very nature are apostolic. We arrive, after a long detour, back to the humble and ancient *age quod agis,* now made more precise and situated in its historical context.

Of course, there is nothing which says we cannot continue to divide priestly activities into two groups: religious and apostolic. The essential thing is for the priest to accept them both as his. But is there not here an absence of profound unity?

4. The "Auxiliaries" of the Church

It is possible to go further in this direction and widen even more the field of formally apostolic activities. We are setting forth a few considerations which flow from the reflection of those interested in certain adjustments, without, however, attaching any major importance to them; it is a matter of fixing a doctrinal position rather than insuring the quality of the sacerdotal life.

It would not be false to say, for example, that, without being formally apostolic occupations, the supervision and management conducted by a diocesan priest are nevertheless a real method of professional collaboration in the activities of the Church. This would assume that it has been established that the Church officially recognizes various means of authentic collaboration, of which the formal apostolate would be the most elevated though not the only one. To be convinced of this, one has but to glance at the situation of the Church in apostolic times and to examine more closely the constitution of the ecclesiastical society.

GROWTH OF THE CHURCH

The Church is not an immutable fact; while remaining substantially identical, she appears to our eyes under different forms in the year 64 and the year 1964. To fulfil her task, she calls the baptized and asks them to place themselves at her disposal; she solemnly entrusts them with a part of her work and gives them the powers needed to carry it out. In short, she turns them into authentic auxiliaries.

But what will be the tasks of these auxiliaries of Christ in the twentieth century? Is the "apostle" type whom we find in the New Testament writings the sole, immutable type of official auxiliary that the Church has ever recognized, just as she has only recognized a sole and immutable "substance" of the sacraments? Or else is he already *one* type of auxiliary created at the outset of the Christian era to protect the first steps of the infant Church? In that event, "apostolic" activity will not be that which every auxiliary of Christ must necessarily perform, but *one* of the means of such collaboration — a permanent means, the most excellent, if you will, even the most specific, but not the exclusive one. And it will be understood that under other circumstances, and in view of the transformations which may affect the life and organization of the Church in the course of the centuries — notably from the fact of her growth — *one or more new types* of cooperation, one or more new forms of collaboration become necessary for her existence. Thus, those who would come to her assistance could call themselves in all truth "auxiliaries of the Church by profession," because they would be prolonging her action, authentically and officially, but according to a format imposed by their own times.

Now, it is certain that in the early stages of the Church, the apostolate was not the only type of collaboration known and officially recognized in Christian communities. From the very first century, alongside "apostles," we note "prophets," "doctors," "evangelists," "helpers of the sick," "alms-gatherers."

God has established in the Church, St. Paul writes, first apostles, then prophets, then teachers, and after that, those who have the gift of healing, helping, governing or speaking diverse tongues. Are all apostles? All

prophets? All teachers? All workers of miracles? Do
all have the grace of healing? Do all speak in tongues?
Do all interpret? (1 Cor. 12:28-30). And in another
epistle: "And he himself gave some men as apostles,
and some as prophets, others again as evangelists, and
others as pastors and teachers, in order to perfect the
saints for a work of ministry, for building up the body
of Christ" (Eph. 4:11-13). In short, there are varieties
of operations, varieties of charisms, varieties of ministries; but there is one Spirit, one same Lord, one same
God who works all things in all (1 Cor. 12:4-6). The
extraordinary origin of several charismatic ministries
did not prevent their being received and recognized by
the hierarchical Church: there is nothing contradictory
in that.

Consequently, the foundation and particular needs of
the early Church already justified the existence of various auxiliaries, officially and authentically constituted,
new conditions could also explain and justify the presence of new types of professional auxiliaries. The Church
of the twentieth century still needs prophets who go
forth to console, but she also needs professors and super-
visors, something which the first century could obviously not anticipate.

DISTRIBUTION OF TASKS

An examination of the *organic* character of ecclesiastical society leads us to a similar conclusion; we have
already mentioned this above, pointing out the danger
of wanting to copy the life-style of the Apostles too ma-
terially. Certainly, the bishop possesses the whole range
of the apostolic powers, but not all priests exercise
them in an equal and uniform manner, so that each
would be acting in the manner of a "miniature" bishop
over a portion of the diocesan territory. As in every
society, the distribution of tasks is made on an organic
basis. Each organ of the human body is not a body "in
miniature, but a part perfectly adapted to the requirements of its function. It is the same for the various

priests of a diocese; some receive as their share more
ministry than others, some more teaching, others more
governing duties. Finally, some, while fulfilling many
apostolic obligations in the strict sense, must also provide all that the ministry of souls necessarily requires,
notably, the subsistence of ecclesiastical society.

Perhaps the day will come when one will call apostolic by nature not only those activities which pertain
essentially and directly to the apostolic function, because
of the fact that they are constitutive elements thereof,
but also those which arise accidentally and indirectly
from this mission, because they guarantee the indispensable conditions therefor.

In saying "accidentally and indirectly," we clearly
recognize that these rather mundane activities are, for
the priest, "marginal." And in this sense, it is well that
they remain, as much as possible, exceptional, temporary,
transitory. These mundane tasks can be accomplished by
those who have not been ordained priests, and they
call for qualities and competencies which a priest does
not necessarily have and does not receive along with the
imposition of hands. A layman more competent in bookkeeping will be a much better steward than a priest
less up to date. A better-educated layman will be a much
better teacher than a priest who is unprepared to teach
the same subject. The fact of ordination does not, of itself, provide technical competence, pedagogical talents,
and scientific erudition. Perhaps someday a revitalized
deaconate will conduct many tasks which today devolve
upon priests. And there is no question that the laity
will be given a more extensive role in the Church of the
future. On that day, laity, deacons, and priests, grouped
around the bishop, will conduct the work of Christ in
each individual Church.

CHAPTER TWO

THE APOSTOLIC SPIRIT

Unless one has transcended their activities to penetrate into their heart, their spirit, the soul which vivifies them, one has not exhausted the contents of the personal revelation which the Apostles themselves constitute. To overlook this factor would be to deprive the doctrine of the early apostolate of its most beautiful flower; it would even be, quite simply, to betray the truth. By *spirit*, we understand primarily the whole range of virtuous psychological dispositions which must adorn the innermost personality of him who participates in the Lord's apostolate. We will understand also and especially, the very soul of apostolic life, that hidden source of all zeal and fruitfulness.

1. THE VIRTUES OF THE APOSTLE

PASTORAL QUALITIES

If one were to sum up all the qualities which St. John Chrysostom, in his *De Sacerdotio*, or St. Gregory the Great in his *Pastoral*, requires in the bishop and also the priest, one would produce an impressive picture. Still, such a portrait is traditional in the Church.

34

Thirty years after the Lord's death, the recommendations of Paul to Titus and Timothy were already inau-
gurating literature on the priesthood with instructions
which all the Apostles unquestionably gave to the presbyters, the bishops, and their other helpers. "If anyone
is eager for the office of bishop," Paul wrote, "he desires
a good work. A bishop, then, must be blameless . . . reserved, prudent, of good conduct, hospitable, a teacher,
not a drinker or a brawler, but moderate, not quarrel-
some or avaricious. He should rule well his own household . . . for if a man cannot rule his own household,
how can he take care of the church of God? . . . He
must have a good reputation with those who are outside, that he may not fall into disgrace" (1 Tim. 3:1-7).
Later on, Paul exhorts Timothy, before God and Christ,
to preach the revealed word with zeal: "Be urgent in
season, out of season; reprove, entreat, rebuke with all
patience and teaching. For there will come a time when
they will not endure the sound doctrine, but . . . will
turn away their hearing from the truth and turn aside
rather to fables. But do thou be watchful in all things,
bear with tribulation patiently, work as a preacher of
the gospel, fulfill thy ministry" (2 Tim. 4:2-5). Finally,
the Epistle to Titus repeats and fills out the list of the
virtues required of presbyters and bishops. "I left thee
in Crete," writes Paul, "that thou shouldst set right anything that is defective and shouldst appoint presbyters
in every city." A man chosen for this position must be
"blameless, not proud or ill-tempered, or a drinker, or
a brawler, or greedy . . . but hospitable, gentle, reserved, just, holy, continent; holding fast the faithful
word which is in accordance with the teaching, that he
may be able both to exhort in sound doctrine and to
confute opponents" (Tit. 1:5-9). What diocesan priest
today could not profit from these recommendations
formulated some nineteen hundred years ago?

Paul does not distinguish between supernatural and
natural virtues for the presbyters or elders. His criterion is always the same and always a single one: the
apostolate. He demands of all his aides that they have

all the virtues which may be useful and *all* the aptitudes necessary to their apostolic task, whether these be natural or supernatural, so that they might carry it out fully. This wholesome pragmatism of the Apostles will be found in the bishops of all ages as well as in the Roman Pontifical.

Examining the situation more closely, Paul even insists especially on the qualities indispensable to the wise management of the churches; he is speaking above all to the "pastor" of the flock of the faithful. Bardy emphasizes this healthy prudence, and even the apparent reticence of the Apostle, who is otherwise so exultant in the captivity epistles which nevertheless are of the same period. He notes that "many pagan writers used to draw up catalogs rather similar to those which appear in the pastoral epistles, when they spoke of the qualities of the general, of the dancer, of the physician. Onosander, for example, wanted the strategist to be prudent, master of himself, temperate, simple, accustomed to fatigue, gifted with intelligence, disinterested, neither too young nor too old, father of a family, capable of speaking, a friend to glory"[1] Almost none of these qualities would be out of place in the portrait of the bishop as drawn by St. Paul.

APOSTOLIC QUALITIES

Thus far, this portrait of the clergy is an attractive one but not one as God-centered as we might want today. However, let us make no mistake. The exhortations of the Apostles to the spiritual heads of the early communities bear on the qualities of a pastor and the virtues which are indispensable thereto. But one cannot overlook other exhortations, other appeals by the hierarchy, or, especially, the great examples which have been preserved for us from these ancient times.

Paul wrote some very forceful pages on apostolic mentality. In his First Epistle to the Corinthians, he shows how much the apostle is God's instrument, acting

[1] Cf. *Vie Spirituelle, art. cit.,* vol. 47, p. 26.

with Him, under His motion, according to His wishes. As a result, he demands humility of them: "neither he who plants is anything, nor he who waters, but God who gives the growth" (3:7). He demands of them a heroic fidelity capable of any test: "Here it is required in stewards that a man be found trustworthy" (4:2). He takes note of all that is miserable and contemptible in the eyes of the world about their way of life: "As the refuse of this world, the offscouring of all, even until now" (4:13). How can one live all this without a profound, intense, truly interior life? His Second Epistle to the Corinthians is no less demanding. How could apostles truly be the ministers of the new covenant, *non littera sed Spiritu,* if they did not live an ardent, strong, interior life (3:6)? How are they going to call reality that which is invisible without an astonishing, piercing, faith: " . . . we look not at the things that are seen, but at the things that are not seen. For the things that are seen are temporal, but the things that are not seen are eternal" (4:18)? And we could go on. No, it is certainly not possible to separate the pastoral from the captivity epistles, or to divide up Paul's teaching on the spirit of the apostolate in the world.

Following the Apostles and in the same spirit, some ecclesiastical writers demanded of the diocesan priest an intense inner life, a serious life of union with God, in view of the sacred functions entrusted to him. But, even more than these exhortations, the very lives of these early apostles are eloquent. Then, as now, the clergy was hardly a writing clergy, and no one was there to tell its story. We have barely preserved the account of the last days of Ignatius of Antioch, in whom generations sought a model and support. In his letters, Ignatius always recalls the necessity of union between the priests and the bishop; but he nourishes in his heart an even more intimate union with the Lord Jesus. Nothing reveals the temper of this soul like these few lines of his Epistle to the Romans:

"When, therefore, will I be face to face with these

beasts which await me? May they throw themselves on
me right away! If I need to, I shall pat them so that
they will devour me on the spot and not do what they
have done with some whom they were afraid of touching. If they seem unwilling, I will force them. Please,
let me be; I know what is best for me. Now I am beginning to be a true disciple. Let no creature, visible
or invisible, seek to take from me the possession of
Jesus Christ! Fire, cross, ferocious beasts, laceration,
quartering, dislocation of bones, mutilation of members,
crushing of my entire body: let the most cruel tortures
of the devil fall upon me, provided that I finally possess
Jesus Christ.

"Of what use would it be to me to possess the whole
world? What have I to do with the kingdoms of this
world? It is far more glorious for me to die for Christ
Jesus, than to rule even to the confines of the earth.
He it is whom I seek, this Jesus who died for us! It is
He Whom I want, this Jesus who rose again for us."[2]

Bardy writes of this passage:

"What is particularly moving about these pages,
now eighteen centuries old, is the intense current of life
which runs through them. They have no literary value;
a translation could not render the breathless roughness,
the circuitous constructions, the bold neologisms; but
one senses in them a soul which bares itself, and that
is more beautiful than anything else. The Bishop of
Antioch had not known Jesus Christ; yet he has for
Him a most profound love, even to a desire to die for
Him. We would perhaps be even more astounded at such
a great love and such a passionate desire if in all the
Christian generations the Savior had not found similar
witnesses and if, among the ancient saints, Ignatius were
anything but the representative of a great multitude."[3]

Here we have come to the very root of the apostolic
spirit. Qualities, virtues, talents, to be sure — we have
summed them up as we will sum them up again. But
the profound source of apostolic life and zeal is more
intimate still. And, in order to grasp it in its first fresh-

---

[2] Chap. V, 2 — VI, 1.
[3] *En lisant les Pères*, p. 17.

ness, we shall attempt to come upon it in the hearts of those who first lived it intensely, the Apostles themselves.

2. FOLLOWING CHRIST

THE SCENE AT TIBERIAS

The scene is laid along the banks of the Lake of Tiberias during a Palestinian spring. Jesus passes two brothers, Simon and Andrew, who are casting their nets into the lake, and He says to them: "Come, follow me, and I will make you fishers of men." And at once, St. Matthew tells us, they left the nets, and followed Him (Matt. 4:18-22). Later, Jesus meets two other brothers, James and John, sitting with their father Zebedee in a boat, mending their nets. He calls them, and at once, abandoning their father and their property, they follow Him.

This humble "Come" of the Gospels sums up all the kindness of the Father with respect to men. It is a call of special favor given to those whom Christ wished to make His auxiliaries, His intimates, and His friends, the confidants of all His thoughts, the heralds of His work, a work announced since the beginning of time. It is a call of loving benevolence addressed to all those who would someday like to be the bearers of His message, the performers of His mysteries, the instruments of His life.

No one will ever exhaust these simple words, "and they followed him," which, in the spirit of the early faithful, characterized the attitude assumed immediately by His disciples. To follow Jesus is much more than merely to accept Him like the faithful and the believers: "To as many as received Him He gave the power of becoming sons of God." The exegetes are well aware of the fulness of meaning which the *recipere* of biblical theology encompasses: personal act, total commitment toward the Lord, oath of allegiance to His person, adherence to His entire doctrine, submission to the rites of His religion, subordination of one's sentiments to

His love, putting the whole man in the service of the Word of God.

Following Christ in the manner of the Apostles goes beyond the crisis of faith, the first stage of Christianity. A believer may return to his secular pursuits, resume the thread of his daily life and continue the worldly tasks which are his. But an apostle puts himself in the service of a Lord, in the school of a Rabbi: he attaches himself to a person, to a Master whose features he will attempt to reproduce faithfully. To follow Christ is to accompany Him in His distant preaching, to assist at His miraculous actions and attend His prophetic laments; it is to live in contact with Him, learning to think like Him, to judge like Him, in order to bear witness to the truth among the "brethren"; it is to live in unison with Him, both internally and externally, in one's actions and with one's heart, in love and humility, in order to announce to all men the appearance of the Word of God in the flesh, the resplendence of paternal glory in a human person.

To follow Christ is to give Him one's reply after hearing His call. And what will this reply be?

OUR REPLY

It is a *loving* reply in the Gospels, without question, with a love which grows even as the marvelous and fascinating personality of Christ reveals itself to the dazzled Apostles, and as the dramatic mystery of salvation, on being unveiled, requires of them a more pure, more disinterested, more self-denying attachment.

A *personal* response. The Gospels ignore the necessary but subtle distinctions introduced later in theology to dissociate intellectual adherence and the acquiescence of the will: "they" follow Him. An act of man: "We come!" An ardent and youthful act, performed by brothers who had previously been carried away by a long conversation with Christ (John 1:35-39). A free and spontaneous act which Christ was to test on numerous occasions to give it greater solidity:

"Do you also wish to go away?" (John 6:68). A virile,
mature, and quite conscious act of those who soon are
to cry out their, "We are unable not to speak," and who
will rejoice to be, because of their Master, the target
of the intrigues and deceits of the perjurers of Israel:
"They departed . . . rejoicing that they had been counted
worthy to suffer disgrace for the name of Jesus." A
determined, immediate act: "Statim! — At once!" This
one word of St. Matthew's says enough.

A *total* response, therefore. In following Jesus, the
Apostles were entrusting themselves entirely to Him and
giving themselves entirely to His work. The Gospel story,
by its very brevity and ingenuousness, powerfully underlines the fulness of this generous gift, the daily sight
of which the early community had before its eyes. The
fulness of universal and unconditional commitment was
in this response. For to follow the Master is to repeat
His divine gestures, reproduce the religious rituals inaugurated by Him or hinted at by His active wisdom,
to repeat on the housetops the words which He spoke
in the shadows of Palestinian dwellings or in the pul-
pits of the incredulous synagogues; it is to be the way
the truth, and the life with Him, and to break the
eucharistic bread for souls hungering for Him. It is to
prolong the sorrowful mystery of His saving Passion as
well as the glorious exaltation of His Resurrection. It
is also to be united with His intimate intentions as Redeemer, to accept with Him the task of salvation, to desire with all one's soul the "hour" fixed by the will of
an all-loving Father, to await anxiously the completion
of the masterpiece of divine mercy, to call with all one's
strength for the constitution and growth of this Christian
fulness, to hate the malign forces which temporarily
check the expansion of the Church: Satan, unbelief,
pride and impurity, the works of the flesh and of death.

This is a response pregnant with the mysterious
increases of divine grace. Like a simple and initial acquiescence, it remains forever profound and radical,
encompassing in its first gesture all the apostolic en-
deavors to come, animating and informing from within

the details of all sacerdotal activities, expanding outward
through the efforts of an unlimited zeal, and becoming
interiorized through an ever more conscious and joyous
gift of the self. For the consequences of this gift were
only gradually manifested. In deciding to follow Jesus,
in the spring of 28 A.D., the disciples were no doubt
expecting to share in the messianic triumph — an ex-
pectation which was primarily spiritual but one not entirely free from earthly hopes. Certainly John was not
already contemplating the great themes he was to reveal some seventy years later in his Apocalypse; nor was
he already enjoying the profound interior life of which
his first epistle has preserved for us a few reflections.
The sublimity, the intensity, and the extent of the love
which the simple *Ecce* was inevitably to arouse, were
not yet revealed to Christ's followers. It was enough for
Christ that they were faithful, that they were found
trustworthy, and that they followed Him step by step in
His work and spirit. If they remained faithful, they
would clearly see that the act of "following" would
take the supernatural path of a mysterious development and would signify at each turn, new perspectives
of growth and of progress.

ECCE! . . . ADSUM!

Arising from the very center of their being and involving all of their powers, the response of the first
disciples would thus soon become *the most basic and
most permanent state of soul* that all apostles would
know in the course of their laborious existence. This
state of readiness, of spiritual alertness, is constantly
called into action by the thousand and one exigencies
of daily life. The apostle responds to these exigencies
with the charity which descends from the Father of
mercies and which, through the Word, is spread in his
heart by the Holy Spirit. For this response indeed prolongs that which is made from all eternity in the bosom
of the Father: "Sacrifice and oblation thou wouldst
not; but a body thou hast fitted out to me; then I said:

Behold I come that I may do thy will, O God." The assent
of love which the Word pronounces *in sinu Patris* is
repeated by those who are swept along in the same current of supernatural fruitfulness. Is it not this very
response, as a matter of fact, which the Church, a wise
and sure interpreter, will require of candidates for the
priesthood, at the beginning of every ordination? To
the *Venite* corresponds the *Accedant* of the archdeacon,
signifying to each candidate to the priesthood that the
bishop is calling them in the name of the Lord: "who
are called by the Church." To the *Ecce* of the Apostles
there is the reply *Adsum,* by which each ordinand commits himself publicly to follow Christ in His work, in
the spirit which animated Him and forever animates
Him in heaven. From the *Ecce venio* of Christ to the
Adsum of candidates to the priesthood, there is a direct
connection; an identical spirit animates both responses
— divine love. This explains the divine fecundity in the
infinite exchanges of Trinitarian life, it takes into account the superabundant divine fruitfulness in the work
of creation, it alone can justify the unspeakable con-
descension of God in the work of the redemption and in
the glorification of humanity and of the cosmos for all
eternity.

This response was the first event in the apostolic
life of the Twelve; it was to remain, for each of them,
the first of their redemptive efforts. A human and complete act, their donation to Christ was to remain permanent and primary. Every apostolic act is first of all a
loving *Ecce,* a devoted *Adsum,* with infinite perspectives
like the divine love which inspires it. The *Adsum* is like
the very breathing of the apostle, the point of departure
of his supernatural dynamism, the shock which sets him
in motion.

And this first apostolic act is completely directed
toward Christ, the Son of God delivered up for men. At
the moment the Apostles were pronouncing their *Veni-
mus,* they were thinking only of Christ Himself; this
moment was fully and joyously "Christocentric," we
would say nowadays. Their eyes beheld the Lord, and

they responded to Him; their ears heard His voice, their hands were in His; it was He alone who was the object of their concern and interest. Everything else — His discourses, His apostolic journeys, His miracles, His work — all that came after Him, with Him, in Him. All that was but an extension of His Person, a derivation of the riches which He possessed, a consequence of the decision which He had made. All that was secondary to the Person of the Word Incarnate. To be faithful to its origins the apostolic life should imitate, even today, the first efforts of the Twelve and be directed toward the beloved person of our Lord Jesus Christ: "Put nothing ahead of the love of Christ."

LEAVING ALL

In responding to the call of the Lord, the Apostles necessarily committed themselves to abandoning anything which might conflict with their commitment to Christ. To be sure, those who believed in Him and desired to be counted among the number of His faithful were bound to be converted, to change their mentality, μετάνοια, to bid farewell to the prince of darkness and to submit themselves to the laws of the invisible Kingdom of Light. But could they retain their habits, their families, their property, their occupations, the free disposition of their lives and of their futures? Christ demands more from those whom He chooses as His apostles and who agree to follow Him; His requirements are more precise, or rather, the personal gift is required with such fulness that it involves, of itself, the renunciation of everything which is not oriented in the direction of the Christian work of praise and of redemption. And tradition, summing up with the heroic simplicity of the humble this act of abandon, suggested these few words to St. Matthew: "Immediately they left their nets and their father, and followed him."[4]

---

[4] The recommendations made by Christ to the disciples in Matt. 10 also imply the idea of an absolute disinterestedness and a complete detachment. Cf. A. Medebielle, "Apostolat d'après l'Evangile," in *Dict. Bible, Suppl.*, vol. 1, cc. 544-555.

As a whole, this loving and affectionate detachment is but the obverse of the gift of self made to the Lord. For to choose, is to abandon; to make up one's mind is to leave behind. And our God, writes the Bible, is a jealous God.

Voluntary, generous, swift and spontaneous renunciation — *statim*. One can see the Galilean fishermen throw down nets and needles, climb over the boats and rush to the Lord's side. And yet, this renunciation was hard; it lead to the witness of blood, even to the supreme witness, martyrdom.

Absolute detachment. To follow Christ, they forgot the rest, they no longer took it into account, they abandoned it to others, to their families. A new epoch began for them; they turned a page of the great book of their lives. They left everything, quite simply. Without any subtle distinctions, they displayed that disposition of the apostolic spirit which is poverty, universal availability, radical independence with regard to all earthly goods, whatever they might be, when they are not those which Christ demands for Himself or for His work.

As basic as the gift of which it is the counterpart, this detachment of the apostle affects *all his faculties*, his wishes and his desires, his tastes and his wants, his views and his judgments. It affects the innermost part of his being and is visibly translated in his efforts. Thus it was with the Incarnate Word. A general and universal abnegation is required — of profession and family traditions, parents and friends, favorite activities and, sometimes, even talents. This is a generous gesture which no shadow can tarnish: "No one who looks behind him is worthy of me."

Such abnegation is quite precise in its purpose and far removed from mere verbalizing; everything which prevents in us the realization of the desires of Christ for the world, everything which hinders the expansion of the Spirit here below is eliminated. Ideas which do not coincide with those of the Lord: How many times did Jesus have to speak to His disciples those words of impatience which the evangelists have preserved for us —

"but have you not yet understood, even you?" How slow you are to grasp my teachings! The sentiments which the Old Law perhaps tolerated are no longer worthy of those who live under the rule of the new covenant and who are its leaders: "You have heard that it was said . . . but I say to you. . . ." A disposition of spirit is needed such that the Spirit may ask whatever He wishes and the apostle will follow. Several times, Paul was prevented by the Spirit from going up north into Asia Minor, or from going back down the Mediterranean coast: the ways of God are not always ours, and the apostle must be pliant to the wishes of the Spirit. Finally, hatred must be had for everything which harms Jesus, His work, for everything which holds back the growth of the spiritual tree planted by Him.

There must be a renunciation total in principle and in its first step, one whose successive phases will be revealed gradually. In leaving behind their nets, did Andrew and Simon perceive completely that they would also have to leave behind certain of their messianic hopes, their narrow concepts, their doctrine of salvation, their brethren by race? Were they fully aware that they would have to bear the witness of blood and that another "would bind them and lead them where they would not"?

And just as commitment to Christ involves an initial movement of love and charity, so too every apostolic action involves a first moment of detachment from all that is not Him and from everything that is not possessed according to His desires and laws. If love unleashes every apostolic act, detachment assures that this motion will be carried out to perfection.

3. THE APOSTLE'S LOVE

Why follow Jesus to the end? Why renounce everything which is not Him? Another episode in the life of the Twelve shows us why. This time, we are no longer at the beginning of the Lord's public life, but at the end of His visible manifestation, shortly before His

Ascension, on the shore of that same sea of Tiberias whose waves had heard the first replies of the disciples. After having breakfasted together at a meal miraculously prepared by Jesus, the latter poses to Peter a question which must have greatly hurt his colleagues and put him ill at ease: "Simon, son of John, dost thou love me more than these do?" Prudently, Peter, who had not forgotten the denial and his tears of repentance, declares: "Lord, thou knowest that I love thee." We know the rest of the account, the triple question on the part of Christ, and these words of St. John's: "Peter was grieved because he said to him for the third time, 'Dost thou love me?' And he said to him, 'Lord, thou knowest all things, thou knowest that I love thee'" (John 21:15-17).

Is it possible to state more accurately the union between love of our Lord and the apostolate? Three times, the Apostle shows us that they are indissolubly linked. Is it by accident that Jesus, wishing to give Peter the responsibility for the entire flock, demands of him a love greater than that of all the disciples? Greater, even, than the love of the disciple "whom Jesus loved," who designated himself by these words? The wellspring of the apostolic response and sense of renunciation is here clearly expressed and required by Christ. If we had but these three verses of John's Gospel, it would remain a blessed testimony to the spirit of the Apostles.

And Paul? Could he have written his captivity epistles without having ever before his eyes, before his heart, the person of his glorified Lord? How else is his "For me, to live is Christ" or his "I desire to be dissolved and to be with Christ" to be explained? And the reader of these epistles is well aware that these expressions do not result from any artificial or unnatural state of soul; his love of the Lord is visible throughout his correspondence and throughout his life.

Even before the somewhat mystical period of the captivity in Rome, from the time of the great epistles to the Corinthians and to the Romans, Paul is already greatly attached to Christ, and it could be said of him:

cor Pauli, cor Christi. In the First Epistle to the Corinthians, he has given us an unforgettable picture of
charity. At the end of this same epistle, he writes these
words, which until now have perhaps been too frequently overlooked: "If any man does not love the Lord
Jesus Christ, let him be anathema." Finally, in the
Epistle to the Romans, at the end of the long and rich
description of the justification of the unbeliever, a doctrinal passage which has nourished the meditation of
innumerable generations, he bursts forth in a chant of
triumph, because the certitude which he has of being
loved by God in Christ is manifested to him with unique
clarity: "Who shall separate us from the love of Christ?
Shall tribulation, or distress, or persecution, or hunger,
or nakedness, or danger, or the sword? . . . But in all
these things we overcome because of him who has loved
us. For I am sure that neither death, nor life, nor angels,
nor principalities, nor things present, nor things to come,
nor powers, nor height, nor depth, nor any other creature
will be able to separate us from the love of God, which
is in Christ Jesus" (Rom. 8:35-39).

The beautiful epistles of John could also be quoted.
There we read of the God who fills his heart, the God
whose definition is "love." This is the Word of God whom
he has touched: "What we have seen . . . what we have
looked upon and our hands have handled . . . the Word
of Life." This is the living manifestation of paternal
charity in the midst of men. But why continue? What
one needs to do is reread these passages following the
manifestations of this love of the Apostles for their
Master, in the first hours of their apostolate.

4. THE APOSTLE'S VISION

It would hardly be correct to state that the fundamental virtues of the Apostle are all of the volitional
order. While the Twelve renounced all things and attached themselves to Christ unto death, they also lived
in the light of the new economy. Their hearts were
ardent, but their eyes, the eyes of faith, remained un-

shakeably fixed on the Redeemer and, in Him, on all
phases of the redemptive work.

This faith of the Apostles is unquestionably a firm
attachment to one Person, an ineradicable confidence
in His power, a permanent recourse to His mercy. The
Lord tells them: "If you have faith even like a mustard
seed, you will say to this mulberry tree, 'Be uprooted and
be planted in the sea,' and it will obey you. And the
apostles said to the Lord: 'Increase our faith' " (Luke
17:5-6). But there is more.

Faith is also an intellectual grasping of the new dispensation, a grasping of the wisdom of God as it exists
in Him and unfolds itself down through the ages in
the creation, the restoration, and the consummation of
the universe. It is an encounter with the gigantic drama
of salvation, which occurs in the hearts of all men and
on the stage of universal humanity. In the same way that
God, in His omnipresence, looks upon the universe, so
too, by infused faith, the apostle also considers it, "as
in the eyes of God." He lives in the fascination of the
supernatural phenomena which unfold before him, he
advances in the work of Christ in the light of this daz-
zling vision, and he endures all the hardships of the road
in order to reach the desired goal.

Ascetic literature has perhaps over-neglected this
explicit faith of the apostle in the work of the restoration of the world in Christ, which is nothing else than
Christian wisdom itself. For we have not completely
described the soul of the apostolate if we stop at good
dispositions, immense desires. New Testament thought
is not a mysticism without doctrinal content; the apostle
lives in his "Christian view of the world" as intensely
as he does in the love of men.

Christ Himself awaited "his hour." Are we to believe
that this "hour" did not represent for Him a vision of
the drama of salvation as it was to be played visibly at
a moment in time in Jerusalem; just as it was also going
to be played invisibly down through the centuries in
every corner of the world? Was it not, above all, this
spectacle of mankind and the universe reappearing with-

out respite before His eyes, that plunged the Lord into
the depths of the agony at Gethsemane, the consummation of the sorrow of the crucified Messias?

This must be the apostle's vision. It is more than the
γνῶσις of all the believers, it is wisdom reserved for
the perfect: σοφία (1 Cor. 2:6). The γνῶσις is rather an
intelligent, enlightened, religion; it is a serious knowledge of the truth transmitted through revelation, at least
in those passages where it is clearly distinguished from
wisdom. The latter, on the contrary, is the redemptive
plan considered in its eternal predestination and temporal accomplishment. These are the secrets hidden before the centuries in the divine counsels, the immense
weight of glory which must compensate our tribulations of the moment; these things which the eye has
not seen, which the ear has not heard, which have not
entered the heart of man. It is the crushing enigma of
evil ravaging the whole human race, to be finally con-
quered in the predestined by the superabundance of the
grace of Christ. It is God shutting all men up in sin,
in order to show mercy to all (Rom. 11:32). This wisdom is the meaning of the history of Israel, the figure
and preparation of the true covenant; it is the mystery
of the rejection of the chosen race, and the grafting of
the wild olive onto the trunk descending from Abraham; it is the call of two peoples — Jews and Gentiles
— into a single body by Christ who, destroying all en-
mities in His flesh, reconciles heaven and earth, men and
God. Paul — and, we could add, every apostle — likes
to fix his regard on the bottomless abyss where from all
eternity the destinies of the world are in development.
As a result he experiences, at least at the beginning, a
sort of sacred horror (Rom. 11:33-36) which seems not
to have been known to the contemplators of the Logos.

"Then, from this sphere of inaccessible light his regard is directed onto the darkened and confused world
where the children of men move about; and suddenly,
everything is lighted up, the behavior of Israel, and the
gropings of the nations, and the inner conflicts of the
soul. Neither philosopher nor historian, St. Paul none

the less, by his profound intuition, conceived the seed of the Christian philosophy of history. From what seemed to be nothing but an incoherent chaos there arises, clearly discernible structure, because Paul's spirit, supernaturally enlightened, discovered the cornerstone which holds everything together (Col. 1:17). For it is Christ who forms the center of all this wisdom, Christ pacifying all things by the blood of His Cross.[5]

This wisdom cannot come to the apostle except through the work of the Spirit. Only the Holy Spirit searches the depths of divinity, and He alone can transmit to the elect the fruit of His eternal contemplation (1 Cor. 2:10-11). The σοφία of the apostle surpasses the θεωρία of the Greek sages in the same degree that the Spirit of God surpasses the spirit of man. And in the Spirit, the human intelligence is dilated until it can encompass all the dimensions of the divine designs.

Thus, seeing God in Himself and the universe in God, the apostle will bear within him the ideal image of a world at once degraded and unceasingly redeemed. Instead of being content to juxtapose an unreal religion and an inhuman earth, he will render Christian and spiritual a burdened, fallen world. Thanks to his vision of faith, the drama of life may be unraveled; the moving spectacle of a regenerated world will lead him to restore effectively in Christ the realities of this earth.

It is pointless to prolong these considerations; their implications are clear and their necessity overwhelming.

---

[5] Fr. de Finance, "La Σοφία chez saint Paul," in *Rech. de sc. rel.*, 1935, pp. 404-405.

PART TWO

THE FORMULAS OF THE
ROMAN PONTIFICAL

CHAPTER THREE

THE CLERICAL STATE
AND MINOR ORDERS

When the bishops of the early ages laid hands on the young men who presented themselves before them for the service of the Church, they took advantage of the liturgical ceremonies to remind them solemnly of the significance of their actions, the seriousness of ecclesiastical responsibilities, the virtues which should flourish in the souls of candidates for Orders. Thus, the supernatural wisdom expressed in the New Testament and in patristic literature, or simply lived in the very history of the Church, penetrated the Temple and attained the "very definite" rites of which Ignatius speaks. From the free and spontaneous form which they undoubtedly enjoyed in the beginnings of the Church, the episcopal admonitions moved into a more fixed and soon stereotyped pattern; certain among them prevailed because of their doctrinal richness or their poetry. The *Sacramentaria* assured their expansion and finally, the "most beautiful liturgical book of the Church," the Roman Pontifical, was born, a monument of wisdom and

Roman solidity which Gallic grace adorned with numerous embellishments.

What does the Roman Pontifical think of the diocesan
clergy? Does the text of the consecrating formulas for
Sacred Orders truly describe the whole range of sacerdotal activity? Will we find in these formulas a reference
to the illuminating function of him who represents Christ
the teacher? Will we find an indication of the role of the
good shepherd which priests must play in this world?
Fortunately, the Roman Pontifical was not composed
out of whole cloth by a theoretician concerned with
making the ordination rites signify only the power of
Orders. Arising from the concrete life of the Church,
an expression of her history and of her initial steps,
the Roman Pontifical reproduces the image of the
apostle as the works of the sacred authors and the
Fathers presented him to us. This fact is full of significance and promise for those who wish to profit from it;
along with the Scriptures, the Pontifical is the authentic
mirror of the apostolate as the Church desires and understands it.

These episcopal admonitions cover with their religious symbolism each of the stages which lead the young
man to the foot of the altar; on eight occasions, from
his entrance into the clerical state up to the priesthood,
the candidate for the priesthood kneels before the pastor
of his diocese to hear his grave and solemn warnings.
It would have been possible to group in categories the
episcopal admonitions concerning the sacerdotal life of
glorification, the ministry of the sacraments and of the
Eucharist, the task of the instruction and the direction
of the Christian people. But this artificial arrangement
has little to commend it. On the other hand, priest-
readers will rediscover, no doubt with emotion, the
words which they once meditated before hearing them
from their bishop, sacramental words whose power is
never extinguished and whose grace can be revived in
each man's soul. It is therefore better to allow some
disorder to reign in the exposition and to retrace piously
the spiritual itinerary suggested by the Roman Pontifical.

Taken in their temporal order, these stages will present a rather disparate aspect; but all it will take to reduce them to unity is to make them pass through the prism of the priesthood; for the priest forever remains truly deacon, subdeacon, holder of minor orders, and cleric of the Holy Church.

1. THE CLERICAL STATE

DE FORO ECCLESIAE

The priest is first of all a *cleric*: κλῆρος, sors; he has chosen the Lord as his "portion," for a spiritual inheritance: "The Lord is the portion of my inheritance and of my cup; thou art he who restoreth the inheritance to me." This official choice, maturely reflected on, solemnly authenticated by the Church, is a decisive step; following it the bishop may proceed to the various ordinations.

The clerical state is not a sacred order: yet it profoundly transforms the state of life of the "pious layman." He now enters into the domain of the Church and takes part in the privileges of clerics: "You should take note that today you have become part of the Church's forum and have been granted the clerical privileges." The clerical state, it has been well said, is "neither a sacrament, nor an order; it is only the official introduction into the great social body of those consecrated to God, the passing from the lay state, from the λαός, to the ecclesiastical state. To receive the tonsure is to be incorporated into the clergy."[1] A clean break with the world, its views, its tastes, its motives for action, its initiatives; an entrance into the body of those consecrated to God for the praise of the Father and the redemption of men.

In order to mark well the separation which henceforth will characterize the spirit and actions of the clerics, the Church has them set aside the "less honorable" livery which they wore then: "They lay aside the

---

[1] R. Dubosq, *Les étapes du sacerdoce*, p. 23.

ignominy of the secular garb." She detaches them from
the real servitude which the lay state always implies
and of which the secular garb was but the symbol:
"Cleanse these thy servants from all servitude of secular
garb." Then she imposes on them a new and holy livery,
symbol of their religious gift: "That thy servants who
have now put on the garment, may be found worthy also
to put on thee."

The cassock, the ancient Roman toga, abandoned by
laymen in the sixth century for the shortened garb of
the barbarians, became the uniform of the clergy. Uniform, because the clergy was enrolled in the sacred
militia of those who, according to the Pauline expression, offer to the Lord their arms and their hearts,
that He may make of them living weapons in the combat
waged against the powers of darkness. The uniform
of those who struggle under the banner of a victorious
leader from whom they expect, not pay, but the free
gift of life (Rom. 6).

But the cassock, like every uniform, has a symbolic
value ("that thy servants who now have put on thy
garment, may be found worthy also to put on thee").
The outer garment signifies inner renewal. As a symbol
it is a kind of echo of Christian justification as it is
presented to us in the Sacred Books: *induere Christum*,
to put on Christ. And in fact, during the whole ceremony,
baptismal themes are repeated time and again by the
bishop, while the *schola* repeats the same themes. It is
hardly surprising, then, that some have seen in the
ceremony of entering the clerical state, a kind of renewal of Baptism.

SIGNS OF INCORPORATION

To complete the symbolism of the ceremonies, the bishop
cuts from each candidate's head five locks of hair in
the form of a cross, so that all clerics might bear visibly
before the world the image of the crown of the divine
Crucified: "We cause them to wear the likeness of your
crown on their heads."

This "tonsure" is not the total tonsure of monks and penitents, but that of the clerics, the "tonsure of St. Peter." It symbolizes the adoption of the "pious layman" by the Church. The latter, "finding in civilian life a rite of adoption, did not deem it necessary to seek another; she accepted and sanctified it by introducing it into her institutions. The tonsure ceremony was then, originally and essentially, the symbol of the contract by which the tonsured person committed himself to live in the service of the Church. Tonsure ennobled him by causing him to pass from the common race to the sacerdotal one; it delivered him from civil jurisdiction and placed him under the power and protection of the Church whose livery he wore."[2]

It is not surprising, therefore, to hear the bishop state, in the formula of acceptance and incorporation: "Dominus pars haereditatis meae et calicis mei." And the *schola* during this time sings the entire psalm from which the bishop's words have been taken: Psalm 15, the hymn par excellence of consecration to God:

> Keep me, O God, for in you I take refuge;
> I say to the Lord, "My Lord are you.
> Apart from you I have no good."
>
> . . . .
>
> O Lord, my allotted portion and my cup,
> you it is who hold fast my lot.
> For me the measuring lines have fallen on pleasant sites;
> fair to me indeed is my inheritance.

Finally, the bishop places the surplice on the candidate, the shortened alb with flowing sleeves, intended to be worn in cold climates on top of furred garments: the "superpelliceum." The surplice is the symbol of the immaculate whiteness and purity of those who are henceforth, step by step, to approach the eucharistic mysteries and the fire of divine love. It is the sign of the mercy which comes down from God and covers the race of those

[2] R. Dubosq, *Les étapes du sacerdoce*, pp. 23-24.

who seek the Lord: "They will receive a blessing from
the Lord and mercy from God their savior," says the
bishop as he puts on the surplice, "for this is the generation of those who seek the Lord."

During this time, the *schola* intones Psalm 23, the
"Lord's" hymn, for in it the Psalmist sings the glory
of the King entering the temple through the ancient
gates. And who will be able to accompany him, to
climb with him the path which leads to the holy mountain
and to stand in the holy places?

> He whose hands are sinless, whose heart is clean,
>   who desires not what is vain,
>   nor swears deceitfully to his neighbor.
> He shall receive a blessing from the Lord.

If one were to seek in the Pontifical the motive which
inspires these young laymen to separate themselves
from the life which they have lead up to that moment,
in order to put on a livery which does not recommend
itself to the uses and interests of this world, it would
reply, like the Apostles, like the saints of any age,
"the love of Christ." This is the explanation of their
action and the meaning of their gift: "They hurry for
his love."

"STRIVE TO PLEASE GOD"

All ecclesiastical rituals of this ceremony, therefore,
signify clearly the desires of the hierarchy: before going on, the young aspirant to the priesthood is made
aware of the spirit which must animate his apostolate:
separation from worldly interests, a consecration to
the Lord and to His work — in short, acceptance of a
way of life similar to that which the Incarnate Word
chose, a redemptive "state of life."

The bishop assumes that the candidates to the priesthood nourish such aspirations. Before concluding his
final admonition, he invites them to try to please God
by their exterior dignity, by their conduct and good
works: "Strive to please God." This is indeed the tenor

of all ecclesiastical documents addressed to clerics. We are familiar with Canon 124: "Clerics should lead a holier outer and inner life than the laity, and provide a better example in virtue and good works." Here is a tone, a firmness and a good sense similar to those of the apostolic Fathers. The *Decretum de reformatione* of the Council of Trent could also be quoted:

"There is nothing which provides better instruction for others unto piety and worship of God than the life and example of those who have dedicated themselves to the divine ministry. For when they, removed from the things of the world, look upon a higher place, the rest cast their eyes on them, as in a mirror, and learn from them what they should imitate; wherefore, it behooves clerics, called unto the Lord's portion, so to order their lives and all their ways as to display only what is grave, moderate and full of religion in dress, in manner, in conduct, in speech and all other things; let them avoid even slight sins, which in them would be very grave; that their actions might bring the veneration of all."

2. THE MINOR ORDERS

From stage to stage, the aspirant to the priesthood is reminded of the various functions which he will later carry out and of the obligations which he will have to meet. Each sacred order unveils for him an aspect of the life he will soon have to lead, a task which will fall to him, virtues which he will have to possess, qualities he will have to maintain. Despite their real interest and importance, the minor orders today certainly do not enjoy an exaggerated esteem: no seminarian, indeed, expects to remain a porter or even an acolyte all his life, nor does anyone contemplate that he will still be only an exorcist at the age of fifty. Since the function represented by the order no longer exists, the ordination for it necessarily suffers from a certain lack of concern.

Still, the spirit of these orders remains the sacerdotal one: the care of the Church must concern every pastor worthy of the name; the service of the altar must be given all the attention appropriate to eucharistic worship; the priestly life is a struggle waged with perseverance against the Evil Spirit in order to dislodge him from matter and remove from him all control over men. In this sense, the minor orders retain at all times their meaning and contemporary quality.

PORTERS

The episcopal admonition addressed to those about to be ordained to the *Ostiariate* has lost none of its value: "See to it that nothing in the Church deteriorates through your negligence, open the house of God to the faithful at the hours set, and keep it always closed to the unbelievers." These "guardians of the Church," *janitores ecclesiae,* faithful watchmen by day and by night, "diebus et noctibus," who call the people at the hours set to invoke the name of the Lord, have a solemn religious task to fulfill. This task, moreover, is the symbol of a more general and more spiritual work imposed this time on the professor-priest as well as on the parish priest: it consists in opening up the living and invisible temple of souls in order to permit Christian truth to penetrate, and also to close it when the devil threatens to introduce into it the seeds of corruption and error: "Strive also that, just as you open and close the visible Church with material keys, you may so close to the devil and open to God the invisible house of God, namely, the hearts of the faithful, by your words and example, that they may retain in their hearts the divine words which they have heard, and complement them with deeds."

The "porter" must also sound the joyous bell of baptisms and marriages, the somber tolling for the deceased, so that the material sound carried by the air quickly changes into a spiritual echo; this echo, reaching the souls of the parishioners, will communicate to them their pastor's concern for religion, for the practice of the sacraments, spiritual joy, a reminder of the last things.

These sacred functions presuppose certain qualities, both natural and supernatural, both human and sacerdotal. The "porter" cannot be negligent, he must be faithful and punctual "in the house of God." The care of all ecclesiastical furniture is entrusted to him. And these few qualities imply many others, such as neatness, competence even in the appreciation of the values of the Church's furnishings, the courage to put in order everything that pertains to worship, the art of being a perfect sacristan. It is all this which the bishop sums up with one word in pronouncing the solemn words which constitute a cleric in this degree: "So act as if you were going to account to God for those things which are enclosed with these keys."

LECTORS

If we wished to translate into modern terms the word "lector," writes H. Martin,[3] "we would have to say that he is like a catechist, but an official catechist, who has both power and grace to teach in the name of the hierarchy of which he is already a member. Though, according to the *Summa Theologica,* Suppl., q. 37, he has been entrusted especially with the first rudiments of the faith, and more precisely, the reading of the Old Testament, yet one can see what a great responsibility has been given to him, for he has no other model, in truth, than our Lord Himself explaining in the synagogue at Nazareth, from the scroll of Isaias, the words which pertained to Him."

The lessons which can be learned from the prayers of ordination to the lectorate are very practical, and any priest can find in them ample matter for reflection. Of course, priests today no longer have to read a text which will later be commented on by a preacher, or sing frequently the lessons of the Divine Office, or bless bread and new fruits. But they do explain and sing, frequently, in other circumstances, the word of God; they are the "communicators of the word of God." The "truth of the divine lessons" must be interpreted by them before the people of God. The function of

---

[3] *La Paternité spirituelle du prêtre,* Paris, 1930, p. 50.

"magisterium" which the priest will receive in full with ordination and jurisdiction could hardly be introduced more solemnly than by this conferring of the lectorate.

The lectorate presupposes and implies many qualities and talents; and the Church, once again, reminds the future lector of the natural gifts and supernatural virtues which the exercising of his function demands.

Apply yourself, therefore, she says to him, "to reading the word of God . . . in a distinct and clear manner," *distincte et aperte,* "so that the faithful may be instructed and edified, and so that the truth may never be altered by your fault to the detriment of the hearers." Here one clearly sees the criterion which regulates the demands of the Church: all qualities useful and necessary for carrying out the apostolate are required, and all these qualities are apostolic. The episcopal admonitions give peremptory proof of this fact.

To communicate divine truth fruitfully by reading the Gospels, pastoral letters, catechetical texts, extracts from spiritual authors, resumés of Christian doctrine, etc., calls for more than oratorical gifts. The faithful can expect from him who sets forth the doctrine of life, warm words from a priestly heart, carrying a profound conviction, a burning faith, and supported by a life which does not contradict the values which are being preached. Desirous of effective preaching, the Church reminds her lectors of its conditions, in terms applicable to priests as well:

"That which your lips announce, believe it in your heart and practice it; thus you will be able to instruct your hearers both by word and by example. When therefore you read in an elevated place in the church, position yourself so as to be seen and heard by all, showing by this raised position of the body that you must live in a high degree of virtue, in order to be for all those who see and hear you, the example and model of a heavenly life." Thus, the lectors will carry out their function as the bishop desires, *utiliter.* By their lives as well as their words they will be a lesson: "The life of the clergy is the book of the laity." This is, in fact, the meaning which the bishop gives to the conferring of the order: "Accept," he says, "and be ye the communicators of the word of God who will share, if you have faithfully and usefully carried out your office, with those who ministered well to the word of God from the beginning." Thus we have found our way back to the apostles of the early ages of the Church, to the evangelists and preachers who planted the Church of God and made her fruitful with their blood; it is their action which the lector must today continue, in the spirit which was theirs.

A candidate for the priesthood can only arrive at this ideal — and the priest can only maintain himself at this level — if he consents fully to a life of study and of religious reflection. The bishop makes this point in the final prayer of ordination: " . . . deign to bless these servants unto the office of lectors, that they may be instructed by the assiduity of their lessons . . ." We could prolong the considerations that can be made on this theme and the conclusions to be drawn therefrom for the priestly life. It will no doubt be enough to have recalled here to priests those words which, as Péguy would say, "temporally and carnally" they heard from their bishop's lips.

Sacred reading is, above all, the study of the Bible, which remains the great religious book of mankind despite the neglect of it by many. Also to be read are works which contain the most beautiful examples of the wisdom of the world, such as the personal writings of the great spiritual figures of Christianity and of the non-Christian religions; and works which deal in a realistic manner with basic theological questions, such as the life of God and grace in man, as well as the salvation of mankind — in short, everything which is necessary "that they may faithfully and usefully carry out their office."

By way of a postscript, a phrase from the instruction preparatory to ordination can be added: "and to sing the lessons." The lector must be able to chant his readings. No one requires the prodigious trills of a *Panis Angelicus!* But it is desirable that he not offend the ears of those who are attending the funeral of a relative or a friend with a voice and a chanting which are unworthy of the religious service being celebrated.

EXORCISTS

In his Apocalypse, John reveals to us the profound explanation of the history of the Church: the struggle of Christ and His followers against Satan and his supporters. Above and beyond the visible persecutions and tribulations which affect the Church militant and afflict her, there rages a furious and silent conflict in the world of the spirit. Initiated into this invisible mystery, the priest takes part in the battle and fights in the front line. Bearer of the seeds of divine life, he seeks out and annihilates the germs of corruption. At all times the role of the *exorcist* is truly his.

Today, in fact, only priests (or rather certain priests) are authorized to pronounce the liberating words over the possessed. But does not the task of chasing the Devil from souls pertain to all those who have received the priesthood? What, then, do the numerous prayers and exorcisms of the baptismal rites mean otherwise? What is the priest doing when, in the confessional, he absolves a penitent who has let himself be seriously carried away by the Prince of Darkness? To what end are his encouragements and his exhortations? Finally, how explain his entire life of struggle for the reign of substantial Truth? "Spiritual leaders capable of chasing from the bodies of the possessed demons with their malice in all its forms," priests, certainly are this by virtue of their ordination itself, even though the exercise of this power is reserved to certain ones among them. But all are "spiritual physicians experienced in the art of healing men by the power from on high," and they must be such throughout their entire lives.

The priest must "command" the satanic legions. Liturgical texts in this regard are forceful and numerous.

"Learn to command," says the bishop, and repeats: "You shall command the demons." The exorcist is not to argue with the Prince of this World: he commands him, at the very least, "by the grace of the Holy Spirit."

This is because in point of fact, the Devil has acquired by his own astuteness and through human weakness, a certain empire over men, and particularly over their bodies, over the flesh and the world. This is why the usage of holy water and the care of the baptismal water, both purifying waters, also pertain to the exorcist. Since the reign of Satan extends even to matter, the Church, in the name of Christ, had to sanctify matter and protect it against Satan's empire. Whence the priestly blessings which affect the order of things and inanimate beings. Whence also the use of holy water, which brings even into the houses of Christians the protective gesture of the minister of the Church and thus removes Satan from those locations. Perhaps the exorcist should have a better understanding of the profound theology of the sacramentals and live more fully the dogma of the universal kingship of our Lord Jesus Christ. These themes should pass through his mind at the moment he hears the bishop say solemnly to him: "and to pour water in the ministry."

To be sincere and loyal with himself, the priest will also attack the Devil in himself, whenever the latter wants to trouble his spirit or disturb his body. "In chasing the devil from your brethren," remarks the bishop, "take care to reject from your spirit and from your flesh all stain and all iniquity, so as not to become yourselves the slaves of him from whom you deliver others. Learn through your charge to command your passions so that the enemy might find nothing in your conduct to claim as his own. For you will successfully command the devil only when you yourselves have foiled his manifold wickedness." The asceticism of the diocesan priest is directly apostolic because it places us in a position to carry out our functions perfectly, or more perfectly. This function of exorcism becomes for us a special requirement for strengthening the asceticism of perfection, of spiritual progress. Here, as in many other situations, the function calls for moral perfection, and this moral perfection itself renders the function more perfect. This will not be forgotten when, in subsequent chapters, we see that the apostolic spirit is an integral part, and not merely a condition, of the Christian apostolate.

ACOLYTES

The lector, as the bishop explained to the ordinand, must be a living book ever open before the eyes of men; the acolyte must be a living light forever shining in the darkness of the world and of sin. The final minor order is ancient, as its Greek etymology indicates: "acolyte," that is, companion, follower; in the early days he was indeed constantly at the service of the higher clergy to help them in their sacred and apostolic functions. Today these tasks are entrusted to laymen, not only to adults or to well-trained young men, but even to small children.

The acolyte, first of all, "bears the torch" so that the temple of the Lord might always be well lit: "you should know how to be of service in lighting the lamps of the church." Taken in its most material sense, this role is still that of the priest today. Formerly, the Roman church, sober and simple as always, was content to add to the conferring of this order the second final prayer: "Lord, who didst ask Moses and Aaron to maintain lights in the Tabernacle of the Ancient Law, vouchsafe to bless thy servants that they might be worthy acolytes in thy Church." Such sobriety could hardly suffice for Gallic customs, and a long symbolism began to be developed.

The material light is the "obvious symbol of the spiritual light" which the acolyte must represent throughout his life. To present the light is to present the splendor of the virtuous life, to present Christ Himself, the true Light which came into this world. Regarding this symbolism, the present texts of the ordination are

inexhaustible, after the fashion of the ancient chains
of scripture or patristic texts:

"For you shall not be able to please God if, while
bearing the light to God in your hands, you serve the
works of darkness and therefore give to others an example of perfidy. But as the Truth has said: Let your
light shine before men that they may see your good
works and glorify your father who is in heaven. And
as the apostle Paul says: In the midst of a wicked and
perverse nation, shine forth like lamps in the world,
holding fast to the word of life. Therefore let your
reins be girt and have lamps burning in your hands.
Be ye as children of the light. Therefore cast aside the
works of the darkness and put on the armor of light.
Formerly you were darkness, now, however, light in the
Lord; walk as the children of the light."

In short, says the bishop after the conferring of
the order: "As often as they bear the visible light in
their hands, may they also show forth spiritual light in
their lives." References to this spiritual light are so
numerous that one cannot fail to apply them seriously
to himself. The priest, even more than the acolyte, must
illuminate the Church of God and the faithful by the
splendor of his life.

The acolyte is also called upon to unite himself in a
more direct manner with the eucharistic sacrifice; he
takes a first step toward the altar itself and the power of
Orders. Just as formerly he was entrusted with the
distribution of the *eulogia* — the blessed bread which
the prelates gave one another as a sign of union and
brotherhood — just as he was on occasion entrusted with
the sacred species intended for the absent or sick; now
he is asked to present to the priest the water and the
wine necessary for the sacrifice of the Mass: "to furnish
wine and water for the Eucharist."

But, adds the Pontifical, the acolytes must apply
themselves to carrying out this religious work with
dignity, "strive therefore to fulfill worthily the office
received." Also, the bishop asks them to purify themselves, to be virtuous and concerned with making them-

selves more perfect: "Be ye therefore solicitous in all
justice, goodness and truth so that you may enlighten
yourselves, others and the Church of God. For you will
worthily offer wine and water in sacrifice to God at
such time as you yourselves are offered as a sacrifice to
God through a chaste life and good works."

One cannot avoid thinking at this point of the ceremonies of priestly ordination and of these very striking
words: "Recognize what you are doing, imitate what
you are handling," words which have moved more than
one ordinand. In conferring the order of acolyte, the
Roman Pontifical calls to mind the profound perfection
required by the sacred function of the priesthood. The
priest is bound to take seriously the work of his own
perfection, because he is charged with renewing here
below the eucharistic sacrifice. The self-sacrifice which
Christian asceticism implies is demanded of him on a
special basis: because he sacrifices the eucharistic Christ.
A life of oblation, *oblati fueritis,* is expressly required of
him, because he is in the service of the oblation par
excellence, that of the Word Incarnate. The words of
the Pontifical: "vos ipsi Deo sacrificium per castam
vitam et bona opera oblati fueritis" are among the
strongest and clearest in reminding the priest that the
celebration of the Mass calls him to a higher perfection.
Also, more than the other minor ordinations, this one
affirms that the reception of Orders establishes the
candidate for the priesthood in an ever greater likeness
to our Lord Jesus Christ. In the final orations, the bishop
addresses himself to God the Father on behalf of the
young ordained and prays in these words: "Holy Lord,
Father Almighty, who, through Jesus Christ, thy Son
and Our Lord, as well as through His Apostles, hast
spread forth in this world the splendor of Thy Light;
and who, to abolish the ancient decree of death issued
against us, hast willed that He be nailed to the glorious
standard of His Cross and bathed in the blood and water
which flowed from His sacred side for the salvation of
the human race. . . ." So, too, in the final oration:
"Almighty and eternal God, source of light and fount

of goodness who, through Jesus Christ Thy Son, the
true Light, hast illuminated the world and hast redeemed
it by the mystery of His Passion. . . . " The reference
to Christ the Light and Christ the Redeemer is clear.
There is even a reference to our similarity with the
Apostles — "and through His Apostles" — which, despite its discreetness and its brevity, is full of significance for us.

Henceforth, the successive stages must be even more
binding, more unifying; the major orders, with all their
dignity dominate the simple functions of the minor ones,
and their union with the priesthood is increasingly
marked.

CHAPTER FOUR

THE SUBDIACONATE

The subdiaconate makes an indelible impression on the future priest. Before, it was the renunciation of the world in a sort of youthful and ardent enthusiasm, crowned by the distant vision of a first solemn Mass and a "magnificent" apostolate, that attracted; now it is a more mature and more definitive advance, more aware of the ordinary quality of clerical life, of him who renounces in particular all the legitimate and sacred joys of emotional and family life, in order to serve the Church forever, "to be forever enrolled in the ministry of the Church."

BEFORE THE COMMITMENT

Even before ordination, the future subdeacons have presented themselves before the bishop's delegate. Since they plan henceforward to work in the service of the diocese, it is well for the diocese to concern itself with their means of subsistence. Formerly, clerics were ordained in the "name" of a particular church which therefore was responsible for guaranteeing her own priest's needs, so that he would have to concern himself only with the spiritual interests of his parishioners. Today, clerics are generally ordained in "the name of the diocese" (c. 981), the latter committing itself to them for the future. Thus we see that, over and above the considerations of a temporal nature which it involves, this ordination testifies to the definitive entry of the cleric into the diocesan family, into the body of those who consecrate themselves under the direction of the bishop to work in a specific area. This is the contract between the master of the vineyard and his workers, between the heads of the Church militant and her soldiers.

On the day set for ordination, the candidates approach the bishop dressed in amices and albs and carrying the maniple and the folded tunicle on their left arms. The bishop immediately addresses them with a gravity heretofore unmatched, which, it seems, is a good reflection of the spirit of the most ancient pontifical admonitions. For already in the Roman rite the future subdeacon was asked to swear that he had not committed any of the four great sins against chastity: sodomy, bestiality, violation of virgins and adultery.

"Dearly beloved sons," says the bishop, "you who are about to be advanced to the order of subdeacon, give this careful consideration." The fact of the matter is that the sacred order which they request with all their youthful desires is a burden, at times very heavy — "today you seek a further burden." The subdiaconate involves the renunciation of the freedom enjoyed by those who remain in the world; it regulates their actions, their efforts, their initiatives and their occupations: "Until now you are free and it is permissible for you, at your discretion, to go on to worldly desires."

But, continues the bishop, if you take this step, your decision to persevere in the clerical state and the apostolate assumes a final character. It commits you for the entire duration of this one life which Providence has granted you; its effects will be felt at every moment until your death.

And in what does this step consist? "To serve God

... forever, to observe chaste celibacy, to be dedicated forever in the service of the Church." Then: "while there is time, reflect, and if you wish to persevere in your holy purpose, come forward in the name of the Lord."

"Come forward!" For five years in the seminary, these young men have been able to reflect calmly on the decisiveness of ecclesiastical celibacy and to measure their own spiritual forces. For five years, they have been able to test their renunciation of the legitimate joys of love and of those which accompany married life. At this moment, all the candidates, standing before the bishop, step together toward the altar. A simple step like any other, but one which synthetizes all the giving implicit in perpetual celibacy. Certainly this decision was already included in the act of entering the seminary, and every young man who considers the priesthood knows very well that he is renouncing marriage. But at this time it assumes a sacred character and unforgettable solemnity, on this day when father and mother, brothers and sisters, relatives and friends, contemplate from afar "their" subdeacon with an emotion which is all the more profound the more advanced they are in years and the more they know of life.

In order to inaugurate this life of celibacy under the most favorable auspices, the ordinandi soon prostrate themselves on the floor of the sanctuary in a gesture of powerless weakness and suppliant misery, while the lengthy invocations of the Litany of the Saints go on, imploring mercy: *miserere nobis!* After having beseeched the Holy Trinity itself, the *schola* calls upon all the heavenly forces: the Virgin and the angels, the patriarchs and the prophets, the Apostles and the Evangelists, the martyrs and the confessors, the doctors and the priests, the monks and the virgins, until the bishop himself, alone, turning toward the ordinandi, blesses them three times: "That you may vouchsafe to bless, sanctify, and consecrate these chosen ones." Every priest recalls with deep emotion these moments of the prostration, remembering with a tender joy the sight of his colleagues stretched out in the innocent whiteness of their albs, on the carpets of the sanctuary.

1. THE CELIBATE STATE

We cannot proceed in the explanation of the ceremonies of the subdiaconate without pausing on the significance of the "step" which the ordinandi have just taken.

In the Latin Church the priestly vocation and celibacy have been united and even intimately linked for centuries, to the point that the faithful are just as scandalized by a breach of celibacy as they are by unfaithfulness in the performance of the burdensome priestly duties. Actually, these are distinct realities, and perhaps in the future the existence of deacons not held to the law of celibacy will distinguish the domains more clearly. However, we have not yet come to that, and we can describe the scope of this step according to the present usages of the Church. First of all, we shall set forth that which appears most decisively in this gesture of the subdeacon, then we shall move on to the profound theological significance of the celibate state, which must retain its primordial value in the mind of the subdeacon.

THE RENUNCIATIONS

The "step," first of all, is a commitment to perpetual continence, that is, absolute abstention from every legitimate satisfaction which is linked with the work of human generation. But it is much more than that, and without wanting to dramatize the clerical life, one cannot lose sight of the fact that the detachment required by celibacy far exceeds the restrictive obligations of continence. This step in fact, signifies that the priest must live alone, not in family society like the majority of men and according to the laws inscribed in the utmost depths of the human instinct. To live "alone" presupposes a host of renunciations which affect the priest at all stages of life and at every moment of his existence.

Through celibacy, the young candidate renounces all the sentimental and delightful bonds that can unite the

young man and the young woman in the springtime
of their existence. The seminarian, because he has eyes
and ears, because he himself knows the tendencies of
his heart, because he often is in the company of friends
or brothers who have a fiancée, is well able to measure
the oblation he is making of so many beautiful and noble
values: love itself, tenderness, the signs and testimonials
of friendship and love, sympathy and support, confi-
dences and common concerns; in short, all the bonds
which weave between two young idealistic Christians —
and seminarians would surely be of that number — the
inexpressible web of the life of love.

Soon, however, it is no longer a question of affection
but of a stronger, more powerful love, that which pushes
a man into uniting himself with a woman. Celibacy demands of the young priest that he renounce this love,
with its absolute submission to the psychological and
physical order. It implies a renunciation of marital society, with all its annoyances, certainly, but with all the
tenderness, the little attentions, the grace and freshness,
the devotion and the care, love and understanding, which
a man can find with his wife after the pain and labor
of each day. Has one ever measured all that marital society involves in terms of life together, of expressions of
love, of "life in common"?

And there is more. At a later stage, celibacy imposes on every priest the sorrows of a physical fatherhood without issue. It is also inscribed in the heart of
man that someday he will be a father and will have to
carry out for his children the work of upbringing and
of direction. Children, "his" children! Are they not frequently a great uniting force in the home, a reason for
working, a source of serene relaxation after work, a
prop in the difficulties and annoyances inherent in every
life, an occasion of pride and of joy as they grow up?
But the priest voluntarily renounces establishing a family society: he will never have "his" home, will never be
able to speak of "his" children or of "his" family, that
is, the one he has created. As beautiful and sublime as
the spiritual paternity he assumes may be, it cannot re-

place the sense of another paternity which is called for by nature and by the heart of flesh.

That is not all. Celibacy still affects the aged priest and signifies for him that he must spend his last years without the warmth of a home. A cold solitude: this is the sacrifice imposed by celibacy on the priest who is advanced in years. He has no wife whose comings and goings put a little movement in a life that is becoming inert, whose words and conversation fill an atmosphere otherwise at times quite empty. He has no grandchildren who enable him to use his old man's wisdom and to rediscover occasionally the innocence of childhood. He remains with his physical solitude, his isolation and the miseries which age brings with it.

The things renounced for celibacy are not mere temporary conditions: the affection between young people binds them together continuously; marital life goes on at every moment, and union by way of memory compensates for the inevitable separations which occur; the sense of paternity is with the adult in all his free moments, and his work itself is performed thinking "of the children." The cold physical isolation of one's final years is also permanent. In short, it can be said that the renunciations of celibacy affect the whole life of the priest to the point that they create for him a veritable new "state of life," very different from that of the laity. Laymen are well aware of this, they fully realize it. Celibacy also causes respect for the priest; it surrounds him with a certain aura of purity which lay people avoid tarnishing. But it is also accompanied by some very characteristic faults — pettiness, hardness, selfishness, moodiness, self-importance — which should be avoided at all costs.

The bishop knows, too, by experience, the experience he has of the life of his clergy, that the celibate life represents more than a liturgical "step." He also wants the subdeacon to be rooted in all forms of natural and supernatural temperance. His admonitions on this subject have such realism about them that they sometimes leave one wondering, and it is better to quote them from the original text: "If you have been up to now sleepy, be ye now wakeful. If you have been up to now drunken, be ye now sober. If you have been up to now impure, be ye now chaste." These remarks, of course, are easier to understand if we recall that the Pontifical existed before the institution of seminaries, and that candidates presented themselves to the bishop to receive orders on fairly short notice.

FOR THE KINGDOM OF HEAVEN

But we must extend the thought of the Church in this admonition and see in it her desire to find in subdeacons all the virtues which remove them from things that are too material, too close to carnal realities. The Church would like priests to detach themselves from everything that can weigh them down spiritually, from all that chains their hearts to worldly values instead of enabling them to show toward those values a "sympathy which is radically independent." She would like them to be interested in all that is spiritual, intellectual, noble and beautiful, pure and elevated, "those things which are from above." For everything that makes one independent of matter creates in the soul a climate very much in harmony with the spirituality of the celibate state.

How erroneous is the judgment of those who are unable to appreciate the value of celibacy, like those excellent lay people who silently mourn for the young people who "take orders" and who try, with very unenlightened benevolence, to turn them aside from their plans. Celibacy certainly deprives us of certain true human values; but so does marriage, and to an even greater degree, since the Gospels teach us that whoever does not marry "does a better thing."

Through celibacy the priest enjoys that freedom of spirit, heart and body which is a very real condition of a fruitful apostolate. He reserves his intellect for the things of God, for the work of the Lord, for the concerns of the Church. He consecrates his imagination to the manifold tasks which are involved in the sacred ministry. He opens his heart to the daring impulses of Him who is Charity. He uses his physical forces to work for the extension of God's kingdom. Celibacy more easily enables the priest to be completely at the service of the interests of the Church and souls. Without a home or the cares which affect every father of a family, the priest can more readily be all things to all men, can live a little above the laws of daily prudence and go beyond the practical wisdom which must regulate the life of a man with family responsibilities. Tacitly, the Church thus signifies to us her very deep desire concerning the priestly mode of life.

Through celibacy the priest also attains the equilibrium of a man who joins to a high degree of self-mastery the authentic tenderness of the good shepherd. And this happy mixture in itself attracts the weak, comforts the hesitant, fascinates the strong, and creates around the person of the priest that climate of cordial attachment and respectful veneration which is so propitious for the work of spiritual mediation.

Through celibacy the priest disengages himself from the too-material attachments which married life involves, in order to better conduct the activities of religion to which he is dedicated by profession. Every married layman will readily understand that the Church prefers that her priests, because they daily celebrate and administer the sacraments, be established in the celibate state: "Be ye such that ye may serve worthily the divine sacrifice and the Church of God, that is, the Body of Christ . . . and *therefore,* if up to now. . . ." The priest must be entirely consecrated to divine worship. Natural law itself seems to require that one "reserve," that one "set apart" everything which is necessary for worship: temples, chalices, priestly vestments. The same law affects the persons who place themselves in the service of the Church and her sacrifice: they are separated from all that is profane and, according to the rather unusual expression of a seminary professor, "expropriated for the sake of public utility." Here the

Church joins in the advice of the Apostle: "He who is unmarried is concerned about the things of the Lord, how he may please God. Whereas he who is married is concerned about the things of the world, how he may please his wife; and he is divided. And the unmarried woman, and the virgin, thinks about the things of the Lord, that she may be holy in body and in spirit" (1 Cor. 7:32-34). The Church, at least the Church of the Latin rite, prefers that her priests not be "divided" between two loves.

AT THE LEVEL OF THE COUNSELS

"That they may not be divided": this is the best way to determine the spirit of ecclesiastical celibacy. By means of the precept of continence and celibacy, the Church elevates her future priests to the level of the evangelical counsels, to the threshold of the Holy of Holies, where the Spirit speaks a language which only those who are able to understand, understand.[1]

Christianity, in fact, as it was set forth by Christ in the Gospels, distinguishes the way of the Commandments from that of the Counsels. The first permits all men to attain to a perfect Christian life and the *total* love of sanctity, but by *including* the means which the believing reason calls "normal": family life, disposal of oneself, the use of external goods, a judicious wisdom compounded of prudence and balance. The second path is destined for some — "he who can understand, let him understand," the Gospels say — who wish to live a Christianity of sanctity and total love but without certain authentic worldly values. This is the path followed, for example, by those who practice perpetual chastity or celibacy; it is of these that St. Paul, speaking of authority, writes that "they do the better thing." In the presence of mere reason, even in a Christian, this appreciation of celibacy remains necessarily mysterious and strange. Hence our minds, always in quest of intrinsic proofs, feel a certain malaise, a lack of assurance,

[1] Cf. *Santidad cristiana*, Salamanca, 1960, pp. 356-360.

from the uncertainty and the painful impression of unbalance which such states of soul involve. In wanting celibacy for her priest, the Church wants for him an act suffused by the Spirit. The Lord had said, "He who understands, understands," and the Church affirms that all her ministers have "understood" the Master: "Come forward!"

2. THE RITES OF ORDINATION

THE SACRED FUNCTION

Each order adds something to the apostolic ideal of the priest and through the power of Orders, brings the candidate closer to the altar and the eucharistic sacrifice. The subdeacon, explains the bishop, must assist the deacon, present the paten, the chalice, and the water for the sacrifice; he must wash the palls, and the corporals. Attentive to her mission and to the life of her ministers, the Church takes care to suggest at all times the symbolism of the least of their cultual activities; she wants them to realize fully what their sacred functions signify. The altar of the holy church is Christ Himself: John states this in telling us in his Apocalypse that he saw before the throne of God a "golden altar" on which the offerings of the faithful were presented to God the Father. The cloths and the corporals are the members of Christ, that is, the faithful, whom the Lord puts on like a precious cloak, according to the words of the Psalmist: "the Lord is a king arrayed in majesty. . . . " This is why "if heretofore you have been barely attracted to the Church, henceforth you will be assiduous therein." Without wishing to force the symbolism of these actions, the priest will use them to help him perform with diligent care the tasks of his order: "that these visible ministries may be brilliantly and most diligently performed."

Then, in testimony and as a sign of the order conferred, the bishop causes the candidate to touch the chalice and the paten, sacred instruments of the eucharistic sacrifice, destined to receive the body and blood of

Jesus Christ: "see what ministry is entrusted to you: show yourselves therefore in such wise as to please God!"

To please God! Especially by fidelity in the service of the Lord, for this is the virtue which the bishop, immediately after the rite of ordination, implores from heaven for his new subdeacons: may God bestow on His servants the grace of His benediction, "that they may serve faithfully in his sight." Then, in the final oration: "Grant that they may be in thy Church as courageous and vigilant sentinels of the heavenly militia, and as faithful ministers of thy holy altars." To obtain this blessing, the Holy Spirit with His seven gifts is called upon, directly and at length; something quite rare in the ordination ceremonies: "let fall upon them the spirit of wisdom and of understanding, the spirit of counsel and of fortitude, the spirit of knowledge and of piety, and fill them with the spirit of thy fear." This time, too, as for celibacy, it is to a life "according to the Spirit" that the Church calls her ordained, so that "obeying the words and demonstrating with deeds . . . [they] might be able to please God."

VESTMENTS OF THE ORDER

After invoking the Holy Spirit, the bishop resumes his miter and places on the ordinandi the vestments of their Order.

Already they have put on the alb, the long toga which the noble Romans wore for several centuries of our era, and which the Church then accepted as the liturgical vestment of clerics, even those in minor orders. By its whiteness, the alb offered an obvious symbolism: the purity which must shine in the whole person of the minister of the altar. A medieval author explains himself on this subject with all the realistic simplicity one could attain at that time: "This (tunic) of linen should restrict the hands and arms so that they can do only that which is useful; the breast, so that it may not think inane thoughts; the stomach, that by desiring delights beyond what is proper it might not become gluttonous; the lower parts of the belly, lest by lusting, they corrupt the whole beauty of the sacerdotal habit; the knees, that they might not desist from prayer; the feet, lest they run toward evil."[2] In fact, the Church herself places on our lips every day words to the same effect: "Cleanse me, O Lord, and purify my heart; that, cleansed in the blood of the Lamb, I might enjoy eternal joys."

The alb of innocence is gathered at the waist by the cincture. Here again, an obvious symbolism was commonly accepted by medieval writers: "The alb is gathered by the cincture, so that all carnal desire is understood to be restrained."[3] This symbolism has come down to us in the prayer which the priest recites each morning while putting on the liturgical vestments: "Gird me, O Lord, with the cincture of purity, and extinguish in my loins the fire of lust, so that the virtue of continence and of chastity may remain in me."

Now the bishop moves on to the imposition of the amice. Introduced rather late among the liturgical vestments, the amice has retained the symbolism which its etymology suggests: *amicire* — "to cover." It was used to cover the head, just as today nuns cover their heads with the coif as a sign of modesty, prudence, and humility. "It is a defense which the Church provides for our weakness, and armor for our infirmity; we must wear it with a great mistrust of self, fearing to be reborn to the unhappy life of Adam and sin, which the Devil usually revives in us by his ordinary illusions and especially by thoughts of pride";[4] or by vain or improper words — "receive the amice, which designates chastisement of the voice." Also, each morning, before ascending the altar, the priest puts on this "helmet" of faith and salvation: "Place upon my head, O Lord, the helmet of salvation, to drive off the attacks of the

[2] Amal. Fortun., *De eccles. offic.*, lib. 2, c. 18; according to J. J. Olier, *Traité des saints ordres*, p. 369, n. 1.

[3] Durand, *De divin. off.*, lib. 2, cap. 3, n. 4; according to J. J. Olier, *op. cit.*, p. 371.

[4] J. J. Olier, *Traité des saints ordres*, p. 365-366.

Devil." There is nothing to prevent the priest from occasionally thinking during the day about this religious rite which he will repeat the following morning before pronouncing the consecrating words of the Eucharist.

Now the bishop places the maniple on the left arm of the ordained. Originally, the maniple was only a cloth worn on the left arm so that the priest could perhaps wipe his face. It has become, however, the rich and fruitful symbol of priestly ardor in the fulfilling of the duties of state: "by which is designated the fruit of good works."

Finally, the tunicle is placed over the subdeacon. Also of very recent origin, since it has been reserved to the subdeacon only since the nineteenth century, the tunicle seems to have as its source the garment of free men, whence its name of "tunic of joy and garment of gladness." Henceforward, the ordained is prepared to carry out the liturgical functions of his order; but he must still receive the book of the Epistles.

THE BOOK OF THE EPISTLES

This final ceremony is not without importance. The bishop, taking the book of Epistles, gives it to the ordained and pronounces these words: "Receive the book of the Epistles and have the power of reading them in the holy Church of God." In the Middle Ages, indeed, the subdeacon replaced the lector in this function.

Certainly every lay person can read the Epistles of the Mass, and, in case of necessity, a minor cleric can put on the tunicle and sing the Epistle of the day; but the words, "accept the power," are addressed to the subdeacon only. In these words, the theologian sees more than a pious ritual; he discerns therein an official invocation of the Church imploring the illuminating grace of the Spirit on all those who will hear the "words of salvation" read by the newly ordained. This reading, performed by him, will be accompanied by a special divine grace linked to the blessing which we call the grace of state, because to read the Epistles is the duty and the profession of the subdeacon. Of course, the grace of state of the subdeacon does not replace the other qualities which he needs, it does not replace the natural talents which are indispensable for him; still it is given to him alone, and not to those who are not ordained like him.

Thus enlightened, the faithful will be able to have a better understanding of their role in Christianity and eucharistic worship; they will have a better perception of the fact that they must be pure in soul when they participate in the holy mysteries. "If therefore," the bishop says in the oration preceding the conferring of the order, "If therefore through human weakness it should happen that the faithful are somewhat stained, the water of heavenly doctrine must be offered by you so that, purified thereby, they may return to adorn the altar and to the worship of the divine sacrifice."

3. THE BREVIARY

Along with the Epistle book, there is another book which the subdeacons will henceforth have in hand, and even more frequently: the Divine Office or Breviary. Born of the ancient tradition of prayers proper to the high priests of the old Law and to the Apostles who went up to the Temple "at the hour of prayer," the Divine Office assumed its definitive form before the Middle Ages; from the end of the fifth century, the broad outlines of our daily office were fixed in the *Ordo romanus,* and the interventions of St. Benedict or of the sons of St. Francis brought no essential changes therein. During the thirteenth century, the various parts of the Office were brought together into a small volume and slightly abridged: hence the name *breviarum,* which has remained. There is nothing, therefore, to prevent the introduction at various times of certain changes in the text and even in the format of the Breviary, so that the principle itself of priestly prayer might be incarnated in a "book of prayers" less strictly delimited by monastic Office and more organically united to pastoral life.

Until now, no liturgical formula has come down to give a religious consecration to the work of prayer entrusted by the Church to all her priests; however, there is nothing to prevent this from happening someday. In the ceremonial of the profession of nuns of the Order of St. Benedict, the ritual of the "handing over of the breviary" exists: "and the [prelate] hands the Breviary to her or to them, touching it with both hands and saying: Receive the book that you may begin the canonical hours and read the office in the Church, in the name of the Father, and of the Son and of the Holy Spirit. Amen."[5]

A TRUE PRAYER

The Breviary is a *prayer*. Just as it behooves everyone from time to time, both outwardly and inwardly, to recognize the essential dependence which binds him entirely to God, so, too, collectivities have the strict obligation of acknowledging the sovereign dominion of God over all that constitutes them. But a collectivity has no voice or no proper intellect; it must express itself with the lips of living persons and cause itself to be represented by them before the face of the Holy Trinity. The Church, too, authentically delegates her clerics to the function of praise, petition, adoration and thanksgiving which she must fulfill here below. Thus, the subdeacon is the bearer of a very sacred portion of the sacerdotal mediation which shortly will be incumbent in its totality on the priest: the authentic glorification of the holy Trinity, the official supplication of the Church. The subdeacon is thereby truly the organ of the Church, her "voice," "bearing the person of the Church."

In this manner, the Church reminds priests of the new covenant that their mediation also involves a looking toward God; that while their arms must be stretched out toward the human harvest to be gathered for the glory of the Father, they must also at times raise them

[5] Cf. *Cérémonial de la vêture et de la profession des Moniales de l'ordre de S. Benoît*, Paris, Monast. Bénéd. du Temple.

toward heaven, in the manner of the beseechers of old. The virtue of religion is as essential to a mediator's soul as apostolic zeal; for Christ, the perfect mediator, is the perfect praise of the Trinity, the permanent supplication, the unique human adoration, the personal thanksgiving most pleasing to God.

The Church desires that this prayer be truly prayer. Certainly works on moral theology must determine the *minimum* required to satisfy the essentials of the obligation the subdeacons have of reciting the holy Office every day, and they reply: "To satisfy the substance of the ecclesiastical precept, spiritual attention, or literal attention, is not required, but superficial attention (which attends to the words, lest there be a mistake in them) even tenuous and remiss, with the intention of praying." One does not sin against the ecclesiastical precept by contenting oneself with this *minimum;* but one can want more than this. In her prayer "Aperi," the Church, always herself, does ask for a little more: "Cleanse my heart of all vain, perverse and strange thoughts; enlighten my mind, inflame my heart, that I might be worthy to recite this office worthily, attentively and devotedly, and that I might deserve to be heard in the sight of thy divine majesty." *Digne:* that is, with external respect, in the mental and corporal physical attitude which is suitable for a prayer, in surroundings where profane noises, shouts, do not disturb one. *Devote:* with sentiments of profound adoration and of intense interior recollection which are characteristic of those who are conscious of being in a state of prayer, "elevating the mind to God." *Attente:* not only to the words of the text, not merely to the ideas which are expressed, but even more to God to whom one is praying: "attention to the words, attention to the meaning, attention to God,"[6] so that our soul may be in harmony with our voice.[7]

The prayer of the Breviary is fully mediational. At times it rises up toward God to sing His grandeurs, His

[6] *Summa theologica*, IIaIIae, q. 83, a. 13,c.
[7] *Règle de S. Benoît* (Coll. "Pax"), Maredsous, 1933, p. 66.

beauty, and His marvelous attributes: "Praise the Lord, all ye nations, praise him all ye peoples. . . ." Occasionally, this prayer bows respectfully before the infinite majesty of the Lord whose voice is as terrifying as the thunder and roaring of great waters. Or else it pours out in cries of confidence in the help and support which the soul will unquestionably find in Him in whom it places all its hope: "O Lord, my hope and my refuge!" At other times, it groans with the penitent soul of the Psalmist, who weeps at length over his sins or those of his people: "Out of the depths I have cried to thee, O Lord." Now it implores the divine help and becomes suppliant in order to ask of the Lord the blessings of soul and body on behalf of all those who have been placed on earth to please God; now it expands in prolonged thanksgiving for all the blessings, temporal and spiritual, with which the Lord has gratified His people: "for his mercy is forever." At times, too, it wants to make up for the faults and the sins of others, and breaks into expiatory laments to sovereign Justice. Thus, all the religious sentiments of redemptive mediation are represented in the Breviary: it is a prayer which rises toward God, beseeching as well as praising, expiating as well as adoring; in short, a prayer which fuses all the sentiments of the Church, which expresses her most varied states of soul. This is why Augustine could write: "When the psalm prays, pray; when it groans, groan; when it rejoices, rejoice; when it hopes, hope; when it fears, fear."[8]

PRAYER OF THE CHURCH

The Breviary is a prayer of the Church. It is the Church which received from her divine Founder the mission of continuing the perfect mediation of the God-Man and the insistent supplication which His soul expressed here below from the moment of the Incarnation. Like Christ, the Church wants a prayer to rise continuously from her heart, and she does this through the voices of her innumerable ministers scattered

[8] *Enarr. in Psalm., P.L.*, vol. 36, c. 248.

throughout the world. She presents them with her
own formulas to recite; through her *directorium,* she
indicates to them the order to be followed in reciting
them. She even establishes their arrangements and ordination herself, "according to the rite of the holy Roman
Church." She confides to them her intentions, her desires, her hopes, and tells them, as one day the Lord
told His Apostles: "thus shall you pray." Is it too much
to conclude that the Church wants to see us consciously
united with her when we open the book of her prayer?
It is up to us to take on her universal personality, to
gather in our souls her intentions, to collect into a sheaf
the chant of praise or the suppliant misery of all mankind, to give a Christian sense to the ontological and
unconscious glorification of all inanimate creation. When
we act thus, we will merely have rediscovered the intentions of our Lord Himself, those which He had and
in which He lived here below: "In union with that
divine intention with which thou didst praise God on
earth."

Spoken in the name of the Church, the prayer of
the Breviary has value *ex opere operantis Ecclesiae.* The
Divine Office is truly prayer even if the minister reciting it does not, unfortunately, find himself in a state of
prayer. Christ assured the permanence and validity of
His worship despite the unstable and sometimes mediocre dispositions of those whom He boldly called to
carry it out. Also, He is the first Priest of every Mass,
and the first Giver of every sacramental blessing. Likewise, the Church, which we personify, is always beautiful, holy, and worthy. Praying in her name, the subdeacon is always praying in the name of a living Christian community which can take pride in its numerous
saints and its supernatural fervor. The formal "glorification" constituted by the Breviary can always presume
upon an imposing "ontological" foundation: the holiness
of the entire Church, the Communion of Saints.

Also, the Church that we represent is not an immobile, inert entity. Though united already to the community of those who take part in the spiritual rites of

the heavenly liturgy described in the Apocalypse, the
earthly community is susceptible to change, and can be
more or less holy, therefore, more or less glorifying or
sanctifying, because the degree of internal mediation is
measured exactly by the degree of participation in the
life of the Spirit. That is why the Church must always
have a very intense personal holiness, so that all the
religious and apostolic functions carried on in her name
may be supported and fructified by an overflowing
sanctifying virtue.

Coming from the Church, the prayer of the Divine
Office embraces all change. The Church is changing at
all times; baptized persons are passing into the final
state, while new beings see the light of day and are
inserted into the Church by the waters of Baptism. We
pray in the name of a living collectivity, always in the
state of evolution and of renewal. Our prayer never remains completely identical with itself. The "new" Church
always calls for mediators to represent her: this keeps
the Divine Office constantly fresh and rejuvenated.

UNIVERSAL PRAYER

Finally, this prayer needs to be fully universal, to
have dominion over the day and the night as it has over
space and over mankind. The prayer of the Church
organized in this way surrounds everything temporal,
envelops it with religion, in order to remind it continuously that it is "relative" to God and "ordered" to
eternity. This is why the Divine Office must permeate
our days. Even when it is not possible for us to recite
the different hours at the ideal times, it is always possible
to place ourselves in spirit at the time of day corresponding to the "hour" we are reciting, and to offer to the
Lord the Church, mankind, and the time of midnight,
of dawn, of noontime, or of evening. Of course, the
totality of our apostolic task will in fact determine the
manner in which we are to organize our time; for the
Church exercises her sway over our time as well as
over our bodies. But we shall place the Divine Office,

as much as possible, in the position which it occupies among those whose lives are completely consecrated to the work of religion.

As universal as the Church, the prayer of the Divine Office must not for all that become abstract, uprooted from the preoccupations of the city of God in combat. Dom Columba Marmion used to reply to his disciples who questioned him on this point:

"Before the Divine Office, after making an act of faith in Christ present in my heart by grace, I unite myself with Him in the praise which He gives to His Father; I ask Him to glorify His holy Mother, the saints, particularly those of the day, and my holy patrons. Then, I unite myself with Him as Head of the Church, as the Supreme Pontiff, to plead the cause of the whole Church. To this end, I cast a glance on all that the earth holds of needs and miseries: the sick, the dying, the tempted, the despairing, the sinners, the afflicted; I take into my heart the sorrows, the anguish, the hopes of each soul; I direct my intention also toward the works of zeal undertaken to glorify God and to save the world: the missions, the preaching. . . . Finally, I take the intentions of those who have recommended themselves to my prayers, of those whom I love, of the souls who are united with me, and thus I prepare myself to intercede for all with Christ, who is 'always living to intercede for us.' Then I say to the heavenly Father: 'Father, I am unworthy to appear before you; but I have absolute confidence in the holy humanity of your only Son united to His divinity. Leaning on your Son, I dare present myself before You and, united with the Word, to sing your praises.' "

If a monk could live his mediation so concretely, how much more should the diocesan priest, attached to a specific community redeemed by our Lord, be able to adore, implore, thank or praise, in the name of men, in the name of the Church, for the suffering and the vigorous — all need it! — the weak and the strong, the unfortunate and the privileged, so that God may be glorified in all and by all in the universe.

This is the spirit which should animate the reading or recitation of our Breviary, and these are our reasons for giving the Divine Office very special esteem. If our daily "meditation" must often be the object of a more vigilant concern because it especially can nourish the soul of our apostolic life, including the recitation of the Breviary, the latter has precedence over the former in the hierarchy of our religious activities. Meditation is the exercise in which the theological spirit is prepared and developed, the spirit which must shine forth in all our activities; the Divine Office is one of the mediating activities entrusted to us by the Church. We cannot, therefore, see how these two prayers should get in each other's way; nor can we see how one could replace the other. Without meditation, the Breviary soon risks becoming a purely verbal exercise; without the Breviary, the priestly life would lose one of its most noble features. This is why nothing will be able to diminish in us the taste, the esteem, the interest, and therefore the study which we shall give to the prayer of the Church so that it may be, in all truth, in the face of God and of His saints, "praise, honor, virtue and glory from every creature, and to us, the remission of all sins."

CHAPTER FIVE

THE DIACONATE

There is question at the present time of a diaconate independent of the priesthood, and desired for itself as a particular ministry in the Church. "The idea, today at least, has not ripened," said Pius XII at the Congress of the Lay Apostolate in Rome, in October, 1957. This implies that in the future, the idea could become mature. At first glance its realization is actually more complex than one might think: A professional or part-time diaconate? A diaconate with or without celibacy? What functions to attribute to it? But all that could someday be clarified and give rise to a broadening of the "spirituality of the diaconate." For the moment, let us content ourselves with establishing what the major order received by all future priests involves. It will be seen that this ministry is a great one and that its organic position is very important in the life of the Church.

Indeed, the reception of the diaconate passes rather unnoticed, because of the fact that the subdiaconate and the priesthood alone capture the whole religious interest and all the attention of the ordinandi. For the subdiaconate marks a notable change in the life of the cleric in minor orders: this decisive step has opened to him the unlimited perspectives of perpetual chastity

and a life of celibacy, while the Divine Office which envelops henceforth all priestly activity, permits him to
consecrate in the name of the baptized all the hours of
the day. For its part, the priesthood, because it is the
consummation of Orders and also assures its immediate
exercise, attracts to it the desires and burning hopes
of the young ordinandi: in their eyes it is the image of
a proximate ideal that one contemplates with emotion,
the anticipated possession of which gives intense joy.
Between these two stages, the diaconate seems to constitute a very humble progression, a necessary step: the
beauty which it harbors is veiled and its splendor more
or less fused into the forthcoming priesthood.

Yet, upon considering the reality of things, the diaconate appears far superior to the subdiaconate. A true
beginning of Orders, it is directly linked to the priesthood itself, and it is from this relationship that it derives its grandeur. Accordingly, one can without hesitation reason as follows: Just as the priest, because he
is consecrated to the interests of the eucharistic Body
and to those of the Mystical Body of Christ, is held to
an interior perfection superior to that of the simple
religious (IIa IIae, q. 184, a. 8, c.), so too the real, though
incomplete possession of the priesthood represents for
the deacon, and to the same extent, a special requirement for inner perfection. A cleric who might remain
a deacon during his entire life, as, for example, is permitted in the Eastern rites, would logically be held by
the fact of his diaconate to acquire and maintain the
high perfection required by the priestly state.

1. The Ordination Rites

Along with the subdeacons, the future deacons had
prostrated themselves while the *schola* sang the Litanies.
Now they advance toward the bishop, clad in the vestments of their previous ordination, and kneel in a semi-
circle before him. Now there takes place, between the
bishop and the archdeacon, a short symbolic dialogue
on the subject of the aptitude of the ordinandi to bear

the burdens of the new charge which they plan to take
on: *onus diaconatus, onus officii*. Then, the prelate addresses to them a final instruction on the nature of the
diaconate.

THE FUNCTIONS

What is a deacon? In outlining his features, the
Church refers to the "levitical order" — *leviticum or-
dinem* — the chosen tribe to which had been entrusted
on an exclusive basis the protection of the Tabernacle
of the Most High. "It is from this tribe, dearly beloved
sons, that you will receive your name and functions, since
you also have been chosen for the levitical office: the
defense of the Tabernacle of the Witness, otherwise
known as the Church of God which, always on the defensive, must fight without respite against her enemies.
. . . You, too, therefore, must carry and especially defend the Church of God, symbolized by the ancient Tabernacle, by the holiness of your lives, the virtue of your
words, and the brilliance of your example." Then, the
bishop calls twice upon the name of Stephen, the antitype of the Levite of the ancient covenant, who had the
privilege of being chosen by the Apostles to be their
closest helper.

What is a deacon? "It belongs to the deacon to minister at the altar, to baptize, and to preach." Such is the
real participation of the deacon in the specifically mediational and sacerdotal activities, those which the bishop
himself sums up in the course of the ceremony of ordination to the priesthood: "For it also belongs to the
priest to offer, to bless, to be in charge, to preach, and
to baptize." Truly, the diaconate is a real beginning of
priestly action.

To minister at the altar. Since the power of Orders
is essentially related to the eucharistic sacrifice and by
this very fact, links the priest to the Eucharist, so too
the deacon becomes directly linked with the priest who
is consecrating and offering the Divine Victim. The
rubrics of the liturgy already show the deacon approach-

ing more and more closely the center of the altar, the place reserved for the priest. The bishop explains it thus: "Tabernaculo Dei ejusque sacrificiis ritu perpetuo deservire," and, further on, using words which would seem reserved to the priest: "Ministers of Christ and dispensers of the mysteries of God." In fact, canon law (c. 845, 2) specifies that the deacon is the normal though extraordinary, minister, of the Eucharist.

To baptize. By his mission and by his own power, the deacon may baptize — not merely as an occasional minister, in the manner of the lay person who confers the sacrament in case of necessity, nor, to be sure, after the fashion of the priest who is the normal and ordinary minister of the sacrament, but as a true, though extraordinary, minister of Baptism. Though restricted in its exercise, the task of baptizing is proper to him — natural, if one may say so. Administering the sacrament of Baptism has become a *potestas:* "the extraordinary minister of solemn Baptism is the deacon; nevertheless, he may not make use of this power without permission either of the Ordinary or the pastor of the place" (c. 741). The deacon is therefore constituted an organ of the Church in the gradual formation of the Body of Christ: "for the deacon must . . . baptize."

To preach. This is another assimilation to the priesthood, as appears from the way in which the jurisdiction to preach is granted: "the faculty of preaching belongs only to priests or deacons, not, however, to the other clerics, except for a reasonable cause, at the discretion of the Ordinary, and for individual cases" (c. 1342).

As can be seen, the function of deacon, initially limited to the "serving of tables and of widows" (Acts 6:1-7), rapidly evolved in a more spiritual sense:

"According to the *Didascalia Apostolorum,* which dates from the end of the third century, the deacons are the ears, mouth, heart, and soul of the bishop, with whom, so to speak, they are one; they are his ears, to report to him the requests of the laity and to be intermediaries between them and the bishop; his heart, to provide for the needs of the poor, the sick, of all those in need. They also have a power of surveillance: over the church, where they act as a kind of police and place everyone properly; outside the church, they inform themselves of the conduct and trials of each believer, in order to give the bishop an accurate report about him. They themselves decide the less important cases; the others, they decide along with the bishop and the priests. They command the deaconnesses. In short, in the then eclipsed state of the priesthood, they are the right arm of the bishop who seems to carry out only through them his functions as administrator of the community's goods, watchman, almsgiver. . . . But all that is now but a memory."[1]

THE RITES

After a double invitation to prayer, the bishop uncovers his head, extends his arms, and chants the long and profound eucharistic prayer which forms the very heart of the ordination: "We give Thee thanks, above all, that Thou hast granted to this mystical body of Jesus Thy Son, the Church, so rich in heavenly gifts, so clearly one despite the multitude of her members, to grow unceasingly in order to complete that admirable temple of which Thou art the base and the foundation, and in which three orders of ministers distribute among themselves the holiest functions, just as formerly the children of Levi were chosen to serve at the altar and gather the eternal inheritance of the blessing promised their Father." Then, after placing his right hand on the head of each ordinand and pronouncing the well-known formula: "receive the Holy Spirit unto strength," he continues his prayer of consecration, the text of which is so beautiful and to which priests will gladly listen once more: "Send forth upon them, we beseech Thee, O Lord, the Holy Spirit by whom they may be strengthened by the gift of Thy sevenfold grace unto the faithful carrying out of the work of Thy ministry. Let there abound in them the form of every virtue, mod-

---

[1] Cf. E. Dubosq, *Les étapes du sacerdoce*, pp. 102-103.

est authority, constant purity, the holiness of innocence, and the observance of spiritual discipline."

Then there remains a twofold task for the bishop: to place on the new deacons the sacred vestments and to hand them the Holy Gospels.

For a long time, the stole was called the *orarium* (*os* means "face"), because it consisted of a kind of cloth which people of a certain rank, orators, for example, used to wipe their faces. It is understood that bishops, priests and deacons also used them. This cloth soon became part of the liturgical garments and was called the stole, στολή signifying the vestment. In fact, the formula for placing on the stole seems to allude to the work of the apostolate: "Receive the white stole from the hand of God; fulfill thy ministry; for God has the power to increase your grace." Perhaps the priest, as he puts on the stole each morning, could occasionally think of the apostolic labors and the sweat that went into them, which are recalled by the history of the ancient *orarium*.

As for the dalmatic, this was formerly a large white garment worn by persons of high rank who came from Dalmatia. Initially reserved for bishops, it was given to deacons in the fourth century by Pope Sylvester. Today, this liturgical vestment still unquestionably symbolizes grandeur, dignity, and high station.

But the priest, along with his ministry of worship, performs a teaching task of the highest importance. After the lectorate and the subdiaconate, the diaconate renews the memory of this task by means of the delivery of the book of the Gospels: "Receive the power of reading the Gospels in the Church of God." On this subject, one should repeat everything that was just said about the subdeacon, to whom the bishop gave the book of the Epistles.

2. The Spirit of the Diaconate

The Church does not customarily entrust to men tasks to which she is committed without at the same

time recalling the moral exigencies which these functions involve and the inner perfection which they call
for. "Handle holy things in a holy manner": this is
the principle which guides her conduct. She does not
link the efficacy of the sacramental rites absolutely to the
sanctity of her ministers (Christian worship and the
sanctification of the baptized must be guaranteed social-
ly despite the possible deficiencies of those who are the
instruments thereof) but she repeats that Orders call
for, in the subject who exercises it, a perfection in proportion to the dignity with which he is adorned.

The Church offers to the deacons the example of the
Levites of the Old Law and especially, that of the deacon
Stephen: "To be sure, in the Old Law, out of the twelve,
one tribe, that of Levi, was chosen to serve with special
devotion the Tabernacle of God and its sacrifices in a
perpetual rite. And such great dignity was granted it
that no one not of its seed could arise to minister to
that divine worship and office, and therefore, deserve to
be and be called, by a certain great privilege of inheritance, the 'tribe of the Lord.'" As for St. Stephen,
the Church insists prudently: "Think on blessed Stephen
chosen for this office by the Apostles because of his outstanding chastity."

TRIPLE REQUIREMENT

For the deacons of the new covenant, the triple
function which consecrates them to the work of the altar, of Baptism and of preaching, implies a triple bond,
a triple requirement for virtues, qualities, and talents
to be acquired or preserved.

The deacon is, first of all, *co-minister of the eucharistic sacrifice.* You are, says the Pontifical, "co-ministers
and cooperators of the body and blood of the Lord";
can one imagine words more powerful than these? Is
this not a call to make a special study of the doctrine
of the Eucharist as sacrament and sacrifice, in immediate
preparation for the priesthood itself? Is it not also a
call for an ever stronger awareness of the central place

occupied by the Mass in the religious life of mankind? Mysterious and sacramental representation of the unique, universal and eternal act of mediation of the glorified Redeemer, the Mass must necessarily draw to and into itself man's entire religious activity: it is in Christ and with Him that our acts of adoration and expiation can become agreeable in the eyes of the Holy Trinity.

The deacon is also *minister of Baptism*. When the bishop says solemnly: "the deacon must baptize," he is considering not so much the new dignity with which the deacon is invested as the outstanding service which the Church expects of him: the gradual building up of the eucharistic Body of Christ. If he comes closer to the eucharistic Body of the Lord, the deacon also comes closer to His Mystical Body. By baptizing, he ensures the growth of the ecclesiastical community. Whence a greater love in him for the Church than that which animated the subdeacon. Without ceasing to represent the Church in her authentic prayer of mediation, he also helps to build her sacramentally. To the service of the Divine Office he adds that of a fertile love whose goal is the supernatural birth of those whom the Father has called to be grafted onto the True Vine. This is the first stage of spiritual fatherhood, the full prerogatives of which will be granted by the priesthood. This supernatural fruitfulness could logically show itself not only in the isolated act of Baptism, but also by the work of a more "resplendent" life, one more truly generating supernatural strength.

Finally, the deacon *preaches the Gospel* of the Lord. The communication of Christian revelation requires a sure knowledge of Christian thought, an appreciation of its vital values, the qualities necessary for transmitting them faithfully. "Receive the power of reading the Gospel": an evangelical thought which is translated as much in a life lived according to the Gospels as by reading bits of the New Testament in Latin. The bishop insists: "Take care that you show forth by living works to those to whom you preach the Gospel by words, so that it may be said of you: Blessed are the feet of those preaching the Gospel of peace, preaching the Gospel of good things. Have your feet shod with the example of the saints, in the preparation of the Gospel of peace." The Master said: "I am the truth"; the deacon should be able to say: "I am the Gospel."

PURITY AND STRENGTH

The triple consecration of the deacon to the eucharistic Body of Christ, His Mystical Body, and His Word of life, will be able to develop and flourish easily only if it profits from an effort at growth in the "spiritual life." The double phenomenon of spiritual progress and the correlative separation from the profane and the material was already clearly manifest from the time of the subdiaconate. The subdeacon attaches himself definitively to the Church of Christ and the prayer of mediation; accordingly, he separates himself from the very legitimate joys of love and home. In the diaconate, it is the same thing: "Be ye detached and purified," the bishop repeats on a number of occasions, and "Be ye even more subject to the elevating control of the Holy Spirit." Purity and strength, detachment from matter and adherence to the values of the Spirit; these are the themes which all the ordination prayers develop.

Purity and detachment from matter, first of all. The bishop repeats this with what could be astonishing insistence. However, it is less for the sake of the ordinand himself, it would appear, than out of respect for the mysteries of Christian life and truth to which the deacon is so intimately linked. "Levi is interpreted to mean 'added' or 'taken up'; and you, dearly beloved sons, who take your name from your paternal inheritance, be ye 'taken up' from carnal desires, from earthly concupiscences, which war against the soul; be ye clean, bright, pure, chaste . . . that you may be 'worthy to be added' to the number of the ecclesiastical grade; that you may deserve to be the inheritance and the loving tribe of the Lord."

The motive for this purity is expressly recalled: it is

the proximity of the eucharistic Christ. "And *because* you are co-ministers and cooperators of the body and blood of the Lord, be ye strangers to every lust of the flesh, as the Scriptures say: Ye who bear the vessels of the Lord, be ye clean." The motive is also, in general, the dignity required by all the functions of the order received: "Let pure ministers be added to thy holy altars . . . and let them please thee by all the virtues with which it behooves thee to be served."

The bishop also counsels the deacon to seek for *supernatural strength* and attachment to the values of the spirit. The more sacred the function, the more definitive the commitment of the young man, the more insistent the appeals of the Church to strength and perseverance in the Spirit: "Send forth upon them, we beseech Thee, O Lord, the Holy Spirit by whom they may be *strengthened* by the gift of thy sevenfold grace unto the *faithful* carrying out of the work of thy ministry. Let there abound in them the form of every virtue, modest authority, constant purity, the holiness of innocence . . . that they might persevere, *firmly* and with stability, in Christ." Likewise, when he places his hand upon each ordinand: "Receive the Holy Spirit unto strength, for the resisting of the devil and his temptations." The Church must always keep herself on the defensive: "Always standing on the ramparts, she struggles in an unceasing fight against her enemies; whence the Apostle says: Our struggle is not against flesh and blood, but against princes and powers, against the world rulers of this darkness, against the spirit of wickedness on high." To resist her enemies the Church asks the Lord for a special outpouring of His Spirit.

SACRAMENTAL DIGNITY

If the Church proposes to the deacons a spirituality already very similar to what will be demanded of priests, it is precisely because an inner, ontological transformation has taken place in them and that, accustomed to the

agere secundum esse, she wants her ministers to be
consistent with themselves.

The diaconate is, in effect, a *sacrament.* As such it
works in the ordained a real and profound change. By
the character impressed on his soul, the deacon is constituted in a state of similitude with Christ the mediator,
he is united with the action of the glorious Lord. Consequently, he finds himself really distinct from those who
have as yet only received the minor orders, and separated
from any function that might not be in harmony with
the basic requirements of his new status. Moreover,
through sacramental grace, the Holy Spirit helps him to
stabilize in himself the virtuous dispositions required
for the perfect performance of his new apostolic activities: "by whom they can be strengthened by the gift
of thy sevenfold grace unto a faithful carrying out of
the work of thy ministry." This is a final preparation
before the day of ordination to the priesthood: "that
they may be made worthy of grasping more powerful
things than in this lower grade, through thy grace."
Thus, the diaconate not only makes the young Levite
something *more* in the ecclesiastical hierarchy; it also
transforms him in his innermost soul so that he can act
better, that is, more apostolically.

One can therefore understand the bishop's emphasis
on inculcating in the ordinandi the *dignity* of the sacrament he is about to confer upon them: " . . . such great
dignity . . . consider very seriously the high grade of the
Church to which you now ascend." One understands
the special precautions taken before proceeding to the
ordination: "If anyone has anything against these, for
the sake of and on account of God, let him step forward
with confidence and speak." Whence the bishop's profound enthusiasm as he contemplates the future "Levites"
and says to them: "Let them be resplendent with the
Order, and, glowing with spiritual conversation, let them
shine forth in the grace of sanctification." Whence his
prayers, continuously renewed: "That He may pour
forth mercifully upon these, His servants, whom He has

deigned to take unto the office of the diaconate, the grace
of His benediction, and preserve for them the gifts of
the consecration propitiously granted (them)." Whence,
finally, with a touch of fear and powerlessness, his final
and confident supplication: "But, O Lord, those things
which to us are unknown do not escape Thee, hidden
things do not remain concealed from Thee; Thou art the
discoverer of secrets, Thou, 'the searcher of hearts,'
Thou canst examine the lives of these (men) with divine
judgment, by which Thou dost always prevail, and purge
those things which are admitted and grant those which
are yet to be done." After these final precautions, the
bishop confers upon them the order of the diaconate
along with the emblems of their responsibility: the stole
of action, the dalmatic of dignity, the Gospel of salvation: Henceforth and forever, they are the "inheritance
and loving tribe of the Lord."

CHAPTER SIX

PRIESTHOOD AND EPISCOPATE

It would be difficult to introduce the reader into a full understanding of the "diocesan sacerdotal community," without explaining the major phases of ordination to the priesthood, and the principal rites of episcopal consecration. And since the priestly state is defined in the Pontifical itself as a life of collaboration in the work of the bishop, it seemed preferable to collect in one chapter everything related to the priesthood and the episcopate.

1. THE PRIESTHOOD

After years of joyous and sometimes impatient waiting, the date of ordination to the priesthood is suddenly at hand; at its beginning, this preparation seemed endless; on the day of ordination itself, it seems to have been much too short, to have gone by much too rapidly. The following chapters will speak at length of the nature, doctrine, and perfection of this priesthood. But there is nothing to prevent our reviewing briefly the various liturgical ceremonies in the course of which a priest is ordained for eternity.

CONSECRATION OF THE PRIEST

More than the subdiaconate and the diaconate, the priesthood is a heavy responsibility. "The burden of the priesthood": the archdeacon takes pains to repeat this at the beginning of the ceremony. The bishop, for his part, underlines the urgency of the warning, so that no one who is unworthy may come forward presumptuously and receive the imposition of hands in the manner of the ungodly. He consults all the faithful, whoever they may be, and for reasons which clearly reveal the realistic good sense of the Church: "Our fathers have established with reason that the simple faithful should be consulted on the choice of those who are to be placed above them in the service of the altar, for two reasons: first of all, because it often happens that sins unknown to many are nevertheless known to some; also, the faithful more readily obey those priests to whose ordination they have given their assent." And, the prelate adds, with excessive precaution, "it is necessary to ask the advice of a large number, so that our own affection for the ordinandi will not blind us."

These preliminaries ended, the bishop begins his instruction preparatory to the conferring of Orders, and recalls the fundamental obligations of sacerdotal life: "For it behooves the priest to offer, to bless, to direct, to preach, and to baptize" — words of great richness which succinctly suggest the whole range of apostolic activities of the diocesan clergy. He finishes with these sublime words which so many priestly generations have meditated with feeling: "Recognize what you are doing, imitate what you are handling, in such a way that celebrating the mystery of the Lord's death, you may manage to mortify your bodies from all vices and lusts. Let your doctrine be spiritual medicine for God's people; may the odor of your life be the delight of the Church of Christ; so that you may build up the house, that is, the Church of God, by preaching and example; so that neither we, because of your promotion, nor you, by the reception of so great an office, may deserve to be damned by the Lord but rewarded instead."

After this there unfolds the impressive ceremony of the laying on of hands. First of all, the bishop, alone, places his hands upon each ordinand; the silence which accompanies this gesture increases the religious mystery whose supernatural efficacy astonishes and confounds spirits. Then, all the priests present join in the episcopal action. In these decisive moments the young Levites become priests. And, always, silence reigns until, the imposition ceremony completed, the bishop begins the famous eucharistic prayer, the ancient "consecratio presbyteri."

THE BURDEN OF THE PRIESTHOOD

A complete résumé of the priest's apostolic activity, this oration deserves more than a cursory examination; more than any other, it shows that the diocesan priest is assigned authentically, sacramentally, to all the ecclesiastical tasks, all the apostolic activities which theological treatises have customarily classified under the three headings: magisterium, or doctrine; ministry, or worship and sacraments; government, or direction.

The history of the early ages clearly takes into account the state of things presupposed by the Pontifical. Placed at the head of the Christian people, the pontiffs soon had to obtain help from clerics of secondary dignity who unburdened them of a portion of their apostolic obligations, "unto the assistance of their society and work," says the Pontifical rather elegantly. But what are these obligations? First of all, the direction of the Christian people: "just as, in the desert, God communicated the spirit of Moses to seventy prudent men in order that, seconded by them, Moses might be able to govern the multitude of the Israelites." Then, worship and the sacramental rites, "just as Eleazar and Jehmar, the sons of Aaron, were chosen of old in order that all the Hebrews might be able to profit from the sacrifices and the sacred rites, that there might be enough priests

. . . for the sacraments of a more frequent office." Finally, the teaching of the religious truths: "Thou hast
added unto the Apostles of thy Son, teachers, companions
of the faith," so as to bring even to the ends of the earth
the benefits of Christian teaching.

But it is not enough to carry out the sacerdotal functions, or be invested with priestly dignity, *presbyterii
dignitatem;* the Church also requires an inner life which
is on the same plane as this high function. The formula
of consecration determines the nature of this life: "Renew in their hearts the spirit of holiness. Let the form
of total justice shine forth in them so that they may
give a good accounting of their dispensation to Him and
obtain the rewards of eternal beatitude." Thus will they
be the alert and prudent auxiliaries of the bishop's
work: "prudent cooperators of our Order." There is
nothing missing in this consecratory formula: a reminder of priestly dignity, requirements of sanctity,
union with the bishop and the promise of reward for
eternal life. Thus is concluded the eucharistic prayer of
ordination, as methodical as a treatise of theology, but
as significant as one might wish, truly summing up the
total work of the diocesan apostolate.

The marvel has been accomplished. A new corps of
Levites will continue the work of *reparatio*, continually
renewed. Thus it has been since the beginning of the
Christian era and thus it will be until the end of time.
The mystery of faith, *mysterium* fidei, in spite of everything, in spite of its improbability, is prolonged. All it
requires is a laying on of hands, affirmed to be efficacious by the authority of the Church. Henceforth the
faithful will admit that these men are truly priests;
they ask of them Baptism and entry into the ecclesiastical
community, they accept from their hands the Host consecrated by them, they receive serenely the sign of their
pardon. Still, the Church, rich in worldly experience,
knows very well that it is useful to surround the essential
rites of religion with exceptional brilliance and detailed
explanation. This is why, to the essential ceremony of
ordination, she adds the supplementary rites which, if

one may say so, interpret the sacramental act of the imposition of hands.

SUPPLEMENTARY RITES

The *investiture,* first of all, is highly significant. After seating himself, the bishop has each of the ordinandi pass before him, and he places upon them the stole, emblem of dignity but also of a heavy responsibility: "Receive the yoke of the Lord; for his yoke is sweet and his burden light." Then he places on them the chasuble, still folded up in back. Originally a civilian garment, a sort of cloak formed of a large piece of material with an opening in the center to permit passage of the head, the *paenula* or *planeta,* later became the *casula* or chasuble of liturgical ceremonies. The traditional symbolism of this vestment is revealed by the Pontifical itself: "Receive the priestly vestment, by which charity is signified." The priest, indeed, because he is assigned the work of redemption, must have an intense love for God and his neighbor: "(they) should be ministers of the Church perfect in faith and works, that is, rooted in the virtue of a twin love, of God and of neighbor."

The bishop next confers the power of celebrating the Holy Mass. Standing and facing those whom he has just raised to the honor of the priesthood, he calls down upon them the blessing of the Lord, who alone is capable of truly consecrating and blessing perfectly His new servants, so that they may have the maturity of age — "prove themselves elders." It is from the Lord also that they receive the glorious power of celebrating the eucharistic sacrifice: "(transforming) bread and wine into the body and blood of Thy son, by an immaculate blessing." And for what purpose? For their own personal consolation? For the beauty of religion? The Pontifical emphasizes the following motive: for the needs of Thy people, "unto the service of thy people."

But this is not enough. The bishop's prayer becomes insistent: kneeling on the steps of the altar, he himself intones the *Veni Creator*, which the *schola* will repeat several times, so long as the anointing of the hands goes on. From the end of the first strophe, as a matter of fact, the bishop has turned back toward the young ordinandi who, one by one, kneel before him to receive the *unction*. They offer him the palms of their juxtaposed hands so that he may trace a large cross thereon: "vouchsafe, O Lord, to consecrate and sanctify these hands through this anointing and our blessing, so that whatsoever they may bless shall be blessed, and whatsoever they consecrate shall be consecrated and sanctified."

The anointing of the hands is followed by the *delivery of the instruments*. Hands bound, the newly ordained come up and touch a chalice containing wine and water, as well as the paten which holds a host: characteristic signs of the power of celebrating Holy Mass. At the precise moment of the handing over of the instruments the bishop says to the ordinandi: "Receive the power of offering sacrifice and of celebrating Masses both for the living as well as for the dead."

All the rites preparatory to the Mass having been accomplished, the newly ordained will henceforth exercise along with the bishop the sacred power they have just received: the *concelebration of the Mass* begins. Every priest still remembers those first prayers said out loud, together, following the rhythm of group recitation. All still remember the first "Hoc . . . est . . . enim . . . corpus . . . meum," so new, so sacred and at the same time, so prosaic: *mysterium fidei* in all the force of that term. All remember the first Memento of the Living and the first Memento of the Dead, that silent moment of ecclesiastical origin. Thus is terminated the propitiatory sacrifice of the New Law, the holocaust of religious and Christian expiation, "that you may be blessed in the religious Orders and may offer pleasing victims for the sins and offenses of the people."

However, before closing this impressive ceremony, the bishop wishes again to emphasize two aspects of the priesthood which he has just conferred: the power of hearing confessions and the duty of obedience.

It is a considerable source of astonishment for the laity, who are quite up-to-date on the darker aspects of human life, to see a young priest, less than twenty-five years old, enter a confessional to listen to people reveal discreetly, but clearly all the same, the weaknesses and baseness of sin. Although young seminarians are usually shielded from some of the less edifying aspects of life, here is the bishop sending his newly ordained priests into the midst of sinners, because his people must be purified and because the Lord wants the work of salvation to be accomplished. The power of the keys — "whose sins you shall forgive, they are forgiven them; and whose sins you shall retain, they are retained" — is a service and a manifestation of spiritual charity.

Now that the bishop has given the new young priests all the powers of the priesthood, and has rendered them capable of working in the Lord's vineyard, he reminds them, by way of conclusion, of one of the important conditions of this work: unity, order and discipline. So that their apostolic labor can be ordered, well organized and thereby fertile and salutary, there has to be a supreme authority who arranges its various phases, like a chief of staff in an army; for the Church is, on earth, militant. The bishop, desirous of insuring the perfection of the apostolate in his diocese, before saying farewell to his young priests, demands of them a promise of obedience. Affectionately pressing their joined hands in his, he tells them: "Do you promise to me and my successors, reverence and obedience?" To which each one replies: "I promise." On this basis, the bishop will have excellent helpers united in one and the same zeal, one and the same drive, one and the same pastoral charity. A final sign, the kiss of peace, expresses his joy and his happiness: "May the peace of the Lord be always with you!"

COLLABORATORS OF OUR ORDER

Excellent helpers, we say. The diocesan priest in

fact, has in the eyes of the Church a very obvious significance which springs forth out of history as well as from
the sacred words of the Pontifical: he is the collaborator
of the bishop, *cooperator ordinis nostri.*

A mere glance at early Christianity demonstrates
this with certainty. Overseers and presbyters were placed
in charge of certain communities. But these grew; individual and common needs became greater, more diverse and pressing. The faithful became too numerous.
Places of worship had to be multiplied. The chair of
Christian teaching reserved for the bishop, no longer
sufficed. What was there to do except use the apostolic
faculties and ordain priests in order to confide to them
a portion of the apostolic task? What is such a priest
except a subordinate collaborator of the bishop, his
helper in assisting the growth of God's kingdom?

On each page the Pontifical presupposes the existence
of such a situation. The priests are the "aids" of the
bishop: "We beseech thee, O Lord, to grant to our weakness these *aids,* whom we need all the more the weaker
we are." They are instituted in order to live by his side
and work in concert with him: "Since Thou hast set
the supreme pontiffs to rule over the people, Thou didst
choose as an aid *for their society and their work,* men of
a lesser order and a lower dignity." They are wise collaborators with the bishop: "prudent collaborators of
our Order." For long ago, explains the bishop, when
Moses could not provide all the needs of his divine
mission, the Lord ordered him to choose out of Israel
seventy helpers and aids on whom He would send His
Spirit, seventy Elders, πρεσβύτεροι. Now, he goes on, today it is you who are the successors of those eminent
elders, if you at least show that you are virtuous and enjoy a true maturity in doctrine and action. Likewise, the
bishop continues, our Lord chose seventy-two disciples
whom He sent to preach ahead of Him, so that they
might help the Apostles. Today, in your turn, you will
be of help to the bishop, the successor to the Twelve:
"Therefore strive to be such that you may be able to
be chosen worthily through the grace of God to help

Moses and the twelve Apostles, namely the Catholic bishops represented by Moses and the Apostles." Following many other writers, Cardinal Mercier concluded from these passages, that: "You are the life companions and assistants of your Bishop; the weaker he is, the more he needs you; Providence has placed you at his side to propagate the Faith together with him, and also so that you might provide an echo of the apostolic preaching in the world."[1]

There is more. The Pontifical almost makes this respectful collaboration the very definition of the diocesan priest. "It is a remarkable fact," writes E. Masure, "that the ancient prayers from the Pontifical for the consecration of priests and deacons, at the time when the imposition of hands originally took place, do not speak of eucharistic powers (for the deacons there is a simple allusion to the altar; for the priests, nothing whatever is said), but strongly emphasize their quality as *subordinate auxiliaries of the Bishop*. This is their great title to glory, their definition."[2]

In these perspectives, the doctrinal status of the diocesan clergy, its spirit as well as its functions, is put into a special light: it is with his bishop and under his authority that the priest exercises a certain spiritual stewardship, preaches the *verba salutis* and while glorifying the Holy Trinity gives the world the life of God.

2. THE EPISCOPATE

Occasionally, the Holy Church brings together her faithful and her priests for a solemn ceremony, the consecration of a bishop, the ascent to the "highest priesthood," to the "ministry of the highest priesthood," to the "dignity of the pontificate." And she sums up, in a succinct phrase typical of her, the task which will thenceforth be incumbent upon her chosen one: "The bishop

---

[1] *Fraternité sacerdotale des amis de Jésus*, Bruges, Desclée, p. 90.
[2] *Parish Priest*, pp. 67-68.

must judge, interpret, consecrate, ordain, offer, baptize, and confirm."

DIGNITY OF THE PONTIFICATE

On the day appointed for the ceremony, the "electus" presents himself before the consecrating bishop, who is aided by two assistant bishops. The rites follow, at times austere, often moving and always solemn. First, there is the reading of the "apostolic decree" announcing the election to the episcopate of a priest of the area; then follows the long formula of the "juramentum," through which the new bishop binds himself under oath to remain faithful to the Sovereign Pontiff, to the decrees and prescriptions of the Holy Roman Church; then, the dialogue of the long "examination" to which the consecrating bishop subjects the chosen one, to assure himself of the beliefs and virtues of the latter. These preliminaries over, the sacrifice of the Mass begins.

As in the other ordinations, the Mass is soon interrupted by sacramental rituals. No sooner has the Gradual been completed than the consecrating bishop turns toward the new bishop to remind him of the functions of his office: burdensome functions, of which he shall have to render an accounting; also, together, they immediately implore the help of all the Saints, in the well-known Litanies of Ordinations. During the singing of the *schola*, the bishop-elect prostrates himself in silence.

When the Litanies are finished, the consecrating bishop extends to the chosen one the book of the Gospels, stretches his hands over him while pronouncing these simple words: "Receive the Holy Spirit." He then anoints the bishop-elect's tonsure, saying: "May your head be anointed and consecrated with a heavenly blessing in the pontifical Order," and his hands: "May these hands be anointed with the sanctified oil and the chrism of sanctification." Henceforth the Church can express her joy: she possesses a new pledge of perpetuity.

All that now remains is to present to the new Bishop

the emblems of his dignity: the cross, the ring, and Gospel. Then the Mass resumes until the benediction: only at this time does the consecrating bishop bless the miter and the episcopal gloves. At that moment, the Te Deum of gratitude bursts forth, and the new bishop, clad in his vestments, is led into the church so that he might give the Christians the first fruits of his blessings.

EPISCOPAL RESPONSIBILITY

Reading the liturgical prayers which surround this ceremony to find out what more they say regarding episcopal responsibility, the *onus episcopatus,* one must conclude, along with tradition, that "the principal task of bishops is instruction."

Unquestionably, the authority of the bishop is underscored. He rules over the community of the faithful: "Grant him, O Lord, the episcopal see, for ruling over Thy Church and the people committed to Thee." He enjoys an authentic authority — "Be Thou his authority, his power, his constancy" — which he places at the service of the growth of the household of God, and not to the uses of personal glory, "that he may use, not glory in, the power which Thou dost grant him, unto building up, not destruction." Such passages clearly establish the "power of government."

Likewise, the rite does not forget to mention the sublime ministry of the bishop: "he must consecrate, ordain, offer up . . . confirm." Each of these words would require a long commentary; but the memory of ordinations, consecrations, and confirmations suffices to convince one of the great power of worship which resides in the episcopate.

Nor does one forget that the bishop is the "good shepherd" of the Christian community over whose destiny he presides: the Church reminds him of fidelity and prudence, zeal and solicitude, humility, truthfulness and incorruptibility: "(that) he may be a faithful and prudent servant whom Thou, O Lord, dost appoint over Thy household that he may give them food in due sea-

son, and show forth every man as perfect. Let him be
untiring in solicitude, fervent in spirit; let him hate
arrogance; let him love humility and truth, and may he
never desert either, being overcome by praise or by fear."

And yet, one cannot fail to point out that the *in-
structional mission* of the bishop is the object of the
Church's first concern. She comes back to it with un-
accustomed insistence from the beginning to the end
of the consecratory ceremonies. An extensive "examination" concerns "Faith in the Holy Trinity," the Divine
Scriptures, the traditions of the Fathers who maintained
orthodoxy, the apostolic constitutions. "Do you believe
in the Holy Trinity? . . . Do you believe in the Son of
God Himself? . . . Do you also believe in the Holy Spirit?
. . . Do you believe that the true Church is one, holy,
catholic and apostolic? . . . Do you also believe in the
true resurrection of the flesh?" The questions follow
one another, crowd upon one another, and to each the
chosen one replies: "Credo." This profession of faith
is followed by numerous counsels: "Let the constancy of
faith abound in him. By your gift let his feet be eager
to preach the Gospel of peace, to bring the good news of
Thy goodness. . . . May his words and his preaching not
be in the persuasive words of human wisdom, but in
the manifestation of the spirit and of virtue. . . . Let
him not make the light darkness, nor the darkness light:
let him not call what is evil, good, nor what is good, evil."

Nevertheless, the bishop has a special role in the
magisterium of the Church: "he must . . . interpret":
a leader of the Mystical Body of Christ, he must guide
Christian thought, distinguish authentic truth from
error, interpret the sources of revelation. The cross
which he receives clearly symbolizes his action in this
area: "exercising judgment without wrath . . . in (his)
calmness not abandoning the censure of severity." What
is more, he must defend the truth furiously and be the
champion of orthodoxy: "May he appear terrifying to
the adversaries of truth . . . and fight strongly as their
attacker." This is the significance of the miter worn by
the "athlete of God," *agonista tuus*.

VIRTUES AND RITES

Can we understand now why the consecratory bishop repeatedly calls for perfection and the most diverse virtues? The *interrogationes* of the preliminary examination refer by name to chastity, sobriety, disinterestedness, humility, patience, affability and mercy. Then, the anointing of the tonsure is the occasion for new supplications: "May this, O Lord, flow freely on his head; may it run down into the parts of his mouth; may it descend to the very ends of his whole body, so that the virtue of Thy Spirit may both fill his inner being and surround his exterior." And what shall be the influence of the coming of the Holy Spirit? "Let the constancy of faith, the purity of love, the sincerity of peace, abound in him. . . . Give him the ministry of reconciliation in word and in deeds. . . . Multiply Thy blessing and Thy grace upon him: that he may be always by Thy gift capable of begging for Thy mercy and, by Thy grace, devoted."

In the assembly of these virtues, a choice place is reserved for the bishop's fidelity to the pope. The reading of the *mandatum apostolicum* implies it. The *juramentum* is its suitably detailed expression, and the "examination" formulates its tone very precisely: "Are you willing to show faith, subservience, and obedience, according to canonical authority, in all things, to blessed Peter the Apostle, to whom God gave the power of binding and loosing, and to his Vicar, Pope N., and to his successors, the Roman pontiffs?"

In order to emphasize certain virtues more vigorously, the Church attaches their value to the symbolism of the insignia of episcopal dignity.

The insignia as a whole, by their splendor and brilliance, express the inner beauty which adorns the spirit and soul of the successors to the Apostles: "And therefore, we beseech Thee, O Lord, grant the grace to this Thy servant whom Thou hast chosen for the ministry of the highest priesthood, that whatsoever these veils may show forth in splendor of gold and brilliance of gems, and the variety of many-faceted work, this (man) may display in his morals and his actions. Fulfill in Thy priest the summation of Thy ministry, and sanctify him who is dressed in the vestments of all glorification with the dew of heavenly balm."

As we have already indicated, the cross symbolizes the combination of firmness and suavity which must reign in the repression of faults and errors: "that you may be piously severe in correcting vice, exercising judgment without wrath; in encountering virtues, soothing the spirits of the hearers, not abandoning in calmness the censure of severity."

The ring, seal of the faith, is for the Church a pledge of integrity: "receive the ring, the seal of faith: so that you may watch over spotlessly, adorned with courageous faith, the spouse of God, that is, the holy Church."

The miter is the sign of the vigorous force which must animate the bishop in his intrepid defense of the truth: "O Lord, we have placed on the head of this bishop and athlete of yours the helmet of defense and of salvation, so . . . that he might appear terrifying to the adversaries of the truth; and by Thy gift of grace, might prove strong as their attacker."

Finally, the gloves symbolize the inner and outer purity of him who carries out the highest functions of the ministry of worship, as well as the prudent and wise activity of the leader of the Christian community. The omnipotent Creator, indeed, has given men "the sign of the hand of discretion as an organ of the intellect, to operate correctly." He has also ordered them to keep them pure, "that he might worthily bear the soul in them, and that they might worthily consecrate Thy mysteries in them."

Such is he who has received the Holy Spirit, source of priestly grace: "Receive the Holy Spirit the cornerstone of priestly grace." Such is he who is entrusted with the heavy responsibility of the episcopate: "onus episcopatus."

PART THREE

THE DIOCESAN PRIEST

CHAPTER SEVEN

APOSTOLIC FUNCTIONS

By simply following the path marked out by the ancient formulas of the Roman Pontifical, we have rediscovered themes which are dear to the early writers of Christianity and to which we shall subsequently return: the work of the diocesan priest is as broad as the entire Christian apostolate; this apostolate involves as a component part, a spirit of sanctity; the apostolic ministry requires a high perfection, and the latter, in turn, renders priestly activity fruitful; finally, exercise of the apostolate is, by its very nature, eminently sanctifying because it involves the activities which Christ undertook and implies that one possesses His spirit.

It is time to penetrate further into the theology of the priesthood in order to determine and describe the functions devolving on the diocesan priest, their ontological and juridical foundation, and finally, the conditions which guarantee their full development.

In doing this, we will attempt to draw from doctrine its moral and ascetical consequences, without any break in continuity; dogma, moral and spiritual life must be, here as everywhere, intimately united. In "living" perfectly all that his vocation involves, the priest necessarily practices the great Christian virtues:

charity and faith, wisdom and justice, religion and repentance. He does not have to look for special occasions
to practice these virtues: his ministry provides them in
abundance. The "care of souls" is the permanent exercise of pastoral charity; the magisterium commits the
priest at all times to lead a life of study; the sacred
ministry often leads him to perform acts of religion;
thus, the idea of the sanctification of the clergy through
the duties of state, or, as people say nowadays, "in and
through the apostolate," will acquire a more vivid
clarity.

1. THE LEADER OF THE CHRISTIAN COMMUNITY

In the spiritual testament which he left to the Elders
of Miletus, Paul asked them to "be shepherds of the
Church redeemed in the blood of Jesus." Diocesan priests
are, above all, and in a high sense, the "fathers" of the
Christian community, because for their subjects they
are the source of innumerable blessings.[1] It is this religious and moral paternity, which is also doctrinal and
directive, which gives proper direction to each priestly
effort.

" . . . NOT TO BE MINISTERED UNTO
BUT TO MINISTER"

Nevertheless, these shepherds are the real leaders,
the spiritual heads of the community. "The priest must
be in charge," says the consecrating bishop. And consequently the priest presides over the destinies of his flock.

The authority which the priest enjoys in the sector
of the diocese entrusted to his care, is not a sort of
"private property" which he is free to use as he pleases;
or a privilege which pleasantly accompanies his state in
life; or an easy means of imposing himself on the
faithful or of working for his personal interests. In
the strict sense of the word, it is a "service." "All things
are yours," the Apostle exclaimed, echoing the "I have

[1] See p. 269.

come not to be ministered unto but to minister" of Jesus Christ.

In the image of the Lord who came to serve and not to be served, the diocesan priests are good shepherds: "You are a shepherd," writes Origen. "You see the little lambs of the Lord thrown into chasms because of their ignorance and you do not run to them? You do not call them back? You do not stop them by your cries of alarm? You do not inspire fear in them by your threats?"[2]

Heavy indeed is the responsibility of the shepherd of souls: what will the Lord say to those who have not been devoted to their flocks, if Yahweh could already let fall His lash against the evil shepherds of the Old Covenant? We are familiar with the famous Chapter 34 of Ezechiel:

"Thus says the Lord GOD: Woe to the shepherds of Israel who have been pasturing themselves! Should not shepherds, rather, pasture sheep? You have fed off their milk, worn their wool, and slaughtered the fatlings, but the sheep you have not pastured. You did not strengthen the weak nor heal the sick nor bind up the injured. You did not bring back the strayed nor seek the lost, but you lorded it over them harshly and brutally. So they were scattered for lack of a shepherd, and became food for all the wild beasts. My sheep were scattered and wandered over all the mountains and high hills; my sheep were scattered over the whole earth, with no one to look after them or to search for them. Therefore, shepherds, hear the word of the LORD. . . . . . . I myself will look after and tend my sheep . . . I myself will pasture my sheep; I myself will give them rest. . . . The lost I will seek out, the strayed I will bring back, the injured I will bind up, the sick I will heal [but the sleek and the strong I will destroy], shepherding them rightly."

He who is called to the episcopate, explains G. Bardy — and he is undoubtedly thinking of the whole priest-

---

[2] *In Jesu Nave, Hom.* VII, 6; according to G. Bardy, *art. cit.*, vol. 53, p. 162.

hood — "is not only called unto the government but to the *service* of the whole Church, and not merely humility is required of him; it is truly service, one might even say slavery."[3] Those who govern "must find their happiness not in themselves commanding men, but in being useful to them."[4] Still, priests enjoy an incontestable authority in the entire domain of Christian life and not only in matters which concern the soul and the heart. If they can sin through an arrogant and touchy authoritarianism, their faithful people can sin just as much by a self-sufficiency quite as arrogant and touchy.

This authority gains by being exercised with the expansiveness which characterizes powerful spirits. It is called "governing" and not just administering. He who administers is concerned with putting order in all the procedures which the parish ministry involves, the less causes of difficulties and bother there are, the better: "what is in order should not be disturbed," and the phrase is accurate. He who governs considers the job to be done, reflects on it, forces its execution through all the vicissitudes of life, to the limit of his forces, and brings along in his wake all his subordinates. Government and administration are, moreover, at the service of the apostolate and determined by the latter.

QUALITIES OF THE GOOD SHEPHERD

The priest must doubtless be a leader. Not, however by always exacting recognition of his privileged position; it is pointless to attempt this. Nor only by displaying a great forcefulness of character; we no longer define a leader primarily by his qualities of will. The leader, first of all, must know where we come from and where we are going; he must possess a philosophy of history which is sure and accurate, so that he will not be a blind man leading other blind men to the abyss. His predominant quality is *prudence* in the theological sense of the

---

[3] G. Bardy, *art. cit.*, vol. 53, p. 156.
[4] St. Gregory the Great, *Regula Pastoralis*, Coll. "Pax," ed., Maredsous, 1928, p. 60.

term: the art of perfectly adapting given means to a goal pursued and desired. The role of the leader is therefore to be a source of order. He has to reflect and foresee, organize and command, coordinate and check.

The good pastor knows where his parish stands, what has succeeded and why, what has failed and why. He is able to reflect on the real situations revealed to him by the "spiritual" map of his apostolic sector; he knows how to provide himself with documentation, to observe, judge, look for the evil and discover the remedy; to compare with other situations, to desire further progress. Capable of precise inspection and imaginative efforts, he knows where he is going and where he is leading others. His directives are clear, though flexible and feasible; they guarantee the continuity and harmony of common efforts.

In charge of souls, he must be able to *organize*, to draw up a picture of the parish and assign each one his place. He must arouse the cooperation which is unaware of itself and develop what is needed, instead of waiting smugly for it to present itself. Then he must assign roles, give promotions and change assignments, or be grateful tactfully, without regard to personalities: for the common good has its rights! "The priest will be sensitive to individual differences. He will never force anyone's hand, but he will, however, suggest and in certain cases be able to make someone want to act. Finally, he will avoid asking for help too late, when the will is already discouraged and resigned to abstaining."

In order to make his aides act effectively and without requiring what is useless or impossible, it is well for the priest to know a little about everything and to be a "specialist in general ideas." Thanks to clear orders and practical points, he communicates understanding of a function, the meaning of a mission, especially as regards lowly but indispensable tasks. Moreover, he opens up a large field for initiative in order to obtain ardor and sustain zeal, instead of nourishing the passivity of some and the indifference of others. Still, he never forgets that his own role consists in bringing within the limits of a fruitful coordination the centrifugal individual forces.

To *coordinate* is to tie together efforts and harmonize activities toward the known and desired goal. It is to nourish the common spirit which makes the work joyous, more spontaneous and more successful. It is to profit from the ideas of others, from their remarks and their experience, in order to perfect constantly the impulse which must come from the center. The good shepherd does not accept every proposal, just as he does not say "no" a priori; he puts everything through the crucible of his supernatural wisdom and keeps what is precious for the work of the Lord.

While giving to his leaders and delegates the capacity for running things by themselves when it is something that comes from them, he is careful that everything is done in accordance with his directions; but he does not block or cut off initiative. He oversees everything with tact and discretion — he has the knack for this — in order to become aware of the work done and to form persons by explanation, by advice, by congratulation. His *checking* is total, sure and competent, impartial and opportune; it is always followed by a judgment or a sanction. To maintain a middle ground between wearisome sameness and delay which make everything useless, to be able to evaluate unobtrusively the methods, the principles, or the performance of a service, is one of the priest's very delicate functions in his role as pastor of a parish.

HUMAN AND SOCIAL VIRTUES

This kind of exercise of authority presupposes in the priest a fine array of natural and human qualities, the same which Paul demanded from Titus or Timothy, which St. Gregory listed in his *Regula pastoralis*.

Every good shepherd possesses a certain power of intellectual work, a good deal of breadth of view and vigor of spirit. He is capable of conceiving something other than what now exists, and he does not resign himself to *de facto* situations, recommending only palliatives. He can see farther than others in order to point out the way to them: for "it is a sheer waste for an army to engage itself actively in pursuit of the enemy if, through the fault of the general in command, it is following a false trail."[5] He sees clearly and dreads letting himself be led astray by easy formulas. Pitilessly realistic, he is docile enough to respect the facts, but also energetic enough to try to guide them. He follows attentively all the stirrings of his environment. Keeping constantly in view the principles of his action, he remains flexible and readapts existing institutions to their goal without any jarring effects. He exerts influence by his judgment, that is, by his sense of proportion, of the possibilities and the opportunities at hand. His good sense is compounded of tact and prudence, of moderation and practical psychology. In addition, he joins an extensive general culture to a respected professional competence.

He is valiant, enterprising and *persevering*. He is also strong enough to drop a cherished undertaking which has proved to be unsuitable to the apostolic goals. He has initiative and courageously supports his responsibilities; he knows how to accept and endure. Every morning, he refreshes this iron will which commands attention, sharpens effort, directs the choice of means, activates decisions and maintains the execution to the end. He knows how to examine calmly, maturely, at length, but without confusing wisdom and slowness. He rejects everything that smacks of pessimism, skepticism, obstructionism. His profound convictions entertain and feed an immense desire for growth and progress. He believes firmly in the possibility of progress and improvement. He is tenacious and holds fast at all times and in spite of all. Every day, he starts up again in little things, without pause or respite, without seeing immediate results. In his action, he proceeds with order and dares to multiply responsibilities by decentralizing. He has the

[5] St. Gregory the Great, *Regula pastoralis*, p. 72.

courage to busy himself only with what he can lead to a successful conclusion, for he prefers to abstain rather than to act by halves.

In his social relations, he is agreeably optimistic and always in good humor, even in times of stress, with no trace of a smug smile or lazy serenity. He radiates enthusiasm and conviction, has an attractive character, is patient and lacks rancor, coldness, and disdain. Wherever he goes, he spreads a spirit of real and serious activity. He is discreet and respects other people's personalities. Always and everywhere he remains himself, without rudeness, but sincerely. He avoids what might discredit him and avoids the slightest gesture that might be in contradiction to the principles he is defending. "The agitated leader wears himself out for mediocre results. The active and calm leader commands every will to the same goal methodically, without great fuss and with few words. He does not allow himself to be bogged down by details which are none of his business. He knows how to distract himself, to provide for air and energy, to keep a cool head. . . . "

Finally, he absolutely avoids that clerical pride so well described by St. Gregory the Great:

"Sometimes the pastor, by the very fact that he is established in dignity above others, becomes puffed up with thoughts of pride. Since everything is at his disposal; since what he commands is promptly executed according to his wishes; since all those who are under his orders load him with praise when what he does is good, but raise no objection to his reprehensible actions; since almost always they go so far as to flatter in him that which they should rather censure; it happens that, led astray by these base tendencies, his soul swells with presumption, and, surrounded externally by unreserved applause, he may be internally void of truth. Ignorant about himself, he falls back on the opinion of others, and believes himself to be just as he hears himself evaluated on the ouside and not as he should judge himself on the inside. He scorns those who are subject to him, forgets that they are his equals in the order of nature, and imagines that by the merits of his life, he has at the same time surpassed those over whom he has been placed by the attribution of power. He flatters himself that he surpasses in wisdom those to whom he sees himself superior in power. In his own opinion, he sets himself up truly on a kind of pedestal."[6]

However, let us not forget that sacerdotal authority is more than a function; it is identified with the person of the priest. Christ defined Himself, for the Apostles, as follows: "I am the good shepherd." In his turn, the diocesan priest in all that concerns the collective and individual direction of his faithful people, is a *pastor bonus*, full of religious sense, paternal severity, ardent zeal, and human understanding. It is not only through his official functions that he comes into contact with Christians, but through his whole person and all his efforts. He must often recall the thousand and one details which weave the web of his life and which may tarnish or brighten the brilliance of his pastoral charity. In governing men, a number of qualities have proved to be precious and indispensable. They are necessary in church and on the street, during visits and on a trip, in meetings and in correspondence, in contacts with superiors and colleagues, relatives and civil authorities, old men and children, rich and poor, the faithful and sinners. They are called tact, humor, attentiveness, sociability, anticipation and propriety, amiability and courtesy, grace and refinement, delicacy without affectation, politeness without pretense, tenderness without sentimentality, sweetness without tastelessness, consideration without obsequiousness, reserve and discretion, deference and *savoir-faire*, vivacity and aplomb. To know how to ask and how to say "thank you"; to congratulate without flattering; to command without a superior air; to correct without smugness; to welcome cordially and to dismiss without brusqueness.[7]

[6] St. Gregory the Great, *Regula pastoralis*, p. 62.
[7] Read especially St. John Chrysostom, *Dialogue sur le sacerdoce*, book III.

2. The Teacher of the Christian People

WORDS OF SALVATION

The collective direction of the parish, if it is well handled, is a precious help for the faithful, and the supernatural profit which they draw therefrom is not small. On the other hand, when parish administration leaves much to be desired, especially when the art of governing paternally is lacking, when contact with the parishioners is broken, the work of the Lord is less easily accomplished.

Still, the task of direction is subordinated to another activity which is more directly apostolic, because it is of itself, a source of grace: that activity whose object is the word of life and the religious rites. We would not go so far as to say, with Charles Héris, that the power of teaching is relative to the power of worship, because it finds its end in itself. He says: "nor must we forget that one of the essential functions of the power of government in the Church is the teaching of the truth; and that this truth is absolutely necessary for Christian worship to ensure its development and full efficacy on souls. For the latter go to God only in the light of faith; and this light can only be communicated to them through the teaching of the Church. Of course, it pertains to worship to communicate to souls, by means of the sacraments, sanctifying grace and along with grace, the virtue of faith which makes them adhere to the word of God. . . . "[8] It would seem that this overlooks the fact that grace is a response to faith, either *with* the sacramental rites which are "sacraments of faith," or *without* the rites, through believing adherence. While Protestants exaggerate this last truth, Catholics may not appreciate it enough.

When a Christian applies to himself religiously the words pronounced by the priest, when he piously reads

[8] *L'Eglise du Christ*, Ed. du Cerf, 1930, pp. 80-81. Cf. also *Préface*, p. v.

Sacred Scripture or a book of sound spirituality, the work of the faith is accomplished, the Word is formed in him, the vitality of the grace in his soul increases and is accentuated. It is not necessary that some ritual crown the act of the believer. This is why preaching is a solemn and sacred ministry to which religious care must be given.

MULTIPLE TESTIMONY

Upon laying his hands on the ordinand, the bishop says to him: "the priest must preach." This is the mission given by Christ Himself to His Apostles: "Go and make disciples of all nations." A doctrine is involved, not some new and subtle philosophy, "persuasive words of human wisdom," but words of life, words of salvation." Paul preaches and travels throughout the communities of Asia Minor and of Greece: "Woe to me if I have not preached the Gospel." All the Apostles assume the responsibility for the apostolate of truth: "We are unable not to speak." They are the witnesses of this truth, and the witnesses of the resurrection of Christ; finally, they will be the witnesses or "martyrs" of the Lord, the substantial Truth.

Thus the Church has the power to teach, and the duty to teach, but primarily in the field of *theology and the spiritual life.* There is a certain arrogance in imagining that some theological knowledge gives one the right to make decisive judgments in all the matters which divide men, particularly in political debate, in the various aspects of social, economic or scientific life: such an attitude is presumptuous and naïve. But it would be lax to neglect, through inconsistency or incompetence, the role of directing wisdom which Christ has entrusted to His Church: she alone, because she knows man's final end, can, in the last analysis, judge the "human" and "progressive" value of all earthly realities which are for men the providential instrument of their personal development. Obviously, a harmonious interplay between this doctrinal modesty and this universal presence is needed.

The priest has been placed in charge of instruction *in all its forms*. Christ and His Apostles mostly preached; their apostolate was exercised through words. But the Evangelists and the Apostles wrote: do we regret the fact today that Mark was asked by Peter to write down his vivid accounts of the Lord's life? Do we regret that Paul, during his captivity in Rome, wrote the Epistle to the Ephesians? The form of teaching is of small importance, so long as Christ is preached. Today, books, novels, newspapers, the press, radio, and films must, in their turn, through the activity of laymen, extend the teaching of the Apostles, thus renewing the application of the one unchanging precept: "Go and make disciples of all nations."

An apostle's words have a special power. All human speech already has the power of arousing in the mind or imagination of its hearers a more vigorous stirring of life than a speaker can foresee. The communication of revelation is a more delicate thing. It terminates in the soul of the faithful where the Holy Spirit lives and works. It is spoken in the name of Christ. The priest is the intermediary, the sign, the echo of the voice of the Word; it is as authentic mediator that he articulates the "words of salvation." And no matter what his skill, he must be distinguished from the ordinary believer, for he is the organ of the Church and the object of illuminating grace.

Finally, the work of instruction is confided to a *person*. Preaching is not only a function, but an act of the whole person. A man's life speaks more effectively than his words. His example, on the whole, is clearer than his explanations and more compelling. *Witnesses*. Christ did not want punctual but impersonal servants, who would speak to the baptized every Sunday and then sow in these same souls seeds of error by the unfortunate example and inconsistency of their lives. He desired apostles who would preach Him at all times. He said "I am the truth," and not "I speak the truth."

NATURAL TALENTS

The teaching mission also calls for many natural and
supernatural talents on the part of the priest. Destined
to preach — on so many occasions and in so many ways
— he must have good training in public speaking. In his
Retraite pastorale, Cardinal Mercier insists on the need
of learning elocution and connects this to the bishop's
charge of "the priest must preach":

"Your role as preacher must make you determine,
especially you younger colleagues, to cultivate your voice,
to watch your diction, to become skilled in elocution. The
formation of young men in the humanities is defective.
It seems, when one looks at the program of literary
studies, that the mature man they are preparing will
have no other social role than to write, whereas, in fact,
those who do write are the exception, and those who
speak, the general rule. Apply yourselves, therefore, to
speaking, that is, to giving your thoughts clear, spontaneous, personal, living expression. That is the price
you must pay for the communicative power of your
words. The public is tired of rhetoric; it tolerates with
impatience and without profit, phrases which are more
or less equally balanced, painfully committed to memory,
and then repeated without feeling or with fictitious
warmth on the day the discourse is finally pronounced.

"Public speaking is the natural expression of a felt
conviction which the orator wishes to transfer from his
own soul into the soul of his hearers. The material word
is only a vehicle and can neither occupy nor hold the
attention for its own sake. The sacred orator more than
any other, must efface himself in order to allow the divine
teachings, of which he is but the interpreter, to pass
through freely. The more his language approaches the
candor and transparency of glass, the less he places
obstacles in the path of the diffusion of the rays of divine
truth, the more it will be that 'fidelis sermo et omni ac-
ceptione dignus,' the faithful discourse worthy of all
belief by Christian gatherings, which St. Paul recommended to his disciple Timothy. Practice your speaking,
therefore, so as to become master of it and not have to

sacrifice, at a critical moment, the faith and the ardor
of the love which animates you, to embarrassing efforts
at material expression."

Progress in public speaking is, for the priest, as
much an apostolic activity as the acquisition of doctrine
through study and reading.

THEOLOGY AND KERYGMA

This eloquence would be in vain if it were hollow
and empty, similar to the "persuasive words" criticized
by the Apostle: indeed, it is necessary that the priest be
doctrinally well prepared, at least if he wants to avoid
the blows of Yahweh's wrath against those shepherds
who "know no discretion" (Is. 56:11) and those who,
though they "[deal] with the law," "[know] me not"
(Jer. 2:8).

First of all, he will pursue his study of the sciences
pertaining to priestly work itself, so that Christ's thinking will become connatural to him: this is the specific
purpose of dogmatic theology and of Holy Scripture.
But it is necessary to be clear here and distinguish
theological science and exegetical science from the
preaching of the Christian mystery. Precisely because
it is scientific, theology is presented impersonally, is
preoccupied with concepts and arguments; discursive
and deductive, it is naturally austere and arid. On the
other hand, let us look at what takes place in the preaching of Christ and His Apostles. They are animated with
unparalleled personal conviction, the famous παρρησία
of the Acts of the Apostles. They are concerned with
affirming mysterious realities of which they say they
are eyewitnesses: for they walk "with their eyes open
to the deific light."[9] They are swift and direct.

It has been written that:

---

[9] *Règle de S. Benoît* (Coll., "Pax," Maredsous, 1933, p. 8: apertis
oculis nostris ad deificum lumen.

"Christ is a witness rather than a man of science. The witness is he who has seen an event and tells of its various phases. Thus it will be in our preaching: to see the supernatural realities and to tell about them (dogmatic theology) ; to see the moral incompatibility between the 'new man' and his actions, and to point it out (moral theology), as St. Paul used to do so powerfully. Christ is more visual than logical in His preaching. He sees what is 'in Patre.' He is more interested in the divine realities themselves than, if we may say so, in their definitions. He gives to men the 'sense' of these realities. He reveals their 'existence' before committing Himself to the path which leads to a rigorous definition of their nature, their 'essence.' He initiates man into religious contact with God rather than attempt to lead his intellect through the maze of reasoning. Before being a man of science, Christ is the great, the unique, the divine witness: *ipse ennaravit.*"

If our preaching bore a closer resemblance to that of Christ and the Apostles, it would unquestionably not deserve the reproaches given to it today. Christ was reproved for proposing an intransigent doctrine, one in opposition to the so-called "traditional" doctrine; such reproaches are hardly addressed to us. But there are others, which do not need to be repeated here. Where we fail, if we reflect on the matter, is in our use of doctrine. We do not need to create a different theology — our task, rather, is to complete and revise what we have — but we do need to make the transition from the level of theory to that of application less clumsily. This difficult skill should be the object of some very searching lessons in "sacred eloquence"; instead, it is quite neglected. It should be the object of scrupulous attention, so that priests would be capable, not of instructing in theology, but of transposing into practical terms theological ideas, principles, concepts, for the benefit of their people. The nature of this practical task, its conditions, its forms, should be minutely examined by every priest, for all are consecrated to the work of the teaching magisterium.

STUDY AND COMPETENCE

After mastering the art of transposing theological truths, the priest should spend effort in completing and, where necessary, revising them.

First, to *complete* them. While safeguarding the knowledge of the essential data given him in the seminary, he will note the fact that certain points, which were only touched on, are of particular interest to him and that he needs to know more about them. He will also note that certain questions are not even answered in the treatises, especially as regards Christian thinking on the meaning of temporal and worldly reality. To be sure, there exists in principle a theology of worldly values since Paul, who wrote to the Colossians that "all things hold together in Him." We still have no "science" built on this foundation stone. We have elements concerning the theology of human societies — civil society, family society, and professional society; we have fragments of a theology of culture, of thought and of the concrete realities which ensure its expression — literature, motion pictures, music; we have fleeting indications regarding a theology of art and technology. But all of this does not add up to an organic and systematic whole to which one could give the name of "theological science."

"A theologian stated twenty-five years ago, that: one must have the courage to recognize that too many questions which are the requests of life itself have remained not only unanswered but undiscussed in the work of theologians. Whereas work is one of the greatest of human facts and modern States are trying to give it status, where do we have a theology of work, and not only of work, but also of what is the necessary complement thereto, a theology of leisure and of rest? Yet, so long as we do not have a theology of work and of rest — *and not merely certain great principles from the Bible or the encyclicals, but a truly scientific, properly theological study,* with research and statistics, historical background and development of the doctrine down to its least elements — I maintain that the theological balance-sheet is absolutely on the debit side as regards what constitutes the immense, the greatest factor in human life. . . . It is essential that we, the clergy, bring our efforts to bear and apply our vocation as the 'salt of the earth' to theology itself, as the human science of the things of the faith or which touch the faith. So long as we have not developed the theology of the great human realities which we must regain for Christ, we will not have done the first of the things that have to be done."

How, in fact, can we work without knowing where we are going?

We must complete our theology and, where necessary, revise it, in order to rejuvenate this ancient science. We must find the words which will suggest clearly the abstract idea which the theological concept involves, in order to permit the discovery of the reality studied by theology. We must identify the present-day errors which are undermining the basis of this or that dogmatic thesis, in order to show men that this thesis possesses today a "presence" in human society, and that it is not necessary to go back fifteen centuries to see it at work in the lives of men. If there are errors nowadays concerning the hereafter, why speak only of Origenism? Let us find the present-day application of moral verities and doctrinal principles: men want to know how the precept of charity can be applied today. Here again, the example of the Apostle Paul is characteristic; he presents Christian thought *in terms* of the thinking of his contemporaries, and especially the Jews, so that from his Epistles alone, one can arrive at the essential elements of Judaism which are in opposition to Christianity. If we were to make the counter-test, might men likewise be able to pick out from our ordinary preaching the larger features of the fundamental errors which mark our century and which are undermining Christian thought? Once again, men might conclude that we are not traditional, at least, if by tradition, we understand the age of the Apostles and of the Lord.

WISDOM OF GOD AND WISDOM OF THE WORLD

But more is needed. Regardless of his skill, the priest must have, on a permanent basis, a mature and sure judgment, that is to say, since he is a Christian, a *judgment regulated according to divine wisdom* and revelation, a judgment in harmony with the work of the Spirit in the intellect, a judgment according to the faith.

What good would it do for the priest to preach the Gospel, if his conversation is ruled by purely human interests, selfish motives, an erroneous vision of the value of creatures?

To be truly the "teacher of his people," the priest must lead a life of intense faith.

Cardinal van Roey writes:

"Faith causes us to enter into communion with the thought of God, revealed by His Word, Christ Jesus, and taught by His Church. To live by faith is to apply to all our reasoning, our judgments and evaluations, the divine criteria such as we know them by revelation, through the formal doctrine of the Church or the directives of her hierarchy. Current ideas and opinions, theories and ideologies, events of a general nature which constitute the history of a nation, of the universe and of the Church, the thousand circumstances of great or minimal importance which form the weft of our life, we must insist on measuring according to the rules of faith, that is, considering them in relation to God: to use a formula which conveys our meaning best, it is necessary to see all things in God. Then does everything appear in a new light: the man of faith understands things differently from the natural man, because his spirit is conformed to the spirit of God."[10]

To believe, says St. Thomas, too, very concretely, is to see with the eyes of God: "Faith is an assimilation to divine knowledge, in that through the faith given us we cleave to the first truth for its own sake, and enlightened

[10] *Collectanea Mechliniensia*, 1939, p. 600.

thus by divine knowledge we see all things as with the eyes of God."[11]

Unfortunately, we often look with eyes of the world and our own interests. The world finds that such and such a book is wonderful and we agree that it is fine indeed. The world prefers extraordinary prowess to the humble duties of state, and we share its admiration. It is fascinated by the talent which shines far more than by hidden virtue, and we share its illusory enthusiasm. It is beclouded by passions, and we follow where it leads. It defends the privileges of caste, of group, and we do the same thing, whereas we represent the transcendent interests of Christ and the Church.

The man of the world prides himself on his balance, but he lacks the equilibrium demanded by the Spirit. He boasts of keeping his sense of proportion and he installs himself smugly in mediocrity. He proclaims his sense of measure, whereas the law of love is to love without limits: this is the measure of the saints! He recommends a prudence that has nothing supernaturally bold about it. The word wisdom is always on his lips, but "the world did not come to know God by 'wisdom'... ; the foolishness of God is wiser than men. The foolish things of the world has God chosen to put to shame the 'wise,' and the weak things of the world has God chosen to put to shame the strong" (1 Cor. 1:21-27).

The world judges according to the *earth;* it takes its standards from men on its side. Its motives and reasons for acting are garnered here below. Its tastes coincide with the tendencies of those who have ensconced themselves in this transitory dwelling place as if they were to remain there forever. But only God renders an absolute, simple, and decisive judgment on things, situations, and persons. And "the sensual man does not perceive the things that are of the Spirit of God, for it is foolishness to him and he cannot understand, because it is examined spiritually" (1 Cor. 2:14).

The worldly man judges in terms of the *visible* crea-

---

[11] *In Boeth. de Trinitate,* q. III, a. 1.

ture. He is impressed by the tangible, captivated by the visible, fascinated by physical beauty. The sight of physical misery moves him far more than the perception of an intellectual disability, and infinitely more than a moral weakness. He will say that certain sinful weaknesses in those whom one loves are gracious and charming. A wound which disfigures the face makes him shudder; he prefers a hundred times over that one besmirch the brilliancy of the image of Christ which the believer bears in his heart. Does he, therefore, deny the existence of invisible reality? Not exactly. But for him it has a secondary value, vague and insubstantial. It has no real place in his world; it entails no consequences for his life; it presents no dangers and is practically nonexistent.

Finally, the worldly man judges in terms of *time*. He ignores the fact that only God and His saints, being constituted in a definitive state, possess the key which opens supernatural secrets, and alone render a judgment of absolute value on the earthly world. But he lacks the perspective of eternity; he occasionally recognizes it, but it is practically inoperative. Indeed, he lives in time and for time. He regulates his conduct, intrigues, and hopes according to the anticipated duration of his life: sixty, eighty years. Everything is done in view of the success to be achieved here below. For the rest, he abstracts from eternity. His greatest desire is to enter it without being obliged to think about all he is leaving behind.

To judge according to faith is to come close to the saints — those authentic models of personality according to the Church — and to see reality as they see it and not as we understand it. It is to think as they thought, and not as the world does. It is to love what they loved, appreciate what they esteemed, taste what delighted them, desire what they possessed, tend toward what attracted them, admire what fascinated them, consider what they contemplated. In short, it is to place ourselves in their path, in their school. To be sure, the worldly man has no interest in the saint, he laughs at him. Yet the saint alone sees clearly: he sees according to God and in God.

Real discernment is that which sees the infinite distance between the lasting and the transitory. True success is measured by the degree of beatifying union that will be publicly proclaimed at the second coming of the glorious Christ. The enlightened man trusts in eternal values. In the last analysis, authentic wisdom comes down to knowing the purpose of life and the best means of attaining it.

The priest is not a man of the world. Nevertheless, to the extent that he has retained in his spirit the taste and vices of the world, he has become useless, like the salt that has lost its savor or the cleric who has become an apostate. He is the accomplice of those Christians whose interests are served by rendering him inoffensive. In all his judgments, he halts and thwarts the expansion of revealed truth and the growth of the Church. This is the gravest sin he can commit against the magisterium with which he is entrusted.

3. THE MINISTER OF GRACE AND OF ADORATION

Preaching the Word is not, for the priest, simply a help, a sacred instrument, in his work of spiritual charity. As with any religious body, the Catholic Church has a network of rites; the role of the Church's rites is to transmit to men the Life which is in God and which spreads from Him to us here below: "the charity of Christ is spread abroad in our hearts." Along with the "Word," the "rites" are holy vehicles, privileged intermediaries through which God comes to men.

THE SALVATION OF THE WORLD

The priest is thus, with Christ, a "savior"; he is sent, like Christ, "that [we] might have life and have it more abundantly." He therefore enjoys a spiritual paternity of a very high order, closer to the divine paternity than that of parents in the order of the flesh.

For the first, "prototypical" paternity is that of God the
Father: a wholly spiritual and supernatural paternity,
one of universal and essential fruitfulness. The priest,
taken up into the work of the Redemption, is "father"
in his turn: he simply expresses in his actions and in his
words the loving sentiments of "our Mother the holy
Church." The priest, instrument of the Lord, gives life:
"The priest must baptize. . . . Ministers of Christ and
dispensers of the Mysteries of God."

Just as the sacred Person of the Lord was the source
of bodily health and salvation — "virtue went out from
him and healed all" — so too the person of the priest is
also like a "sacrament" for the faithful people, a living
sacrament, a sign of mediation, a means by which men
come closer to their Creator. That is what Christ wished:
"I am the Life." He did not institute a business involving certain daily services; He chose Apostles.

The priest is vowed to the sanctification of men; as
such, he exists for men. The Apostles were not chosen
so that there would be in the world a caste endowed
with divine powers, but so that men would receive the
life of Christ. If he is truly apostolic, the priest likes
to remind himself that a divine attentiveness has called
him to serve in the militia of God. He rejoices that he
can administer the sacraments, distribute the Holy
Eucharist, celebrate the eucharistic sacrifice. Also, he
tries to be, in his whole life, a "sacrament" in the broad
sense, in order to carry in all his actions a sanctifying,
converting power. He acquires the habit of formulating
universal and wide-range redemptive intentions, like
those of Christ, as ecumenical as those of the Apostles:
"When St. Paul prayed, he had the map of the Churches
present in his mind; he saw them as shining lights amid
the shadows of paganism."[12]

Moreover, he *eliminates* whatever in him is in opposition to his vocation of doing good. He countenances no
dilettantism in the serious work of the salvation of the

    [12] J. Huby, S.J., *Les épîtres de la captivité*, coll. "Verbum Salu-
tis," VIII, p. 27.

world: Christ was not a dilettante. He shakes off laziness and indolence; "the charity of Christ urges us," as the Apostle said. He rejects temporal occupations that would prevent the carrying out of his sacred ministry. He eliminates all indifference that would make him insensitive to the saving desires of the Lord. He removes all that is vain, worldly, and mediocre — in short, everything that can be a source of death for believers.

If the priest would religiously administer the sacraments, if he would celebrate all the liturgical ceremonies with respect, something would change in the Church; the faithful, and nonbelievers, too, would be attracted in spite of themselves to the mysterious source of such a life of worship. For this to happen will require much self-mastery, much renunciation, many sacrifices, and much intelligent fervor.

SACRAMENTS AND CHRISTIAN LIFE

Let us not be misunderstood when we write that the salvation of men depends on the priest; let no one ascribe to us the kind of clericalism which is so harmful to the religious development of the faithful. The general economy of God's entrance into man's life shows that He wants to give Himself to men: the act of supreme charity which He manifests in the Creation and the Redemption is sufficient proof. For their part, men receive God and His life the moment they open themselves to Him, the moment they turn toward the substantive Light and open themselves to Love. To this point, we have assumed only invisible, interior, or at least personal, links between man and God. This kind of link is a fundamental aspect of the virtue of religion, so important that the vivifying instrumentality of the "word" and of "rites" depends in good measure on it; such a link is presupposed when we say that one must hear Christian preaching and approach the sacraments with "good dispositions."

Why sermons, then, why sacraments and the sacramentals? All religions, we know, because they respect

the visible nature of man and of society, draw up confessions of faith and propose sacred rites. These are
agents designed to effect contact between the soul and
God, to bring one closer to supernatural reality by their
symbolism and to give one the divine life which is attached to their material nature; they are accordingly
called the visible signs of invisible grace. This definition is customarily applied to the sacraments, but,
servatis servandis, it applies to preaching as well.

Because he is the representative of the Catholic
religion, the priest is particularly interested in the
visible, ritual framework of the Church; he is, by definition, the man of the "visible" word and the "ecclesiastical" rites. He is the one charged with ensuring their
performance, from Baptism through Extreme Unction.
One can therefore understand that he likes to see people
come to church, listen to the sermons he preaches there,
and receive the sacraments which he administers. It
is a short step from this to judging the "religious"
worth of his parishioners in terms of their church attendance. It must be acknowledged that the attendance
of the faithful at Church is one index of religious life;
the latter almost spontaneously seeks certain tangible
and sacred manifestations, the living witness of which
is the temple of stone. But the accurate and adequate
measure of religious life depends, above all, on the
quality of the inner life of the faithful, on their authentic
charity, on their union with God or with Christ. Yet
is it obvious that the persons making the greatest use
of sermons and rites are always, in point of fact, the
most charitable, the most united and "bound" to God?

The error would become outrageous if the priest
were to measure not only the religious life but even
the "Christianity" of his parishioners on the basis of
their attendance at sermons and liturgical ceremonies.
Regular presence of Christians at cultual manifestations certainly proves that they practice a visible religion better than others; but can it be legitimately in-
ferred from this that they have ipso facto, in highly
developed form, the virtues of justice, charity, fortitude

or temperance? Here again the priest, because his mission is particularly ecclesiastical and ritual, could be tempted to identify "Christian" values with the virtue of "religion." This is a common mistake. Good "practicing Catholics" refer to themselves as and believe themselves too readily to be, "good Christians." Are they good Christians, these bigots who have no sense of charity, those workers who botch their work, or employers who do not respect the laws of justice? We know the harm this unfortunate and vague use of words and these errors of judgment have done to the Church.

ADORATION AND PRAISE

The work of the ministry of worship does not concern only the sanctification of men; the sacraments are not merely the "channels" of grace, as they are too often considered. The priest also represents mankind in the presence of God, in order to offer Him the tribute of its *adoration* and *praise*, in order to ask His grace and blessing, in order to implore Him humbly for the forgiveness of its sins.

The Epistle to the Hebrews, because it describes the Christian priesthood as an antitype of that of the Temple, touches on this aspect of our apostolate: "For every high priest taken from among men is appointed for men in the things pertaining to God, that he might offer gifts and sacrifices for sins" (5:1-2). Petition, thanksgiving, expiation, and the praise of glorification, such are the ascendant activities which the earthly mediator continues in the name of mankind.

This role and service of praise and glorification is indeed ours: "Come, let us sing praise to the Lord, let us rejoice in God our Savior; let us be occupied before Him in praise, and let us rejoice in Him with psalms." These acts rise up toward God, the only absolute, and lose themselves in Him. It is perfectly useless to expect therefrom in return any concrete advantage for oneself or for mankind; the reward is included in the very act of glorification itself, since it elevates us in performing it; humanity acquires new stature by recognizing that God alone is the absolute toward whom everything must be oriented and in whom everything terminates.

This is priestly prayer. When in the presence of His Apostles Christ solemnly pronounced the words that would defy the attrition of the centuries: "Do this in commemoration of me," He wanted the Catholic priesthood to accept the responsibility for perpetuating the Christian sacrifice, rich in adoration, praise and thanksgiving. When the Church entrusted her priests with the reading of the Divine Office, she wanted to point out to them that the *Opus Dei,* the divine work, is also directed toward heaven. Coming from Christ or the Church, these prayers are particularly worthy and agreeable to God; may we acquire their meaning and value them accordingly.

Do these prayers exclude *private praise* which rises serenely and disinterestedly toward God? They rather demand it as a logical corollary to the direction officially given by Jesus Christ. Gathering therefore all of visible and invisible creation, the material and the immaterial universe, we offer it through the Word to the Father, in filial and grateful homage. Here, if we are not prolonging the visible mediation for mankind of Christ in the world, at least we are carrying out our service of universal mediation. "Bless the Lord, all ye His works."

Glorification, like praise, does not result only from specific acts. Alongside formal glorification which is expressed religiously by our human lips, theologians place ontological glorification, that which is sung silently by the very being of every creature, whose intensity is measured in each case by its degree of perfection. A created being is perfect to the extent that it "is," and it "is" by participation in the being of God, to the extent that, in itself, it proclaims the splendor, the fullness and perfection of the Trinity.

Can we therefore perceive the potential for glorification in the pastoral ministry itself? It is totally directed toward one goal: to make men more like God, to make societies and cultures more Christian. It is completely directed toward increasing the inner power of praise and adoration which creatures conceal. If this apostolic labor is accompanied by a chant of thanksgiving or of humble supplication, does it not constitute a very complete form of Christian praise?

The priest himself is glorification and praise according to his degree of being, that is, of likeness to God through the Spirit. By becoming like unto God, he best represents the divine perfection and more intensely radiates the beauty of the Three Persons. This role seems to fall to him by function; Christ did not charge the Catholic priesthood with speaking His praise by its official actions, and denying it by its life; He did not choose apostolic functionaries, but Apostles in their whole persons, just as He did not say, "I give life," but "I am the life." For the priest personal sanctification is a necessity of function as well as an individual obligation; grace is given him for this purpose. "Let the odor of your lives," the Pontifical repeats, "be the delight of the Church of Christ."

Does not the splendid prayer of Serapion the Bishop spring from a priestly heart?

"It is worthy and just to praise Thee, to sing Thee, to glorify Thee, uncreated Father of the only-begotten Jesus Christ. We praise Thee, uncreated Father, unfathomable, ineffable, incomprehensible to all created beings. We praise Thee, who art known through the only-begotten Son, who art through Him spoken, interpreted and known by created nature. We praise Thee, who dost know the Son and dost reveal to the saints the glory which pertains to Him. We praise Thee, invisible Father, choragus of immortality. Thou art the source of life, the source of light, the source of all grace and all truth, friend of men, friend of the poor, propitious to all, drawing them all to Thee by the coming of Thy beloved Son. We pray Thee, make of us living men. Give us the Spirit of light, so that we may know Thee, the True One, and Him whom Thou hast sent, Jesus

Christ. Give us the Holy Spirit so that we may say and
relate Thy ineffable mysteries. May the Lord speak in
us, as well as the Holy Spirit: let Him praise Thee
through us. . . ." [13]

"May the Lord Jesus speak in us," Serapion exclaimed. These words contain a profound theology. No
matter how saintly the priest may be, his praise nevertheless proceeds from a created heart and lips. Only one
humanity is divine, that of Christ; only one humanity
pronounces temporal words and expresses the sentiments of a heart of flesh, but gives them a superhuman
and boundless dignity and value: that of the Incarnate
Word. But to assure the renewal and visible perpetua-
tion of this unique action, the Incarnate Word has incorporated men with Himself, assuming them into His
efficient causality, uniting them to His activity of praise,
thanks to an ontological transformation which radically
delegates them to the divine worship and "orders" them
in their very being to glorification and adoration. This
is the ontological foundation of the function of praise
with respect to the Holy Trinity, a foundation which
makes the priest suited for carrying out a "Christian"
praise around which all personal prayer will normally
be organized. This is why, strictly speaking, the prayer
of the priest is made *in nomine Domini*.

PRIESTHOOD AND THEOCENTRISM

The priest is therefore dedicated by function and by
profession, to the work of *religion*. He must have an
intense spirit of petition and supplication. With the
psalmist he will repeat unceasingly: "look down from
heaven and see; take care of this vine, and protect what
your right hand has planted" (Ps. 79:15-16). Like
Moses, he will remain with arms outstretched in the
presence of the Divine Majesty, as long as the Church
struggles on earth against the powers of darkness.

He will be able to send up toward God a prayer of

[13] G. Bardy, *En lisant les Pères*, pp. 197-198.

thanksgiving and engage all universal creation in an
explosion of profound gratitude. He will repeat the
eucharistic prayer which the *presbyters* and *episcopes*
of nineteen centuries ago recited, after having renewed
the Lord's Supper:

> We thank Thee, Holy Father, for Thy holy name,
> Which Thou hast made to dwell in our hearts,
> For the knowledge, the faith and the immortality
> Which Thou hast shown us in Jesus Thy servant.
> To Thee be glory in the centuries.
> Thou, all powerful Master,
> Thou hast created all things because of Thy name,
> Thou hast given food and drink to men
> That they may give thanks to Thee.
> But to us Thou hast given spiritual food and drink
> And eternal life, through Thy servant;
> Above all, we give Thee thanks because Thou art
>   powerful,
> To Thee be glory in the centuries. . . .

He will savor and understand this calm and disinterested prayer which loses itself in God. He will have
the sense of the glorifying mediation which extends,
through liturgical acts or life, the actions of Christ; he
will have a predilection for the most worthy praise, of
which we are not the individual source but which has
its origin in Christ. He will have the habit of centering
private prayer around the Divine Office, and the latter
around the unique, universal, and perpetual act of
adoration and thanksgiving of Christ — the eucharistic
sacrifice. He will have the facility of recollecting himself even outside of the mandatory professional acts, to
express to God the glorification which comes from the
animate and inanimate creature — a priestly action *par
excellence*. He will have the desire to kindle in the baptized a sense of adoration and of profound submission
to mysterious Providence.

Consequently, the priest is a *man set apart*, radically
and by function. He should not, therefore, have a men-

tality concerned directly and exclusively with man, as if all prayer were but a "means" of obtaining grace. His manner of judging and acting should not be one that would presuppose a kind of religion of humanity, man becoming an absolute to which everything else is relative and subordinated. He should not search for private prayer in preference to the Christian prayer pronounced *in Christo* in a state of dryness. His should not be a narrowness of view that would limit the whole universe to one corner of it, a view that would render a larger gesture of universal praise impossible.

4. THE SACRIFICER

CALVARY AND THE MASS

The work of the cult of redemption is summed up, in Christianity, in a sacred ceremony: the Sacrifice of the Mass. Considering things in Christ, there is, of course, but one Supreme Pontiff, eternal and perfect, raised up in the heavens in the presence of His Father, showing Him forever the sign of His bloody offering. "He lives always to make intercession for [us] (Heb. 7:25). "By one offering he has perfected forever those who are sanctified. . . . Having offered one sacrifice for sins, [Jesus] has taken his seat forever at the right hand of God" (10:11-14). One pontiff, one victim, one priesthood, one celestial temple: all the doctrinal wealth which the author of the Epistle to the Hebrews delivers to us could be brought together here in a powerful picture. But, if we look at it from the priestly point of view, if we put ourselves at the level of the visible and ritual instrumentality established by Christ in His Church, the thing that is striking is the permanent, continual, and universal presentation of this unique oblation: we leave the horizons of the Hebrews and place ourselves in the perspectives of the ecclesiastical society. Now, in this matter of essential redemptive activity, the priest emerges as the *sacrificer*. At the moment when, sacramentally, the work of the Cross is represented on our altars, the priest performs an act of con-

secration of which he alone is capable, and which puts
him above and beyond the assembled Christian community. The power which he puts into action at that
point is not merely the power of worship which is held
by every baptized person by the very fact of his baptismal character, but the power of worship which belongs exclusively to the "ordained" and which clearly
distinguishes them from the community of Christians
placing them in a sphere of reserved sacramental activity.

When the Mass is truly for the priest the sacramental
representation of the unique redemptive activity carried on in heaven by the glorified Lord, it cannot fail
to be the *very center of the apostolic life*. Since the life
of the apostolate is linked as to its source to the glorious
Person of the eternal and perfect Mediator, how could
the Mass, which visibly captures the saving force,
ἐνέργεια, of this Person at a given time and place, not
be the center of our redemptive action?

Some priests find it difficult to make the Holy Mass
the "center of their apostolic life"; they will surely find
a reason for this difficulty in the manner in which they
conceive of the eucharistic sacrifice. If the Mass is no
more than an individual and private act of piety for
them, even though a profound one, what is astonishing
about the fact that it is not the center of pastoral activity? If the rites, the rubrics, the colors or the chant
cause the primary and unique role played by Christ to
be forgotten; if the visible and the human distract and
hold back, instead of "signifying" the invisible and the
divine — as is required of an instrumental cause completely oriented, in principle, toward the principal cause
— how can the priest see therein the center of all sanctification and glorification? It is Christ, and not the visible
ecclesiastical society, who is the source of all worship.
On the other hand, when the Holy Mass is the visible
and temporal representation of the supreme, universal, and perfect act of the latreutic and salvific mediation
of the Savior, what is more natural, more spontaneous,
than to see therein the core of the apostolate?

SALVATION AND ITS APPLICATION

A distinction, however, is necessary; we must not confuse redemption *in actu primo* and redemption *in actu secundo*. Some emphasize the former: when the Mass is celebrated, they maintain, the mystery of salvation is accomplished. Others, especially those who are responsible for the *cura animarum* recall that so long as the baptized have not "accepted" this redemption, very little has been accomplished: what good is a redemption which is not in fact redemptive, *actu secundo?* And this is why they make the *cura animarum* the center of the apostolate. The work of the apostolate, they say, is to prepare mankind to receive the gift forever offered by the Lord.

It would seem that both sides are correct. What would the apostolate be if it were cut off from its source: the eternal Mediator whose fruitfulness is truly captured by the sacrifice of the Mass? No one would dream of denying this dogmatic fact. But, on the other hand, it is just as certain that an apostolate which did not end in the acceptance of the life of Christ by men, would not fit its own definition. It would be inconceivable to claim that Christ offered Himself on the Cross for the salvation of the world *in actu primo*.[14] Whence the attitude of the priests charged with the ministry, an attitude more "moral" than "dogmatic." When the faithful are well disposed, they say, they will always find Christ in one way or another, either in and through the Mass — which is the best way — or else through faith, charity and good will; for the return to God does

[14] These words of J. J. Olier should be noted: "The religion of Jesus Christ was therefore a perfect one, for He annihilated Himself completely in His Father and also returned entirely in God, as religion demands. For it is not enough to die to oneself and to annihilate oneself, to perform a perfect sacrifice; it is also necessary that the victim return in God. It is not enough to separate the creature from itself, it must be rejoined to its own principle, so that God is only fully satisfied and content, and His plans for religion fully achieved, when He has taken back unto Himself His creature and has caused it to return into His bosom to resume the place whence it had departed" (*Traité des saints Ordres*, III P., cap. V, Paris, 1929, p. 504).

not occur exclusively through the visible instrumentality of Christian rites. We are always sure about Christ, it is pointed out; He is always ready to offer His grace and salvation. We have nothing to fear from that quarter. But men are subject to all the caprices and fluctuations of sin and evil; from that quarter, we are never sure of things. So, the *cura animarum* is the dominant concern and principal occupation of our apostolate as diocesan priests.

It would be profitable to examine closer and specify the respective places occupied in the work of grace by the return to Christ through the Holy Mass and the return to Him through the private or simply inner acts of the theological virtues. It would not be enough to reply that the theological virtues necessarily find their development in the Holy Sacrifice and that the Mass is necessarily animated by faith and charity. It is indispensable to answer this question: What is the scope of the salvific instrumentality of the Mass as such?

"IMITATE WHAT YOU HANDLE"

This act of consecration is, for the priest, a *solemn commitment*. Unquestionably, the religious validity of the consecration is assured by the mere fact that the priest is "ordained"; in this sense, the Lord clearly manifests that the inner efficacy of the Christian life stems from Him and in no way flows from the moral sanctity of the minister. But it is one thing to act validly and another to act perfectly. The human perfection of the act performed calls for inner correspondence, a moral symbiosis, a personal unity. Following Augustine, Thomas writes that "Whoever offers sacrifice, should participate in the sacrifice, because the external sacrifice which is offered is a sign of the interior sacrifice." (IIIa, q. 82, a. 2, c).

Moreover, the supernatural perfection of the priestly act in turn calls for a total personal and religious participation. The reason for this is that the *total* fruitfulness of a sacramental activity is not limited to its

valid efficacy; other supernatural factors are operative
in every religious work. Human and supernatural logic
therefore require that the priest form a unit, become
one body with the act which he performs as sacrificer,
and that he, personally, be a praise, a thanksgiving, a
prayer and an expiatory victim in the presence of God.
Thus will he accomplish in himself the multiple ends
of the eucharistic sacrifice. "Know what you are doing,
imitate what you handle."

The personal commitment which affects the consecrating priest, though relating to all the ends of the
sacrifice, nevertheless concerns the *work of expiation*
more particularly. This is not a mere impression without foundation, a truth vaguely perceived by the Christian who cannot however justify it. The Mass is, above
all, the "memory of his passion." Propitiation is the
"specific end of the Mass," writes Dom B. Capelle:

"the Mass is a propitiatory sacrifice carrying out
the work of Redemption in the Blood of Christ. It is
against this very point of doctrine that sixteenth-cen-
tury Protestantism had bent its most obstinate efforts.
The reformers had no difficulty in admitting the Mass
as a sacrifice of homage wherein the Christian gives
himself to his God, according to the example of Christ,
his leader and model. But that it should be really propitiatory seemed to them intolerable, as taking away
from the uniqueness of the redemptive sacrifice of the
Cross. Armed with the strength of all tradition, the
Council of Trent replied: 'It is truly propitiatory, *vere
propitiatorium'* (Sess. XXII, chap. 2 and can. 3). Amidst
all sacrifices, the Mass belongs not only to the latreutic
species, but also to the propitiatory species, like that
of Golgotha. Can one imagine an explanation of the
sacrifice of the Cross that would not place the stress
on 'the remission of sins.' Yet the Mass is a strictly
similar oblation: 'different only in the manner of its
offering' (Sess. XXII, c. 2). Its prayers, moreover, say
this and repeat it without respite throughout the celebration."[15]

---

[15] "Du sens de la Messe," in *Quest. Liturg. paroiss.*, 1942, p. 18.

The point of view adopted by the author of this article is sufficiently ontological and dogmatic to escape
any danger of anthropocentrism; the Mass is truly a
sacrifice of reparation, one that characterizes our condition: "state of nature, fallen and restored."

Through the consecration, the priest, then, commits himself to "make reparation," to expiate. Just as
the Mass is essential for him, since he has been ordained
to offer it, so is it natural and normal for him to want
to repair what sin has upset and destroyed in the world.
Here again, the profound significance of the Mass joins
that of the whole priestly apostolate. All work accomplished by the priest is marked with the sign of reparation. His whole apostolate is a "setting in order," a
restitution, a renewal. His whole apostolate will therefore be also "expiation." As we can see, expiation is not
added to the priest's apostolate as a chance element, as
a supplement that the more "generous" will accept as
one concern among many others; on the contrary, it
is a constituent part of the apostolate in the sense that
every work undertaken by the priest must bear the mark
thereof. The apostolate of Christ was expiatory throughout its duration. It began with these words: " 'Sacrifice
and oblation thou wouldst not, but a body thou hast
fitted to me: In holocausts . . . thou hast had no pleasure.' Then I said, 'Behold, I come — (in the head of the
book it is written of me) — to do thy will, O God'. . . .
It is in this 'will' that we have been sanctified through
the offering of the body of Jesus Christ once for all"
(Heb. 10:5-10). And He ended His life with the *Con-
summatum est* of the Cross. The priest, in turn, must
live by the logic of his origins: it is by his "witness"
that, like Christ, he will find the Cross.[16]

5. END AND MEANS

When the work of the priesthood is presented as it
just has been, with the help of categories which have
become classic in the treatises on the Church — ministry

---

[16] For an extension of this idea, see p. 330.

of worship, teaching magisterium, direction of the flock — there is always the danger of being misunderstood by the reader, in the sense that the latter may not perceive clearly enough the amplitude of the gigantic task expected of the clergy.

DIMENSIONS OF THE MAGISTERIUM

Thus, when it is a question of the "ecclesiastical magisterium," many priests think only of Sunday sermons, commentaries on the Gospel, catechism classes and the teaching activities which are proper to the personal apostolate in a parish, school, or church. Without noticing it, they lose sight of another "magisterium," of major importance, namely, the press, newspapers, literature and novels, motion pictures and radio programs, speeches and conferences. Every day thousands of priests carry to the baptized, children especially, the most beautiful pages of the Lord's message. But every day, too, newspapers by the hundreds of thousands, novels by the thousand, innumerable films, multiple conferences, are also presenting to millions of men an incisive and fascinating message. What message? Can we say that it is always in the spirit of the Gospels, in line with the thinking of Christ, according to the wishes of God the Father, inspired by the Spirit of truth? Can we say that this formidable universal "magisterium" does not often undo our humble preaching, continuously sterilizing the seeds we laboriously sow, removing with a brutal blast all that our hands have built, the way a cluster of bombs eradicates part of a city?

Should not our conclusion be that the priestly magisterium must also be interested in modern methods of diffusing ideas? Christ did not say that one had to preach the truth only through certain means; He did not give any orders to use only oral, or personal, methods; He did not ask that certain powerful, though recent, techniques, be rejected. He said, "Go and make disciples of all nations." The work of the teaching office will be realistic only if it embraces all the means of spreading the truth; and those who work in one of these influential spheres are doing a very apostolic work. Moreover, the more the work of a priest is diffused, the more apostolic and priestly value it has. The end must not be confused with certain means suitable for achieving it: all honest means are to be put to use, all these means can enrich the Christian apostolate.

DIMENSIONS OF THE MINISTRY

The same is true as regards the ministry. One does not find, of course, alongside Christianity, a secular system for sanctification and purification, with its own oblations and sacrifices. There does exist in the world, however, a certain technique of praise and a complex of attitudes which are in direct opposition to the work of the Christian ministry.

The world praises certain men, certain ways of life, of doing business, of organizing affairs. The religious forces which slumber in the inmost depths of every created soul are aroused and oriented toward created values which the world honors: money, technology, the body, sports, art, the State, the party. Who can deny that false gods are promoted and worshipped today? The world also has its rites, which, in contrast to the sacraments, produce corruption and death. Rites celebrating success, sensual gratification, power are celebrated by society and amount to an anti-Christian ministry, destructive of the Christian ministry.

Again, it is quite clear that the ministry of life entrusted by Christ to His Apostles is not restricted exclusively to certain efficacious signs, certain rites that carry blessings. Christ did not ask that life be given by specific means; He desired that His life be given, that it dwell in the soul of His disciples and grow there, leaving to each generation the task of seeking the best means of ensuring the execution of this wish. He loves those who prevent Satan from destroying the divine life among men as much as those who give it to one of them. All who give, preserve, or safeguard grace in

souls are doing true apostolic work. If the very gift of
life depends on him who has received the power thereof, the preservation and the increase of this life in the
baptized person can find appreciable help in institutions,
public life, traditions, even though all these realities do
not at all depend on the power of Orders. But for all
that, they have no less importance for Christian religious life. And on that basis, it would be inconceivable
for the priest not to give them major attention.

DIRECT AND INDIRECT MEANS

When priests are inattentive to these realities, it may
be because they confuse the redemptive goal with certain means of redemption. They are told to preach the
Gospel, and they act as if this goal could be attained
only through sermons and catechism lessons. They are
asked to give men divine life, and they seem to think
that only the sacramental rites are sources of grace.
Their imagination is defective and not very inventive.
Could their love be in short supply, also?

A glance at history would show that this was
not the attitude adopted by the Church down through
the centuries. One example will suffice. It is well known
that the hierarchy used to act as patrons, during the
Middle Ages and the Renaissance, for a number of cultural and charitable institutions, from schools to burial
societies, to fire-fighting organizations. Many of these
creations of Christian charity were taken over by lay
men or civil society. But why has the hierarchy clung
so tenaciously to the right to operate schools where
humanistic learning is taught? Out of a desire to propagate human culture? It would seem not. But the hierarchy knows very well that along with this culture
there is transmitted a concept of life and the world,
and the latter can be non-Christian, even nontheistic.
There was a time when such schools could be objected
to on the ground that they were not "traditional," and
certainly unknown to the Apostles. But the shepherds
of dioceses, more far-seeing, keeping before their eyes

the goal of the teaching office rather than attaching themselves to certain forms of its manifestation, did not fear to protect this new initiative, which today is so important.

Today the *indirect* work of redemption is just as important to the salvation of the world as that which flows strictly from the power of Orders. Someone may ask, with reason, what could be offered which is superior to Baptism, to sacramental absolution? It is true that the divine life is given normally only through the sacraments or with reference to them; in this sense, they have a fundamental importance. Still, when one considers Christian life as a whole, it is also evident that the conditions necessary for the development of grace in Christians are also of extreme importance. If we were to ask a pastor what is more "important" for the Christian life of his area: an extra curate in a parish or a great Catholic daily that would be read by several thousands of readers, we cannot be sure that the curate would be preferred over the newspaper, even though only a curate can baptize and give absolution.

The priest who is content with his *personal* magisterium and gives no thought to the great universal magisterium of the press or motion pictures, indicates that he has not understood the meaning of his teaching mission. If he is content to give life without helping to combat the institutions and societies which have been organized to destroy it, does he really have the spirit of Jesus Christ? He should read in the Apocalypse, in the Epistles of John and of Paul, regarding the *collective* secular opposition to the establishment of the messianic kingdom.

This kind of apostolate requires well-tempered souls. There is nothing more dangerous than "modern" spirits which at the same time are not solidly rooted in a holy tradition. The more powerful the technique which is set into motion, the more profound must be the mystique which animates it. The richer the methods put to work, the more authentically poor must the priest be who has the responsibility therefor. To appreciate a good con-

cert without having an esteem for prayer, to insist that
young girls, too, have a soul, without being equally convinced that the priest has a body, to participate in sports
while neglecting to think in a Christian manner, are all
forms of modernism which err because of their very
incomplete character and which often ruin the most well-
meant undertakings.

Moreover, in this urgent task of focusing the great
sources of doctrinal and vital influence, *laymen* must
have a large and important part. Since these means of
redemption are intimately linked to temporal efforts and
earthly institutions, it is well for the priest not to assume their immediate direction; he must inspire them,
animate them, enlighten them, support them with his
ardor, orient them according to the Gospels. Thus these
works of apostolic endeavor, though less sacred by nature, though less religious in their essence, can also be,
by their enterprise and their scope, very important in
the redemption of the world. Their international nature will certainly not replace the sublimity of a strictly priestly act, but a sacerdotal act, even while sacred,
can at times have less redemptive effect than a work of
a profane nature. The good order of a State, for example,
is highly favorable to the ascendancy of Christ in souls.
In this sense, and with all the necessary distinctions, it
will sometimes be logical to speak of a primacy of the
political, the social, the economic. This does not signify
a primacy of nature, but rather a primacy of urgency
and of influence.

CHAPTER EIGHT

FOUNDATIONS OF APOSTOLIC ACTION

The structure of the priesthood and the apostolate rest on a broad and solid supernatural foundation. Christ "sent" His disciples with the promise of coming to their assistance in all the necessities of their state. He ordained them and consequently assured them of the graces attached to the reception of this sacrament. These realities, some juridical, others ontological, but all equally apostolic, will be the subject of this chapter.

1. THE "MISSION"

I AM SENDING YOU!

"Behold, all power has been given me on earth and in heaven; and I am sending you." As soon as Christ had pronounced these decisive words, the Twelve were able to disperse throughout the world and spread the good news of salvation. Authentic envoys, they had the right to present themselves as witnesses of the Lord and continuers of the redemptive work.

That which makes the apostle, write Batiffol, Scheeben and, in addition, all the commentators of the

Pauline Epistles, is the fact of *being sent*, of having received a mission from Christ. Actually, one of them
writes:

"Apostle of Christ, as Paul claims to be, signifies
envoy of Christ, sent by Christ, just as apostle of the
churches signifies sent by the churches: Paul speaks of
the ἀπόστολοι Χριστοῦ (2 Cor. 11:13), the way he
speaks of the ἀπόστολοι ἐκκλησιῶν (Id. 8:23). If the
apostle of the church has as credentials a letter given
to him by the church that sends him, the ἀπόστολος
Χριστοῦ could only be accredited by a letter from
Christ. . . . Finally and above all, to be sent by Christ
implies that one has received a mission: on earth from
Christ in person there is the real root of the apostolate.
If Paul is able to proclaim himself an apostle, 'sent
not from men nor by man, but by Jesus Christ and God
the Father who raised him from the dead,' (Gal. 1:1),
it is because there is no apostle of Christ except him
whom Christ designates and sends: '. . . it pleased him
[God] to reveal his Son in me that I might preach him
among the Gentiles,' and, immediately, Paul left for
Arabia. It is in this full sense that Paul is an apostle,
not merely an apostle but 'an apostle of Christ,' called
and sent personally by Christ Himself."[1]

If the etymology of "apostolate" seems clearly
enough to designate a *mission*, a task entrusted to a
messenger, the reason why the Lord chose so to designate His Twelve rather escapes us. Ἀπόστολος is found
once in the Greek version of the Old Testament (2
Kings 14:6). Is this enough for us to conclude as to the
biblical origin of the word chosen by Jesus to designate
His disciples par excellence? Herodotus also uses this
term to signify a "messenger," an "envoy."[2] It is, however, generally supposed that the biblical reference would,
along with the etymology, quite easily have led Christ
to this name.

The origin of the institution remains obscure. Did

---

[1] Batiffol, *L'Eglise naissante et le catholicisme*, 1927, pp. 56-57.
[2] *Hist.* I, 21; V, 38; according to A. Médebielle, art. *Apostolat*,
in *Dict. Bible, Suppl.*, I, c. 533-534.

the Lord derive inspiration from the Jewish ἀπόστολοι, personages living in the service of the ethnarch, whose functions were to serve as couriers for the authorities, to take care of the synagogues or to collect the annual tribute? But we know of these ἀπόστολοι only from rather recent testimony, dating from the third century, long after the destruction of the Temple.[3] It does not seem that the apostolate as it was established by the Lord can really be linked to any already existing institution; it is the natural expression of the will of Christ and the normal means of assuring the existence of the Church.

IMPORTANCE OF THE MISSION

Actually, we forget too easily the importance of the "mission" which is indicated to us by the bishop, because the quality of *envoy* we thereby acquire does not seem to be of any consequence. Still, it gives us, from a juridical point of view — and this is important, since every civil hierarchy is established on a juridical basis — the power of accomplishing the work of the apostolate; while the sacrament of Orders gives us the basic, ontological power to act, the "mission" grants us the right to use it in the name of Christ and the Church. The "mission" guarantees our authority in the ecclesiastical society; when an "envoy" presents himself, he is the minister of Christ, the authentic representative of the Church and of the bishop, who speaks and prays, sanctifies and glorifies. From it we also receive a share of sacerdotal perfection: when we have received, along with the power of Orders, jurisdiction, when a bishop has said "Ite," then we enjoy the maximum blessings any creature may claim in the order of the sacramental priesthood.

Was not the Messiah the Envoy par excellence? After the first man had sinned by refusing divine friendship, God the Father promised him a Savior. From that day forth, man, who had fallen back on himself, possessed

[3] A. Médebielle, *art. cit.,* c. 563.

the pledge of eternal hope: someone would come, an
envoy from heaven. The Incarnate Word, an envoy —
why? I come, replies Christ, that they may have life.
I have come for sinners, and not for those who think
themselves just. I am the Way, the Truth and the Life.
I am the door of the sheepcote; I am the good shepherd.
I am your master, and the only one.

But what is it that characterizes this mission definitively? It is not only because He did this, that or
the other thing that Christ is the perfect Mediator, but
because He, the Man-God, lived according to the wishes
of the Father, in order that the Scriptures might be fulfilled. "As it was pleasing before Thee."

A résumé of the lives of the Apostles leads to the
same conclusion: in their turn, they are pastors of the
flock, teachers of their people, sacrificers, and leaders.
But who can state each one's part in this work, here
and now? Should Paul be an itinerant missionary or a
stationary pastor, administer the sacraments or spread
the revealed doctrine? How are we, in turn, supposed to
choose among these apostolic occupations, if not in consideration of the specific role which is assigned us?

To preach here, to baptize there will be apostolic if
Christ has *sent* us for that purpose. An Apostle who
would have preached the Gospel against the will of
Christ, or a priest who would preach contrary to his
bishop's will, would not be acting as an apostle, even
if he were to communicate the superabundance of his
own contemplation and arouse the religious enthusiasm
of the crowds. He might be eloquent and make conversions; but he would not be an apostle. The overflow of
contemplation cannot suffice to characterize the apostolate adequately. To be an apostle is to be under orders,
to be on a mission; to act as an apostle implies that one
remains within the framework of his assignment.

"Within the *framework of his assignment.*" Here
is something which no doubt is likely to renew the discussion between those who claim that one must occupy
himself only with the tasks imposed and expressly determined by the duty of one's professional state, and

those who maintain that one must accomplish as much as possible, everywhere, on all occasions. When, then, is one working within the framework of one's assignment? To determine this, let us consider what actually happens in the hierarchical Church. The canonical prescriptions given to the episcopacy regarding the direction of a diocese do not change the fact that bishops differ widely in action and thought. Within a diocese, it does not seem that the bishops want to form a "standard" type of priest as there are "standard" types of spare automobile parts. The basic responsibilities, the essential duties, the main concerns are identical, specific; but one can note very many differences among those who are called "good" pastors: differences stemming from their characters, temperaments, methods of work, tastes, even from their preferences for certain tasks. A "good" priest is one who responds to the expectations of his bishop in a given area, both as regards mandatory professional duties *and* that which one can expect from someone who loves Christ. Thus, he will imitate his bishop, whose pastoral charity is expressed in those acts which are positively prescribed, *and* in those things which a paternal heart judges it must do "over and above," in specific circumstances.

For in the area of his own ministry, the diocesan priest is the "good shepherd": he must "feed the Church." How can we detail in advance everything required of a true "shepherd"? One determines exactly the services to be rendered by an employee, by the personnel of a bureau — although, even here, there are employees and employees — but one cannot determine exactly what a father or a mother must do: this would be a gamble and, above all, an insult. Thus is explained the impossibility of exhaustively describing the secondary "duties" of the diocesan priest.

2. THE GRACE OF STATE

In the second nocturne for the Solemnity of St. Joseph we read each year a few pages of St. Bernadine

of Siena, and in particular: "the general rule for each
and every grace communicated to any rational creature
is this, that, whenever the divine grace chooses someone for some sublime status, it gives that person all
charismata which are necessary for the person so chosen
and for its office, and supplies them in abundance."
Though rigorously accurate, this principle must be
judiciously handled. It is enough to look at oneself to
realize that the fact of having this or that function
does not, *ipso facto,* include the gift of unmixed perfection! One does not avoid every error; one does not
conquer every defect; one is not without deficiencies: the
facts, in this area, must not be forced in order to prove
a principle, when the latter is considered to be deduced
from experience itself. On the other hand, it is also
indisputable that the providential call to any function
must go hand-in-hand with a special divine assistance;
avoiding supernaturalism must not lead one to naturalism
— that would be going from Scylla to Charybdis.

FUNCTION AND GRACES

The idea of a special grace attached to every *function*
is traditional in the teaching of the Church: it is found
in theologians and spiritual writers; it is applied in
particular to the Apostles. This is how Journet sums
up the fruit of his research.

"God, says St. Thomas, offers to each a grace in
proportion to the mission for which he has been chosen.
The Christ-Man received the most excellent of graces,
for His nature was destined to be united to a divine
Person. The blessed Mary, after Him, had the highest
fullness of grace, for she was destined to be the Mother
of Christ. Then we must add St. Joseph, to whom, Leo
XIII has said, 'God confided the divine household containing the first-fruits of the infant Church, and St.
John the Baptist.' Among the other saints, St. Thomas
goes on, the Apostles are those who were raised *to the
highest dignity,* namely, that of directly receiving from
Christ those things pertaining to salvation, so that the
Church was in some sense founded by them, according

to what is stated in the Apocalypse, 21:14. The Apostles surpass all the saints, regardless of how the latter excelled — whether in virginity, teaching, martyrdom — for the Apostles received the Holy Spirit with greater abundance. Others may have suffered more and practiced greater austerity; but the Apostles fulfilled their task with greater charity, and if necessary, their hearts were ready to undertake even greater things still. Raised to an unique dignity, they saw in themselves a superabundance of grace, whence we can see the error of those who dare compare the other saints to the Apostles as regards grace and glory."[4]

In this passage, quoted in its entirety from Journet, something seems unclear. St. Thomas, quoted at the beginning, speaks of a "grace in proportion to the mission," which the author ultimately interprets, it seems, as sanctifying grace and charity. But is this really the case? Considering the customary meaning of these "functional" graces, it seems rather that we must look in the direction of the grace of state. In that event, the grace given the priest would be a form of assistance granted by Providence to every state of life, and, especially, to every profession. Every profession involves its special qualities, carries with it specific difficulties, calls for a particular assistance; and one would be truly lacking in supernatural realism to suppose that the specific needs of each profession would not be the object of divine benevolence.

Otherwise, what would be the meaning of the sacramentals pertaining to the professions? The blessing of the abbots, the coronation of emperors or kings, the appeals for the protection of fishermen and bakers, miners and aviators? These innumerable sacramentals, whose highly allusive theological significance should be studied in a more systematic way than has been done until now, show us that the Church believes in the help given by the Lord to the different secular professions and callings. A fortiori, one may conclude that the "priestly profession," the "apostolic calling," will draw

[4] *L'Eglise du Verbe Incarné*, vol. I, pp. 163-164.

down on those who are part of the clergy "functional" blessings and graces, which are particular and specific.

GRACES AND NATURE

These graces are multiple, and varied: insight for the intellect, energy in the apostolate, perseverance in initiative, flexibility in adaptation, judgment in decisions, care in execution. One can find no better way of stating it than by quoting the ancient blessing incorporated in the consecratory Canon of the early Gallican rite:

"O God, the author of all sanctification, whose true consecration is the fullness of benediction, Thou O Lord, pour forth upon these Thy servants whom we are setting aside for the honor of the priesthood, the gift of Thy blessing; that by seriousness of action and probity of life they may prove themselves 'elders,' founded in those disciplines which Paul set forth to Titus and Timothy; that meditating day and night on Thy law, they may believe what they read, teach what they believe, imitate what they teach; that they may show forth in themselves justice, constancy, mercy, fortitude and the other virtues, and may demonstrate by example, confirm them by admonition, and preserve pure and immaculate the gift of their ministry. That they may transform bread and wine into the Body and Blood of Thy Son by means of an immaculate blessing, for the service of Thy people; and that, by inviolable charity 'unto the perfect man in the measure of the fullness of the age of Christ,' they may rise again on the day of the just and eternal judgment of God, pure of conscience, in the true faith, full of the Holy Spirit."

But these graces do not *substitute* themselves for nature. A priest who cannot sing will not acquire as a result of the sacramental graces a new voice; and the man whom nature has endowed with a fine voice will sing just as well even if he is deprived of sacramental graces. He who brings as his dowry to the diocese gifts of boldness or of culture, will be able to make them more fruitful in his apostolate, and the sacramental grace given to a timid or poorly gifted priest will not compensate for his deficiencies. Sacramental grace is *one* special help; it tends to ensure that the apostolate will, first of all, be worthily carried out and, then, be more fruitful.

3. THE SACRAMENTAL CHARACTER OF ORDERS

In order to accomplish his "mission," the priest must possess very extensive sacred powers. He must be made capable of administering the sacraments, of consecrating the Eucharist, of preaching, and of directing his flock. He can acquire by personal effort the qualities of a leader, he can arouse in his heart the sense of pastoral charity, and his long study can put him in a position to understand and to transmit the doctrinal message of Christianity; but he cannot, by his own industry, acquire the capacity for celebrating Mass, for baptizing, for hearing confessions. Only Christ, in His mercy, can grant him these powers; only He can make the priest "apt" for the valid administration of the sacraments. By the hands of the bishop, Christ, indeed, makes him "capable" of performing validly and fruitfully certain religious acts. This basic capacity which the priest possesses is identified by the theologians with the sacramental character of Orders, the cornerstone of the foundations of our apostolate.

THE SACRAMENTAL CHARACTER

The fathers of the Councils of Florence and Trent, summing up the best scholastic analyses of Augustinian thought, expressed themselves clearly on the sacramental character. In the *Decretum pro Armenis* (1439), Eugene IV states that "among the sacraments, there are three — Baptism, Confirmation, and Holy Orders — which imprint a character, a sort of spiritual mark which affects the soul in an unalterable way, and enables men to distinguish those who have received it." A century later, in March, 1547, the fathers of the Council of Trent formulated a doctrinal canon similar to the declaration of Florence: Let him be anathema, they said, who denies that Baptism, Confirmation and Holy Orders imprint a character on the soul, that is, a spiritual and indelible sign, the ultimate reason for the prohibition against repeating these sacraments. Such is the most accurate teaching which the magisterium gives us in its official documents.

The modern theologians who have interpreted this general teaching can be divided into two groups which are clearly defined though of highly unequal numerical importance. Some, basing themselves on Durand of St. Pourçain, see in the sacramental character a mere relation of reason, a purely nominal deputation to the Christian cult. This explanation, which could be called juridical, is difficult to reconcile, it seems to us, with the expressions in the *Decretum pro Armenis* and the canon promulgated at Trent. Still, the Fathers have expressly refrained from condemning it. More in harmony with the Council texts is the interpretation which we would like to call "realistic," and which most authors, following St. Thomas Aquinas, prefer. The character, they say, is a *spiritual*, ontological reality — not a mere relation of reason; a distinctive impression which marks souls, an indelible sign which nothing, not even mortal sin, can erase.

What is the nature of this reality? Let us assume, for the purposes of our inquiry a priest in the state of mortal sin. We know from the traditional teaching of the Church that this priest can "validly" celebrate Mass, and that he can "validly" administer the sacraments; the faithful will not be deprived of the grace of the sacraments because the minister is unworthy. It may be deduced from these traditional beliefs that the priest is "capable" of validly carrying out religious acts, even when his own moral and psychological dispositions are not good. Whence it follows that the "validity" of the Mass and the sacraments does not depend on these dispositions. On the other hand, we know, too, that mere laymen, who have not been "ordained" priests, even if they are extremely holy, will never be able to celebrate a valid Mass, and that their absolution would have no sacramental value. There is nothing more logical than to conclude that the sacrament of Orders renders the priest *capable* of performing religious acts. This sacrament changes something in him, transforms something in his person and powers. But what are the effects of Holy Orders? — the sacramental character and sacramental graces. Since the latter are more designed to guarantee the worthy exercise of the apostolate, it may be conjectured that the sacramental character, the seal impressed on the soul, is precisely that inner transformation which makes the priest "capable" of administering the sacraments. Also, the character is called a *capacitas*, not a *habitus*, like grace or virtue.[5]

To this distinction is added: "the capacity for receiving or acting." What does this mean? It is clear that the character of Baptism makes one *capable of receiving* the sacramental effects of the other sacraments, whereas an unbaptized person, though he were the best man in the world, cannot do so in any way: in order to receive the sacramental effects of Communion or of Confession, one must be baptized. The conclusion is that the sacramental character of Baptism is a "capacity for receiving the effects of the sacraments." As for the priest, he is made capable also of *acting*, of performing acts which have value and fruitfulness: in this sense, the character is also "the capacity for *acting* in the sacramental order."

To what does this *capacitas* refer? To the realities of ecclesiastical worship: the sacraments. The latter are, in fact and above all, the religious rites of the authentic cult of the Christian Church. Whence it is that the theologians say of the sacramental character that it introduces us into an order of sacred things, the order of Christian worship. In the same way, the fact that we are in the state of grace introduces us into another order of spiritual realities, that which we call the communion of saints.

And how do we function in this order of Christian

[5] Cf. Ch. Journet, *L'Eglise du Verbe Incarné*, vol. I, pp. 90-101.

worship? Certainly not as the source and origin of all grace and of all cultual praise: Christ, the unique and universal Mediator, alone assures the fruitfulness of the Church's worship. He alone is "always living to make intercession for us." He alone merited for us "by one oblation" the redemption of all men. If the priest also carries out a certain activity in the order of Christian worship, it cannot be except as an instrument. The classical theory of principal and instrumental causality cannot be applied here without distinctions; but it can be useful in helping us to understand that in the order of Christian worship, there is, in addition to the supreme and principal causality of the glorified Lord, a subordinate, visible and ecclesiastical causality to which the name "instrumental" may be given. This is why the character of Orders, the foundation of the sacerdotal power, is called "an instrumental power."

THE PRIEST AND THE INCARNATE WORD

Participating in the sanctifying and glorifying action which Christ carries on in and through His Church, the priest thereby acquires a certain similarity to Jesus Himself: it is the priest who absolves, baptizes and consecrates. It would unquestionably be erroneous to believe that here "similarity" signifies equivalence, identity: the instrumental causality is not identical, is not equivalent to the principal cause. But it would be a mistake also not to note that the priestly power as it is possessed by the priest gives him an indisputable resemblance to the Incarnate Word. This is why the sacramental character is called an assimilation to the Incarnate Word, a reality of the hypostatic union, an authentic extension of the mediation of Jesus, a participation in the priesthood of Christ — "the priest is another Christ." All these expressions simply mean that the sacramental character is a real participation in the power of *worship* possessed in its fullness by Christ and carried out by Him in His Church.

The sacramental character of Orders, therefore, ele-

vates the action of the human creature to the level of
the divine activity of Christ. The priest prolongs in
time and place the visible action which Jesus carried
out when He roamed the plateaus of Judea and Galilee.
Nothing, of course, changes in the makeup of the intellect or will of the priest who performs a sacramental
rite; but at all times Christ assures him of a superhuman power, a divine efficacy. In every sacramental act
he performs, the priest infallibly sets in motion the action of the eternal Mediator, in order to render to the
Trinity praise which is ever pleasing, or to transmit
life to mankind with certainty.

The views of St. Thomas on the sacramental character, as well as on sacramental effects, are profound
and rich and little has been added to them since. A priest
of his order, a faithful interpreter of his thought, writes:

"The character links priests to the holy humanity
of the Word, and prolongs in the world in a sacramental
way the priesthood of this humanity. Thus the priest is
connected in a very close way with the mystery of the
hypostatic union. For the sacerdotal power of Christ
derives from this union. Jesus is priest by His humanity,
but He is so because this humanity, at the time of the
Incarnation, was taken up by the Word to the point that
it formed but a single person with it. He is priest not
by some added dignity, but by the very mystery of His
being. One cannot conceive of a closer belonging to
God, a more complete consecration. And, consequently,
one cannot imagine a more absolute priestly power. The
human nature of Jesus permits Him to represent His
brethren, men; His personal dignity makes Him their
leader and gives His activity infinite value. Thus, as we
have seen, He can render perfect homage to God, offer
Him superabundant expiation for the sins of the world,
merit grace for all; thus He restores the universal order.

"And, by marking with the priestly character those
whom He calls in order to cause His redemptive work
to be spread, He captures them in turn. A mysterious
capture, but one so real and so active that it gives their
intellects a new capacity. To be sure, there is a tremendous difference between this sacramental capture

and that of the proper human nature of Christ by the Person of the Word. From the fact of the hypostatic union, the humanity of Jesus, while preserving the freedom of its voluntary activity, no longer belongs to itself; all its acts are the human acts of the Word; according to the expression of St. John Damascene, it has become 'the conjoined instrument of the divinity,' its normal organ for action in the created world. The priest is only a 'separate' instrument. His dependence with respect to Christ does not suppress his human personality, nor modify its substance, but is merely added; nor does it give all his acts the value of acts of Christ. And still, despite this essential difference, there remains a striking analogy. . . .

"Finally — and this adds even more to the grandeur of the divine gift — the priest uses this permanent capacity as he wishes. He carries out his ministry freely, just as Christ freely exercises His supreme priesthood. And this is true not only of the priest's ministry of liturgical works and functions, in which he presents to God the homage and the supplications of the Christian community, or distributes to the faithful the graces of the Church; he also retains this liberty in the very rites where his personality seems to be completely effaced before that of Christ. The initiative in these rites is his; if he plays an instrumental role in the hands of the Divine Artist, it is nevertheless he who, at his own discretion and infallibly, begins the action. The power of homage and of sanctification from Christ's priesthood is, as it were, placed in his hands. If he wills the exercise of this power, and acts, it passes through him. And this is true every time he wills it, for whom he wills it, at the instant he wills it. . . . He has the power of taking hold, at his own discretion, of the very life of God, of communicating it to his brethren, of making them into sons of the Most High. This power he holds not because of some mere nominal and revocable delegation to his sacred office. Since his ordination, he really takes part in the sacerdotal power of the Incarnate Word, and this divine gift, deposited in his mind, transfigures his soul for all time."[6]

[6] J. Périnelle, *Le sacerdoce*, Paris, 1936, pp. 48-52.

THE PRIEST AND THE STRUCTURE
OF THE CHURCH

Through the character of Orders, the priest is therefore really the instrument of Christ the Mediator, in His work of salvation and praise. Also through orders, the priest becomes a constituent part of the hierarchical, visible Church. For the latter must have a foundation, a base in each of the members who make her up. What will this be? The life of grace? But this life can be lost and is invisible: one could hardly claim that the supernatural sanctity of the priest is the basis of the visible nature and the hierarchical character of the ecclesiastical cult. Would this basis be simply external adherence of the faithful or the priests? By itself, this could suffice. But, as a matter of fact, the real factor on which worship is supported is the character of the sacrament. Though invisible and spiritual, it is necessarily linked to the visible nature of the sign which produces it. By contrast with grace, it cannot be lost and is indelible. Finally, by its nature, it is a cultual power, a religious potency. It is, therefore, this which is the constituent element of the worship of the Christian community. And if, in this community, the baptized are the subjects, the priests, on the contrary, are constituted the leaders: "In every order whatsoever, someone is constituted leader over the others in divine matters."[7]

It follows that this same character is the generator of *profound unity* among all those who possess it: such unity, whether among the baptized or the "ordained," is a source of solidarity and of cohesiveness, at least in the realm of the religious and liturgical life which is more or less its normal development. Here, as everywhere, Christianity is, ontologically, communitarian: "through Baptism a person becomes a participant in the unity of the Church."[8] It is important to emphasize the profound supernatural and spiritual roots of the unity which unite the baptized, the confirmed and the

---

[7] *Sum. theol.*, Suppl., q. 36, a, 1, c.
[8] *Sum. theol.*, III a, q. 67, a. 2, c.

ordained, through the indelible character by which their
souls are marked.

But, by the same token, the baptized, confirmed, and
ordained find themselves also *distinct from one another*.
The ecclesiastical community of worship is organic, not
uniform. "The character is a sign which distinguishes
one from the others." Alike in the fact that they all
possess a *certain* power for Christian worship, the baptized, the confirmed, and the ordained are, nevertheless,
distinguished one from the other in the same measure
that the power of worship reserved to them differs;
and, in this area, we know that the "ordained" are
privileged: "the ministers of the Church are separated
from the people in order to attend to the divine worship."[9]

SACRAMENTAL CHARACTER AND PREACHING

Strictly speaking, the sacramental character described
above is the foundation of the *ministerium*. Could it not
also constitute an ontological basis for the *magisterium?*
It seems that it can. Two reasons of a theological nature seem to us to favor this hypothesis: a comparison
with the character of Confirmation and the fulness of
the sacramental sign of Holy Orders.

What is the effect of Confirmation? A theological
reflection starting from the sacramental facts would
lead us to conclude that the confirmed person acquires
a participation in the power of Christian worship
through the character of the sacrament. But in what
sense? In view of carrying out certain rites validly?
It does not seem so. His action bears on the nature and
value of the profession of Christian faith. Christ, who
did not leave the validity of the sacraments to chance,
depending on the virtuous dispositions of men, did not,
either, leave to their own powers the defense of the
truth. The Mass celebrated by an "ordained" man is
validly glorifying, because it draws its radical efficacy
from the Mediator, Christ, the priest being but an in-

---

[9] *Sum. theol. Suppl.*, q. 40, a. 2, c.

strument in His hands. Thus, the profession of the faith, the proclamation of the truth and of the holiness of Christianity, coming from a "confirmed" person, are real and agreeable to God, certainly and authentically, because their basic value comes from Christ, the confirmed person being at that moment only His instrument, His powerful voice in the Spirit.

In his long study of the sacramental character of Confirmation, Father Héris explains that: "to the confirmed person and to him alone belongs the duty of confessing his faith before the enemies of the Christian cult; and his confession has a real, sacred, objective value which that of someone merely baptized would not have."[10] But the objection could be raised as to what, in the final analysis, is this "sacred" and "objective" character of the profession of faith? It means exactly what is understood by the "certain" glorification of the eucharistic sacrifice.

The application of this theological doctrine to the preaching of the Christian faith is obvious. Assimilated to Christ, the priest speaks and preaches, but in an authentic and official manner. His word is that of Christ; consequently, it enjoys an inalienable sacred and objective character. Regardless of his dispositions, it remains a profession and affirmation of Catholic belief. It is at all times a saving "testimony," a sacramental outpouring, a "word of salvation."

The sacramental sign of Orders, in its own way, seems to be in harmony with the hypothesis set forth above. During Ordination, the bishop reminds the ordinand several times of his magisterial function: "the priest must preach. . . . " But does not the sacrament effect what it signifies? "The priesthood of Christ, which was communicated to the Apostles through the right that Christ granted them of consecrating the Eucharist," writes M. Masure, "extends far beyond this power, not only in Christ but even in the Apostles. For this power to consecrate is but the sign of the realities it contains

[10] *Le mystère du Christ*, p. 89.

but which extend beyond it."[11] Nevertheless, it will always be difficult to distinguish in the ceremonies of Ordination, the sacramental sign strictly so-called from the rites, prayers, and sacramentals which frame it.

It can therefore be concluded that the sacramental character of Orders constitutes, in its entirety, the radical and ontological basis of the priesthood.

4. THE SACRAMENTAL GRACES

"It is enough for me, Lord, take away my soul; for I am no better than my fathers" (3 Kings 19:4). The massacre of the priests of Baal had brought down on the head of Elias the thunder of Jezabel's wrath. The prophet fled to the desert and asked Yahweh to take him to Himself. This rending cry has nothing in common with the desire "to be dissolved and to be with Christ" (Phil. 1:23). It is heavy with lassitude, dejection, and exhaustion.

The sight of the innumerable obligations which are incumbent upon the priest could discourage us and we could be tempted to let our arms drop. The Scriptures, in reply, send us to the history of Elias. The prophet cast himself down and fell asleep at the foot of the juniper tree, expecting to awaken in the bosom of Abraham. And behold, an angel brought to his side a hearth cake and a vessel of water, and awakened Elias: "Arise and eat, for thou hast yet a great way to go" (3 Kings 19:7). And he walked another forty days and forty nights, as far as the mountain of the Lord, thanks to the strength given him by this providential food.

By means of the sacrament of Orders, Christ commits Himself to giving His priest the strength to hold fast in his way of life and to remain faithful to his sacred vocation. Sacramental grace will provide for this, at least if the priest calls upon its energies and revives it in himself. It will be abundant, though without luxury: Elias received bread and water, and was able to go as

[11] *Parish Priest*, p. 44.

far as God wished to lead him. What then is this support of the sacramental order?

Let us recall briefly what St. Thomas has to say on the Christian economy of the sacraments. "In the use of the sacraments," he notes, "two things can be considered, namely, the divine worship and the sanctification of men,"[12] and, further on, "the sacraments of the New Law are ordered to two things, namely, as a remedy against sin and to perfect the soul in those things which pertain to the worship of God according to the rite of the Christian life."[12] It is necessary to return to this broad and integral thought in order to measure the importance of the sacramental effects and determine their field of action. The sacraments are the religious rites of the Church which place within our reach the worship of Jesus Christ Himself. Sacramental grace helps us to perform these rites well. It is a force of reparation and a balm for our hidden wounds.

Because of the fact of original sin and its consequences, the Word did not become incarnate merely to establish a "Christian" religion on earth; He also had to *repair* human nature, restore the cognitive and affective powers of men. The grace which flows from Calvary is a grace of healing, a divine remedy. The entire sacramental order is marked with this sign. The Postcommunion of the Mass very often places on our lips the word "reparatio," though perhaps we do not realize adequately the large perspectives which it suggests. "May it be to us, O Lord, this heavenly mystery, the reparation of mind and body" (Eighth Sunday after Pentecost). "That those whom Thou dost not cease to repair with the divine sacraments, Thou wilt not in Thy kindness deprive of Thy help" (Tenth Sunday after Pentecost). "Thy medicinal work, O Lord, in us . . ." (Nineteenth Sunday after Pentecost). "That we may anticipate the coming solemnities of our reparation with fitting honors" (First Sunday of Advent). "The sacred mysteries which Thou hast conferred for the strengthen-

---

[12] *Summa theologica*, IIIa, q. 60, a. 5, c.

ing of our reparation" (Ember Saturday in Advent).

The grace of the sacrament, therefore, produces a *restoration* of our weakened powers. It is a true remedy: "the sacrament implies some remedy of man's holiness against sin."[13] It corrects our defects, rectifies our judgments, reforms our tastes, adjusts our impulses, purifies our affections, heals our wounds. In short, "sacramental grace . . . although it has a connection with the grace which is in the virtues and the gifts, nevertheless is different from it, because sacramental grace perfects by removing, first and principally, the defect arising from sin; but the grace of the virtues and gifts perfects by inclining one to the good of the virtues and the gifts."[14] These miseries inherited from sin and from weak nature are: obscurity of intellect, beclouding of judgment, instability of the will, langour in action, aridity in devotion.

HANDLING HOLY THINGS IN A HOLY MANNER

Christ, indeed, desires more than a simply valid ministry on the part of His priests. He wants it careful, holy, and perfect — "handling holy things in a holy manner." "The character directly and proximately disposes the soul to those things which pertain to the performing of the divine worship. And because these things cannot be done *suitably* without the help of grace, the divine bounty bestows grace upon those receiving the character, by which they may *worthily* fulfill those things to which they are delegated."[15] Divine help unique in its nature but manifold in its expressions, sacramental grace disposes the priest to fulfill in impeccable fashion the entire mission which falls to him through the imposition of hands by his bishop.

The grace of Holy Orders, therefore, will be first of all *a grace of religion*. Since the sacraments are ordered directly or indirectly to the Christian worship, the grace

---

[13] *Suppl.*, q. 42, a. 1 and IIIa, q. 61, a. 2, c.
[14] *IV Sent.*, q. 2, a. 2, sol. 2 and *Sum. theol.* IIIa, q. 62, a. 2.
[15] *Sum. theol.*, IIIa, q.63, a.4, ad 1.

which accompanies them is always religious. Holy Orders assures the priest, who is a liturgist par excellence, of a special gift of the Spirit. His intellect will perceive more readily the essential dependence which attaches him to the providential will, both in his being and his action; it will recognize in a very special way its radical and basic disproportion to the work of worship of which Christ is the source. His heart will draw him more spontaneously toward the service of the altar and the visible, authentically Christian and ecclesiastical ministry, toward the liturgical ceremonies of the sacraments and the sacramentals.

"Holy Orders gives this pre-eminence principally to the virtue of religion and the annexed gift of piety. It leads the priest whom it consecrates to render homage to the infinite transcendence of the Most High, and to permeate this homage with filial affection; to carry out his functions of worship with tender inner reverence and great outer care; to apply himself to works of zeal as to a service of the Lord; to give himself with prompt and generous will to his entire ministry, imitating the loving devotion with which Christ offered Himself to all the plans of His Father even unto death and the death of the Cross. The dominant energy of the grace of ordination is an energy of true devotion and piety, of religious devotion to God and filial love toward Him."[16]

The grace of Orders also makes up for the deficiencies which harm the exercise of the priesthood and the apostolate. It attacks inertia and lukewarmness, dissipates the darkness of the intellect and the obscurity of the imagination, lessens the coldness of the heart and the inability to act. It accomplishes in priestly souls the wishes formulated by the consecrating bishop during the ordination ceremonies: a completely heavenly wisdom, *coelestis sapientia;* irreproachable morals, *probi mores;* uprightness and maturity in judgment and in life, *probi et maturi in scientia similiter et opere;* the integrity of a chaste life, *in moribus vestris castae et sanctae vitae*

[16] J. Périnelle, O.P., *Le sacerdoce*, p. 57.

integritatem; a way of acting aware of its seriousness, *agnoscite quod agitis;* the mortification of vices and unwholesome desires, *mortificare membra vestra a vitiis et concupiscentiis omnibus.* Let your preaching be salutary, continues the bishop, *sit doctrina vestra spiritualis medicina populo Dei;* may the perfume of your life rejoice the Church, *sit odor vitae vestrae delectamentum Ecclesiae Christi;* let your conduct be the instrument for the moral reform of the Christian people, *censuramque morum exemplo suae conversationis insinuent;* may sanctity in all its forms shine forth in you, *eluceat in eis totius forma justitiae.*

For all those who call upon it, the sacramental grace of Orders will keep intact the immaculate splendor and divine radiance of the gift which is the priesthood.

CHAPTER NINE

THE SACERDOTAL COMMUNITY

Until now, we have spoken about priests and not about the "clergy," the sacerdotal community. While it is indispensable to determine in a precise manner the duties which are incumbent upon every priest as an individual, the powers that are entrusted to them, the inner transformation which affects them, it is no less necessary to show that, in reality, priests are members of a great diocesan, even universal, community.

1. CLERGY AND COMMUNITY SPIRIT

The priestly mediation of the God-Man was not entrusted to individuals who were isolated and unknown to one another: Christ confided the work of salvation to the Twelve, the College of the Apostles. The apostolic task will be developed together, as a team and in collaboration. True, each effort is personal and isolated — priests are not drawn up in battle formation — but each is also part of an over-all movement directed by an alert leader.

COMMUNITY AND FELLOWSHIP

An insistence upon collaboration should not be regarded as a concession to our times, which are so com-

munitarian-minded. The need for union among priests
has a justification over and above what may be a passing current of thought. The evils which Christians suffer,
and to which we must furnish a reply, are not only individual and local, not even restricted to the boundaries
of a parish; accordingly, would not that apostolic action,
which did not take into account the extent of the sources
of de-Christianization, be unrealistic? The idea of
priestly collaboration, therefore, flows in a direct line
from a realistic view of the religious situation of an
area; it is born of a judicious desire to act reasonably
on behalf of Christ.

This unity in not based only on the need for action;
it comes from the character of Orders itself. It is because
priests enjoy a profound ontological similarity that they
find themselves simultaneously constituted in an indelible
and eternal unity. Unity in being calls for understanding, cohesion in action. "We are brothers, truly brothers,
because we are priests in the sacerdotal Order, through
sacerdotal consecration, in the hierarchy. The characteristic bond for diocesan priests, the strongest one, is the
sacerdotal bond which, through priestly consecration,
unites them, on the one hand, to their bishop as to their
true shepherd and father, and, on the other hand, to
the other priests of the diocese as to their spiritual
brethren, *confratres*."[1]

Also, by nature, the priest is destined and dedicated
to work in common — to cooperation. To this end, he
develops the many small virtues which create unity, in
life, at least in action: he is able to understand, to have
compassion, to concede, to be conciliatory, to adapt himself.

"All priests are members of a single body; all are
fighting in the same army, under the command of Christ
Jesus and His vicar on earth. Also, we urgently ask
each and every one, along with the Apostle Peter, 'that
in brotherly love, with a simple heart, [they] love one

---

[1] E. Poppe, *Entretiens sacerdotaux*, p. 76.

another more thoughtfully,' and with the Apostle Paul, that they 'bear one another's burdens, anticipating one another with honor, solicitous to preserve the unity of the spirit in the bond of peace, savoring the same things and persevering in one same rule.' Though there may be differences of origin, language, environment, responsibility, and others, let us, nevertheless, be one in heart and in spirit."[2]

Hence the priest will be hostile to the individualistic, cramped and particularistic spirit, confined to the limits of a single place, parish, or class. He will be opposed to faults which specifically destroy unity, such as intransigence in details, rancor and self-love, impatience and disdain, wounding indifference, the lack of understanding, self-sufficiency; he will be neither a blunderer nor a scolder nor a pessimist.

MANY-SIDED COLLABORATION

As a matter of fact, the most common form of communitarian life in the clergy is, it would seem, apostolic collaboration. The apostolate makes it possible to concentrate on a single target a host of qualities and talents which otherwise would risk arousing personal opposition. Diversity, when not oriented toward a specific goal, turns easily into divergency. The fact of finding ourselves together under one roof, at the same table, is a guarantee of unity, joy, and support to the extent that the desire for common action, concerted and carried out as a team, gives it a soul. The unity acquired by bringing together different aptitudes toward a definite goal is the best gauge of successful life in common. This is why it is so urgent for diocesan priests to possess, more and more, one and the same ideal, one and the same spirit, one and the same conquering intention, one and the same redemptive desire, in short one and the same general concept of their diocesan priesthood. Thus, though dissimilar in their talents, their tastes,

[2] Stat. dioec. Mechlin., n.6.

their human and supernatural potentialities, they will have a basis for authentic unity.

In the intellectual domain, the possibilities for co-operation are immense: a pastoral theology relating to the various milieux, a study of the psychology proper to different types of persons; an examination of the concrete situation in each region; a reminder of the great doctrinal currents which affect the spirit of the parishioners; reports on theological, social, economic, pedagogical questions; the establishment of parish centers and libraries; days of priestly studies. It has often been noted that this form of collaboration stimulates the most gifted, bolsters those who have less imagination, and, finally, enriches both.

In the domain of action itself, collaboration is extremely valuable: priests doing the same kinds of work can be brought together to exchange ideas; common campaigns can be planned, facilities can be shared, etc. In this area, the episcopacy today gives a striking example. Cardinal Griffin, the late Archbishop of Westminster had prophetic words to say in this regard: "I am convinced that there will be a great innovation in the Church of tomorrow: I mean that she is going to encourage international relations among the Catholic hierarchies of the various nations. We face similar problems, we run into similar difficulties, and I believe that we shall surmount them more easily by concentrating our efforts, comparing our plans, and helping one another in the great work of reconstruction which awaits us."[3] Likewise, in France, the assembly of cardinals and bishops has proposed to all the bishops the text of a survey having to do with the diocesan clergy, its formation, action and pattern of life. Such examples coming from above, will be the point of departure for a more coordinated, more thought-out, more united apostolic life.

Finally, in the realm of the spiritual life, a great deal of good is to be expected from more close-knit

[3] From *The Sword and the Spirit*, November, 1944.

relations among members of the clergy. When priestly attention is drawn to the fundamental necessity of helping one another in the difficulties inherent in every diocesan ministry, such as discouragement, bitterness, spiritual slackness, the loss of the apostolic spirit, forgetfulness of the laws of the Christian apostolate, those who slide toward mediocrity through lack of any serious and regular clerical support, will become the exceptions.

FRIENDSHIP AND ASSOCIATIONS

Unity among priests can take the form of sacerdotal friendship. While it is always true that the priest must be able to live alone, it is certain that everyone does well to impose on himself, according to his own temperament and personal needs, a kind of "regimen" based on social and emotional needs as well as physical and intellectual ones. Priestly friendship can provide support, help, and assurance: it makes it possible to communicate what one considers most intimate to someone who will understand, accept, and sympathize in a heartfelt manner. Experience shows the importance of friendships in the most difficult circumstances of life and in the most decisive hours of one's existence.

Still, it may happen that an error of perspective will harm the development of strong friendships. Some priests seem to include in their idea of perfection the obligation to live without friends. One can to a certain extent understand the origin of this error, but one cannot subscribe to it. Our perfection consists in pastoral charity, and our whole lives must be taken up in nourishing it as much as possible and in developing it. But solitude, as well as friendship, can weaken this charity. Friendship can involve a loss of time, dispersion, exclusiveness, attachment to others; but solitude can, for its part, engender languor, nervousness, discouragement, a moody spirit, obsessions, attachment to self. Solitude aids reflection, meditation, calmness; friendship comforts, revives convictions, gives courage, restores enthusiasm. In short, both can favor charity and harm it.

Today when the difficulties of exterior action, the troubles, labors and annoyances of priestly life are very great, it seems that pastoral charity could benefit a great deal from a fine sacerdotal friendship.

Priestly associations are another form of friendly support in and for the clergy. It serves no purpose to quote the approbations and encouragements relating to them in the Church. Even without being in themselves necessary, or even good for all, for many reasons — scruples with regard to the regulations, personal repugnances, etc. — they can be of real use to many priests. Through the check which they provide, the minimum social framework which they insure, and through the minimal commitment which they impose, they can sustain and strengthen the priest during his whole lifetime: it is from that point of view that they must be evaluated. Indeed, for an adult, the benefit to be gained from these associations can be summed up in two words: few disadvantages and certain appreciable advantages. That is already enough not to reject them without reflection.

2. THE DIOCESAN COMMUNITY

The priests of a diocese do not merely form a community among themselves: the diocese has a keystone, a directing and unifying center, a paternal leader, the bishop. Moreover, to specify the relations which unite priests to their bishop is, at the same time, to recall the organic bonds of the sacerdotal community within a diocese.

THE BISHOP AND HIS PRIESTS

The history of the priesthood and the liturgy itself reveal that the priest is the bishop's *cooperator*, his "co-worker." This is self-evident, once one gives it a moment's thought. When a bishop was placed at the head of an important community, in the early Christian Church, how could he be adequate to the task? Could he do everything himself? Could he prepare catechumens, baptize, hear confessions, help all his subjects? Reflection makes us realize that the bishop soon had to call upon helpers. And not merely deacons, for it was necessary that these helpers be truly able to guarantee the bishop's spiritual presence among his people; he therefore had to give his helpers the power of baptizing, of celebrating the Last Supper, of forgiving sins, of presiding over marriages, of aiding the dying. He had to permit them to speak in his name and transmit authentically the evangelical truth entrusted to his care. This explains, quite naturally, the existence of a numerous clergy called to act with the bishop, under his direction and by his impetus: thus was born the "common" priestly life.

According to Father Masure,

"the priesthood has sprung historically and theologically from the episcopate, or rather from the Apostolate, in the primitive sense of the latter word that designated the powers and the functions of the Twelve. The Apostles conferred upon inferiors a portion of their obligations, so that these inferior priests might exercise them in dependence upon them: it was a participated, derived, and subordinate priesthood.

"The priestly state must be related to the episcopal state, not only as the part to the whole, but as the subordinate and dependent to its principle. The priest accomplishes in an imperfect manner, limited in time, space, and power, what the bishop does in a perfect, absolute, and independent manner. That is why the priestly state must be defined through the episcopal state if it is to be rightly understood. The presbyteral priesthood consists essentially in the subordinate participation in the religious and apostolic functions of the bishop. Seeing himself in this light, the priest will find once again all his value. . . . " [4]

Thus we will find the law of our life, the norm of our action, the foundation of our dependence, the measure of our dignity.

[4] *Parish Priest*, pp. 63-64.

DIOCESAN SPIRIT

The *law of our life* and spirituality. Actually, each time the diocesan priest performs an act of praise or sanctification, teaching or direction, he is acting to "help" his bishop, to cooperate in the latter's work. Every priestly activity is, in this sense, stamped with the mark of collaboration in the apostolate of the bishop. This is a characteristic element of the priest's spirituality.

The *norm of our action*. The nature of the functions to be carried on, their arrangement, their disposition — everything is determined by the intention of the bishop, in whose name and as an extension of whom the priest acts. Whence the effort at cohesiveness, unity, and coordination which is required on the part of diocesan priests.

The *foundation of our dependence*. Since the priest is ordained only to the extent that the bishop has need of him, his activity is carried out under the sign of this subordination. For the bishop, he is a kind of extra arm, an auxiliary who represents him accurately, a delegate who interprets his intentions perfectly, an envoy who faithfully accomplishes his mission. Each act of ministry, of magisterium, or of government bears the seal of this complete dependence.

The *measure of our dignity*. Actually, the work of the bishop is, by definition, a work of charity; to participate in it is to take part in a life of unequalled pastoral charity which establishes the bishop himself in a state of perfection superior to that of religious. The more the diocesan priest reminds himself that he bears a part of the responsibility which rests on the shoulders of his bishop, the more he can take legitimate pride in being called to an eminent and noble task. How the priest should love and esteem "his ecclesiastical state," concludes Masure, "his diocesan state. . . . How beautiful is this state when seen in the light in which we have been trying to restore it. Born of divine charity, in whose service it was created, it elevates priests above all particular asceticisms, and constitutes them as the fathers and servants of the Christian people. It makes them participate in the life and in the state of the bishop, who is the true pontiff. Is there any dignity in the world greater than this?"[5]

The union in the diocese of the bishop and his priests is strengthened by the fact that the apostolate is exercised *visibly and locally*. When two persons of the same family are separated by an ocean, the bonds of blood finally lose some of their vitality; when two industrialists manage the same enterprise, one from Paris, the other from New York, one cannot speak of a common life. When, however, all the members of a family work together on a farm, for example, their union becomes very close, because they are harnessed together, visibly physically one might say, to a common task which they see come into existence, grow, then wither or flourish. The joys and hopes, the regrets and sorrows, are pooled, nourishing life and creating a very real "community" of life. Likewise, he who directs all the efforts of priests toward the same goal, tying together their activities, insuring their cooperation, animating the members of this great sacerdotal body, carefully directing the soldiers of Christ the King, is a creator of profound unity and manifests by that very fact that he is not only the leader of an army, but the father of a family, the soul of a community.

Intimate collaboration, similarity of activities, paternal direction and filial submission, the impetus of the leader and intelligent discipline, common dignity and nobility, coordinated life and action — such are the multiple threads of which the tightly woven fabric of the diocesan community is formed. In a certain sense, it is true to say that all priests are "diocesan," some exclusively so, based on the fact that they have been accepted and formed by the shepherd of a diocese to be totally and uniquely at his disposal in his own diocese; others, in a more or less complete manner, in the measure in which they carry out a ministry which is more or

[5] *Parish Priest*, pp. 103-104.

less independent of the episcopal jurisdiction. But every priest exercising an apostolic ministry in a diocese must have the diocesan spirit and live a diocesan spirituality, for he necessarily belongs to the diocesan community.

3. THE UNIVERSAL COMMUNITY

The affection which unites us to the concrete diocesan community which we see developing before us each day, must not become a sort of exaggerated regionalism. If individual communities can sometimes hurt the parish community, if a certain parochial particularism can disturb the community life of the diocese, a certain diocesan exclusivity can similarly veil some great national, continental, even universal, realities.

UNIVERSAL PROBLEMS

In fact, when one becomes aware of the elements which justify and form the basis of the diocesan community, one realizes that there are a large number of these which all priests, *of all nations*, possess in an identical way. The entire clergy, of East or West, of Europe or Asia, of America or Australia, is attached to the same work, as universal as the Catholic Church herself, as the sacrifice and redemption of the glorified Lord. The whole clergy, throughout the world, evangelizes and preaches the Christian truth, sanctifies the faithful by means of the sacred rites instituted by Jesus Christ, and, in the manner of good shepherds, supports the faltering steps of men. The entire clergy is marked with the indelible sign of the character of Holy Orders, and thus bears in its soul a spiritual image of the Incarnate Word, the "Apostle of our believing," the Source of truth and of life. The entire clergy has received the authentic "mission" of consecrating itself professionally to the ministry of salvation. Finally, the entire clergy nourishes an apostolic spirit in its soul like that demonstrated to us by the Apostles. In short, all the great values which create among the members of the clergy a specific similarity and unity — goal, functions, mission, spirit — belong to the clergy of the entire world. Every priest must then nourish in himself community sentiments as universal as the Church.

Moreover, the very conditions of action call for an ever increasing breadth. A wholesome realism led to the conclusion, above, that the apostolic remedies had to take into consideration the nature of the evils from which the faithful are suffering. And since these woes often have a scope which exceeds the boundaries of one parish, it is reasonable to undertake the work of spiritual restoration on a diocesan basis. But, the evils the faithful are suffering today often exceed even the boundaries of dioceses; some of them are national, continental, world-wide. The wise realism which guided diocesan action will, in its strict logic, have to give way to national, continental, world-wide actions. This is not the place to enter into further detail; but it cannot be held that a work must be limited by the boundaries of a diocese because a bishop's authority does not go further. The principle of action which is valid within a diocese for parishes, is also valid by analogy, it seems to us, within the Church for the dioceses. Once again, all the priests must take part, in fact or by intention, in the great national, continental or world-wide actions which are set into motion in the universal community.

UNIVERSAL INITIATIVES

This sense of the *clergy's universal community* must be reaffirmed by the priest in his own soul. Not only in the celebration of the sacrifice of the Mass, which is universal by definition; not only in the daily recitation of the Breviary, which he prays in the name of all creation; but in all the enterprises which concern the universal clergy and the world-wide apostolate, such as the great campaigns relative to public morality and international means for spreading ideas: the radio, the press, motion pictures, television; the great movements of prayer and of practical projects which pertain particularly to priestly vocations, currents of thought, and Catholic and missionary action.

Even though less immediately perceived than the diocesan community, the universal community has an *authentic reality*. It, too, has its requirements. And it has its chief and father — the pope, vicar of Jesus Christ. This is not the place to determine theologically the relationships which exist between the pope and the episcopate, and the faithful of the entire world. We wish only to stress the inner, intimate, and familial, as it were, aspect of these relations. The diocesan impetus evidenced in the twentieth century does not imply, as a consequence, a lessening of the spirit of universality and catholicity. It seems possible, if one possesses an organic view of the Church, to give greater emphasis to the paternity of the bishop, even while appreciating ever more fully the paternity of the pope. Further progress in all these dimensions is demanded of the priest today.

CHAPTER TEN

THE SOUL OF THE APOSTOLATE

New Testament writings and books on spirituality sometimes give the name "apostle" to certain persons. When we look in these doctrinal sources for the reasons which justify such an appellation, we find three. First of all, that man is an apostle who is, so to speak, attached by profession to all the tasks of teaching, sanctification, and direction which Christ confided to His Church; in this case, the apostolate is determined in terms of function, *activities*. That man is an apostle whom the Lord sends: the authentic *mission* coming from the Lord or the hierarchy, also justifies the title of apostle. Finally, that man is an apostle who possesses to a certain extent an apostolic *soul*, that is, who is one in heart and mind with the Man-God, the Redeemer. This last aspect will be the subject of this chapter; we shall demonstrate the fact that the apostolic masters demand this inner life, and we shall endeavor to determine just how they understand it.

From the outset, let us point out that this "apostolic soul" is a constituent element of the apostolate. It is not only the best means of guaranteeing a fruitful ministry and the best preparation for that ministry, it is also, above all, an essential ingredient of the apostolic

life. Any priest who would fail to maintain it carefully
in himself would not fully deserve the name of "apostle
of Jesus Christ." Certain noteworthy consequences flow
from this, especially in regard to the way in which one
conceives the pastoral ministry and daily meditation.

1. NEED FOR AN INTERIOR
"THEOLOGICAL" ELEMENT

THE APOSTOLATE IS ACTION

The apostolate is *action*. Let us repeat this quite
clearly and explicitly at the beginning of this chapter
which will deal with the apostolic "spirit," that is, the
interior theological element — "contemplative" as it is
sometimes called — of the apostolic life.

When at the moment of His Ascension our Lord said
to the Twelve: "Go ye . . . teach . . . baptize . . . teach
them to keep my commandments," He was talking about
action. When the Apostles from Pentecost Sunday on,
began to preach, visit the cities and villages of Palestine,
baptizing, celebrating the Supper, anointing the sick,
reproving the delinquent, they were fully in action. When
the Holy Scriptures call the apostle an "envoy," a "servant," a "witness," a "dispenser," a "steward of divine
wealth," in each case they have a mind a life of action.
The *ministerium, magisterium,* and *regimen* which sum
up the theology of the Church's apostolate, signify a
mediating action. And when the Pontifical has the bishop
say, "the priest must baptize, preach, offer sacrifice, bless,
govern," it is unquestionably describing the forms of a
life consecrated to action.

Equivocation on this subject is no longer possible
and discussion would be idle. Today, as of old, the best
spiritual writers are repeating, loudly and clearly, the
same truths. We can be excused from quoting them here.

Besides, in this field as in many others, it is preferable
to fall back on the *life* of the Apostles, bishops and
diocesan priests themselves. Consider Paul, Peter, the
Elders and the episcopes; the Apostolic Fathers and the

great bishops of the controversial centuries—Athanasius, Gregory, Augustine; the doctors and thaumaturges; the episcopate of modern times; the "simple" priests of our towns and countryside, of the working-class or middle-class neighborhoods of our cities: everything in them speaks of action.

Let us even penetrate within *contemplative circles,* behind the protective grilles of the Carmelites, or the walls of the Trappists. When these monks and nuns speak of the apostolic value of their charity, of their prayers, or of their penances, they are describing a powerful radiation which transcends the cloister walls and spreads throughout their own countries into far-off missions; and their hearts are filled with the desire of efficaciously extending the great redemptive action perpetually carried on by the Incarnate Word, the glorified Lamb of the Apocalypse. Did not St. Thérèse of Lisieux, a cloistered nun, become the great protectress of the Catholic missions? The *Story of a Soul* quite clearly reveals her redemptive desires. And, in a letter dated February, 1903, Sister Elizabeth of the Trinity wrote to a priest: "Do you not find that in action, while one is apparently carrying out the function of Martha, the soul can always remain, like Magdalene, absorbed in its contemplation, holding fast to this source? This is how I understand the apostolate both for the Carmelite and the priest. Then both can radiate God, give Him to souls, if they only cling to these divine sources."[1]

NEITHER "INACTIVE" NOR "AGITATED"

This is why certain temperaments seem less suited for carrying out an apostolic task, and why it would be desirable that there not be too many of these in the ranks of the diocesan clergy. Among these types are those with an inert, passive, and nonchalant temperament, for instance, those who are capable of straggling along in an idle existence and watching the hours and

[1] M. Philipon, O.P., *La doctrine spirituelle de soeur Elisabeth de la Trinité,* 3rd edition, p. 196.

days drifting before their eyes without worrying about filling them in a human way. There are the dilettantes, who are active but in their own way, according to their own tastes and caprices, not according to the good of the Church. They suffer from a voluptuousness of the spirit as harmful to the apostolate as the voluptuousness of the flesh; for they work at the apostolate merely to keep themselves honestly occupied, just as they dabble in literature, sports, or arts. Then there are the dreamers and morbid esthetes: those moved by the beauty of the apostolic life as described by some capable preacher, rejoicing in advance in the tragedy of souls, the harmony of the liturgical ceremonies, the beauty of works of religious culture. Finally, those whose only concern is to improve themselves personally and live an exclusively intellectual life, for whom knowledge is the absolute, who prefer a book to a man, a system to a life. Apart from certain exceptions, such vocations adjust very poorly to the spirit of action and giving inherent in the apostolic priesthood of which Jesus has furnished the model.

The diocesan priest has been placed in the midst of his flock to be a good "shepherd," alert, informed and wise, but a "shepherd" above all. But what can one expect of a passive, dreaming shepherd primarily preoccupied with himself? What could one expect from a mother of a family, a teacher, and the head of a firm who were lazy, dreamers, desirous above all of improving their own minds? What would become of the home, the school, the factory, in the hands of such people? It would not be very long before there was a catastrophe. And if catastrophes in the apostolic field are more often than not invisible, they are nevertheless real.

However, "practical" men, "anti-intellectuals," "activists," should not prematurely rejoice in reading these lines. We have spoken thus in order to assert vigorously the active nature of the apostolic life, and not to exclude the aspect of interiority, "conscience," and "union with God," about which we shall now speak. For those who are "activists" in the purely external sense of the term, the following lines will be as hard to bear as those which preceded were easy to accept, and they will no doubt often entertain the regret felt by the Apostles: "This is a hard saying. Who can listen to it?"

For while the apostolate is action, it is action of a very special kind, and cannot be compared to any activity which man conducts in the purely temporal domain. It is unique action, for its source is in God; unique action because of the visible instrumentality of the minister who insures its execution; unique action, through the mysterious ways in which it is brought to its fulfillment; unique action from the fact that it results in divine life for others. Unique action, finally, because it finds part of its substance in the soul of him who carries it out.

SOME MODELS

To prove that apostolic action necessarily involves an inner theological or "contemplative," element, we shall examine the life and works of those who are our authentic models. The excerpts we quote from their writings, will, of course, represent moments of fullness; how else can we come to know the life-ideal extolled by them? We cannot after all, take St. Ignatius as a model during the time he was still a soldier, or St. Augustine before his conversion!

Does not Paul, then love the risen and glorious Christ just as directly and as immediately as he does men, his brothers? The "For me to live is Christ" is just as real as the "I wish to spend and be spent for your souls." The "I desire to depart and to be with Christ" is just as ardent as the "to stay on in the flesh is necessary for your sake" (Phil. 1:23-24). Could Paul speak in these tones if his apostolic life were *theocentric* only on an alternating basis — loving God directly in the morning during his meditation, and later concerning himself with his brethren? Or if he were acting simply for the glory of God? The "I am hard pressed from both sides" (Phil. 1:23) tells us something else: an immediate and direct love of Christ and of

Christians, a real attachment to the One and the others.

Today, as of old, the doctrine of the full apostolate is demanding. To live fully the apostolic instrumentality, the spiritual authors write, requires as much inner charity as outer activity, as much love of God as zeal for men. To live the Christian apostolate fully, just as Christ instituted it, involves a living faith as much as technical skill, ardent desire as much as know-how, theocentrism as much as interest in souls. Regardless of the point of view from which it is considered, the fullness of the apostolate calls for the *synchronized and real union of the life of the soul and of action.* This is the message which the spiritual authors have handed down to us over the centuries and which reaches us by the most diverse paths.

We are familiar with these lines of Dom Chautard's: "In the soul of a saint, action and contemplation, blending in perfect harmony, give his life a marvelous unity. Such, for example, is St. Bernard, the most contemplative and, at the same time, the most active man of his century, who was beautifully pictured as follows by one of his contemporaries: in him, contemplation and action were so in tune that the saint seemed at once completely devoted to external works and yet wholly absorbed in the presence and love of his God."[2]

An interpreter of the thought of St. Ignatius thinks along the same lines as the son of St. Bernard. Let us listen to his explanation of the formula which we, personally, find an apt one: "contemplative in action":

"To order a Christian life is not merely to develop a personality harmoniously; it is to place it in its proper rank in the universal plan; it is to make it perfectly suited to carry out with all its resources, in communion with the social life of the Church, the mission assigned by Providence. This mission, as we shall see, is essentially apostolic. We must, therefore, go on to tell how the *Exercises* intend to form perfect apostles by forming perfect contemplatives. Their ideal is summed

---

[2] *L'âme de tout apostolat*, Paris, 1930, 3rd ed., p. 62.

up in the formula which, according to Jérôme Nadal,
already expressed the spiritual life of St. Ignatius: *in
actione contemplativus*. Is not the "what shall I do for
Christ" not more or less the first burst of zeal? This
sacred fire is brought to the world by Christ Himself.
For the Christian, the apostolate is not a virtue of super-
erogation, a counsel graciously offered and freely followed. It is an essential part of the imitation of Jesus
Christ. 'Propter nostram salutem descendit de coelis.'
All the intentions of the Incarnate Word, the details
of His life and virtues, are directed toward the sole goal
of His redemptive mission. How can one be united with
Him, and walk in His footsteps, without collaborating in
His work? Nor is this enough. After having caused the
apostolic spirit to be born, after having fortified, fore-
warned, stimulated it, prayer must, so to speak, inform
it, penetrate it: it must literally become its soul. The
richer and more profound a meaning one gives to this
oft-repeated yet always expressive comparison, the more
one shall approach the ideal envisioned in the *Exercises*.
For St. Ignatius, action and contemplation are not, cannot be, two alternating currents, two movements succeeding one another at more or less regular intervals.
So long as outer work, even undertaken for the sake of
God, distracts one from God and disturbs prayer, or so
long as prayer, still too jealous of its delightful repose,
keeps action at arm's length, there remains a dualism,
the sign of imperfection. . . ." [3]

To these teachings must be added examples from life.
If the Curé of Ars had been asked whether he loved
Christ as directly and as really as men, would he have
replied in the negative? If Cardinal Mercier, at the
end of his life, had been asked for his concept of the
apostolate, would he not have readily talked about uniting the "inner life" and action? Did he not say that
one has to live not only "for" God but also "from" God?
Does not the Breviary suggest the same ideal when it
tells us, regarding St. Elias, in the Second Nocturne:
"while he practiced his trade, his eyes scanned the Holy

[3] L. Peeters, S.J., *Vers l'union divine par les Exercices de S.
Ignace*, Bruges, 1925, pp. 88 ff.

Scriptures, so that his spirit might be occupied with God while his hands devoted themselves to human tasks."

Thus, action and the spiritual life are not attended to in turn by the apostolic person, but are always joined together in his life.

The conclusion can be drawn that a strongly theocentric apostolic spirit is a necessity, with this implying no betrayal of action and interest in men — quite the opposite. If they wish to respond to the appeals of Christ, if they wish to imitate the Apostles and the holy priests who are their models, if they want to lend an ear to the teachings of authorized spiritual writers. diocesan priests will seek to form a full and perfect ideal of apostolic action toward which they will advance stage by stage until the end.

2. NATURE OF THIS INTERIOR ELEMENT

In the diocesan priest the apostolic spirit presupposes a certain inner life, that is, an awareness of the total reality open to him in faith, and an attachment to God and his neighbor on the basis of a redemptive love. This life of awareness of the theological virtues is called, generally, "contemplation," as opposed to the apostolic activities designated by the word "action." Unfortunately, the word "contemplation" was not born along with Christianity. It was not applied to the inner life which the Apostles manifested on the first Pentecost. It was, however particularly dear to the Greek thinkers and it had, among them, its own history, its own value, its own disciples and practitioners. Both the Christian and the Greek traditions remain alive even today, to the point that the term "contemplation" sometimes represents the one tradition, sometimes the other. Since the inner element of the apostolic life is generally called "contemplation," it is necessary now to specify precisely what the term means for us when we say that the apostle is "a contemplative in action."

When it represents the inner aspect of the apostolic life, the term *contemplatio* in no way signifies religious speculation, nor even the exercise of morning prayer, as it was lived with great ardor by the Apostles during the most fervent years of their lives. The Twelve were completely "given" to their Lord, and this giving in view of the redemption included a very perfect act of charity: "Lord, thou knowest that I love Thee!" They had also a very acute perception of the mystery of the inclusion of all men in Christ. What is that except the theological life of faith and charity? The "contemplatio" of the Twelve was nothing else but that. In all the examples that we could adduce from the lives of authentic models of the diocesan clergy, from a Curé d'Ars or an Ignatius of Antioch, the same truth comes to light. When they speak — expressly or in equivalent terms—of uniting action and contemplation, they signify by *actio* the apostolic activities which arise in their mission, and by *contemplatio* the soul which is their innermost constituent part, the divine breath.

In order to define what the spirit of the apostolate involves, it is therefore of supreme importance to understand the nature and mode of action of theological virtues.

THEOLOGICAL VIRTUES

Through theological virtues, man enters into a communion of life with the Holy Trinity — a divine communion in its very nature. It is a mysterious "activation" by the Three Persons of our capacity for comprehension and affection, of our cognitive and voluntary powers. It is an actual insertion of human activity into the vital trinitarian movement, an assumption of man's action into the current of charity which is the very substance of God. One could say of it, with the necessary distinctions, what St. John of the Cross wrote about perfect mystical union:

"Finally, all the movements, operations and inclinations which the soul formerly received from the principle and force of its natural life, are in this union transformed into divine movements, dead to their own proper operation and tendencies, living now in God. For the soul, as a true child of God, finds itself already completely animated by the Spirit of God, as we are taught by St. Paul when he says: 'whoever are led by the Spirit of God, they are the sons of God,' (Rom. 8:14). So that, according to the above, the understanding of such a soul is the understanding of God, its will is the will of God, and its joy, the joy of God. And the substance of this soul, while not the substance of God, because it cannot change itself substantially into the substance of God, yet, united with Him, absorbed in Him, is God by participation."[4]

"Our understanding is the understanding of God," writes St. John of the Cross. By faith, indeed, we see as with the eyes of God; these are the very words of St. Thomas: "Faith is a certain assimilation to the divine knowledge, in that through the faith infused in us we cleave to the first truth for its own sake, and thus enlightened by the divine knowledge, we see all things with the eye of God."[5] The same is true of our charity. On considering more closely the role played by God in the heart of the believer, it seems that divine love is the principal actor. Nevertheless, human love, very active and personal, is made fruitful, is animated, "informed" by the love which is in God to such an extent that the act which arises therefrom is more divine than human or, rather, is essentially divine, since it is a question of an infused theological virtue, and really human, since it is born in my own will and capacity for love.

This *transforming assimilation* of our spiritual activities to the divine activity itself is such that the spiritual authors compare it to the transformation undergone by a metal bar which has remained for some time in a fiery furnace. Nothing appears to remain of the opacity of the metal which, through its stay in the fire, has become altogether like the fire; it radiates heat, it glows. So it is with the soul living under the sway of the divine life, or with our higher activities animated by the Holy Spirit.

[4] *La vive flamme d'amour*, ed. H. Hoonaert, 1937, p. 190.
[5] *In Boeth. de Trinitate*, qu. 3, a. 1.

THEOLOGICAL LIFE

In order to formulate this "inner life" in a more technical manner, it would seem that we must call on the term "fecundation," proposed by Maritain, or even better, the term "activation" preferred by M. de la Taille.[6]

"By act," he writes, "we understand that which in a being determines it to be of a particular essential perfection or to have such perfection added on to its essence. If the subject is its own perfection, we have a subsisting act which is not distinct from the subject. On the other hand there is, over against the act, the receptivity by which the subject is in potency to the act. In this case, then, it can be said that the act is that which, by communicating itself, brings to the imperfect the perfection of which it is capable."[7]

After explaining that there cannot be an "informing" but only "activation" when the uncreated Act of being or intelligibility is united as such with a created potency,[8] the author goes on to various applications: the beatific vision, the life of grace, the hypostatic union. But how does he explain the activation of man by God in the case of sanctifying grace? "There is henceforward among the just an activation of their soul, as the previously existing and living substance of the latter's rational life, but in potency to an increase of divine life by means of an uncreated vital principle which, by communicating itself to the soul, radically empowers it for the functions of this new life of which the beatific vision is the full flowering."[9] And what can this activation in the intellect and the will be? Perhaps we can learn

[6] Cf., J. Maritain, *Les dégrés du savoir*, pp. 489, 615; M. de la Taille, "Actuation créé par Acte Incréé" in *Rech. science relig.*, 1928, pp. 253-268.

[7] *Art. cit.*, p. 253.

[8] Still, there is a question as to whether it has been proved that there is no informing or quasi-informing. Is it certain that this quasi-informing coming from God would imply a strict material causality on our part? Or might this all be just a matter of wording?

[9] *Art. cit.*, pp. 257-258.

a little about it by basing ourselves on what the divine
action in us will be in the beatific vision.

It is impossible to see God as He is

"without an immediate conjunction between the intellect and the uncreated species, which alone represents
God just as He is. There will therefore be, between
God and the intellect, a union which is that of potency
to Act; for the intellect is the act of the knower. The
created intelligible, the impressed or infused species, the
informings regardless of their nature, placed in the
soul at the disposal of the mind, are the act which activates the potency to the true that we bear within us.
The subsisting Truth will be, not less but rather even
more, the Act of the intellect which is united thereto
as to an intelligible which it has at its disposal for knowing God and everything in God."[10]

Something quite similar takes place even here below
in the intelligence "informed" by infused faith and in
the will "informed" by charity. These faculties also live
by the divine life but to a still limited degree and always under the veil of our earthly humanity. In non-
technical language, one would say that it is the divine
life itself which bursts into our souls, into our principle
of life, in order to take it up in its movement and place
us in God, while safeguarding our real and distinct
existence.

In short, in this intimate and ineffable ascendancy,
God already grants to man the goal of his desire: to
become God by participation, to become "deiformed."
For "what God aspires to do is to transform us into
gods, and to give us by participation what He Himself
is by nature."[11] We thus become deiformed not only
in thought and love, but, as a consequence, in our person and action.

This sway of God over the apostle, the insertion of
the latter into trinitarian life, his participation in the
redemptive and outgoing love of God, have been des-

[10] *Art. cit.*, p. 255.
[11] J. Maritain, *Les dégrés du savoir*, p. 636.

cribed so well by Henri Bergson that we have no hesitation in borrowing a page from him. Opposing the ideal of the Christian mystics to that of Plotinus, for whom "action is a weakening of contemplation" (*Enn.*, III, 8, 4), the French philosopher writes:

"The mystical soul wishes to be this instrument. It eliminates from its substance whatever is not pure enough, not tough enough, not supple enough, for God to use it. . . . Now, it is God who acts through it, in it: the union is complete and, consequently, definitive. Then, words such as mechanism and instrument evoke images which are better left to one side. . . . Let us say that henceforth it is a superabundance of life for the soul. It is a tremendous impetus. It is an irresistible drive which throws it into the greatest undertakings. A calm exaltation of all its faculties enables it to have broad visions and, no matter how weak it is, to accomplish things with power. There is nothing which apparently distinguishes such a man essentially from the men among whom he circulates. He alone is aware of the change which raises him to the rank of *adjutores Dei*, passive as far as God is concerned, active with respect to men. . . . He has felt truth flowing in him from its source as an active force. He can no more prevent himself from spreading it than the sun can stop shedding its light. Except that now, it is not with mere words that he will propagate it, for the love which consumes him is no longer only the love of a man for God, it is the love of God for all men. Through God, by God, he loves all of mankind with a divine love. . . . Coinciding with the love of God for His works — a love which made all things — he would reveal to those who might question him the secret of creation. . . . Thus it is with this impulse of life, fully communicated to privileged men who then wish to impress it on all mankind and, in a sort of effective contradiction, convert into a creative effort this created thing which is a species, to make a movement out of what is by definition a stoppage."[12]

And so we are led to a more detailed examination of the contents of this theological activity and its characteristic elements.

[12] *Les deux sources de la morale et de la religion*, pp. 247-51.

OBJECT OF THE THEOLOGICAL LIFE

The very contents of this inner apostolic life are not a sentiment of natural or philanthropic interest, even in the highest sense; nor a spirit of mercy and compassion; nor a desire of accomplishing one's duties of state, of serving. The inner life of the apostle is, above all, *theological.* Its immediate object is God, considered in Himself, and one's neighbor, seen and loved in God.

Such is the content of the *act of faith.* The latter, in an obscure though sure and authentic realization, opens immense perspectives to the supernaturalized spirit: God, source, center and end of all things; the unfathomable Trinity; creation, the image of this divine Trinity and, since the Redemption, the "daughter" of God, by Christ in the Spirit. This is the spectacle which fascinates the elect and the angels: "Into these things angels desire to look" (1 Pet. 1:12).

Such is the object of *hope.* One hopes for "God," above all. It is He who is the first "material" object of this theological virtue, for God is, personally, the very reality of our beatifying union. It is also the supernatural and natural realities, both divine and temporal, which will lead us to God and which are perceived in a single glance, as the countless springboards thanks to which we throw ourselves more vigorously toward the heavens.

This is, finally, the content of *charity.* God again is the primary object of our love, and, in a subsidiary manner, every creature to the very extent to which it is seen in God, crowned with the divine, participating in that which constitutes God. Charity, as a matter of fact, is the divine love itself in which man has been made capable of sharing. How could man, to the extent that he is conscious and logical, love anything else but the absolute good, God? And if he does love the creature, out of charity, it is again to the extent that this creature is deformed, or like unto God, so that God is discovered necessarily in it. To love is to open oneself in the presence of God, to admire the fullness of order, splendor and perfection which is in Him, to allow oneself to be fascinated by His brilliance, to approach His essential goodness, to respond actively to the insistent demands of His appeal, to unite oneself to His love, and, in a heroic gesture, to proclaim that one is giving oneself to Him, that one wants only Him.[13]

In short, the full theological life extends to God considered in Himself, and to the entire universe, considered in God, "insofar as it is for God, in God, of God."

UNITY OF THE THEOLOGICAL LIFE

Does the love of God *and* all creation retain a true and inner unity?

The answer, while very simple, is fraught with practical consequences. Since it is a matter of theological life, it is certain that it is life in God which is primary and fundamental. On this subject there can be no doubt: that would be to deny the very essence of theological virtue. Creation itself is love *in God*. But does not this kind of love dilute creation itself? Apparently not; for what is to be loved is this creature itself, this whole creature, this whole concrete creature. Yet, in being loved, the creature is considered as to what it signifies in the eyes of God: a more or less full participation in Himself. Since theological activity is God's activity in us, it is impossible for our faith, hope, and charity not to espouse, in their movement, the rhythm proper to the life of God Himself.[14]

The apostolic spirit, in its inmost nature, will therefore be above all theocentric, united with the Holy Trinity, the Incarnate Word, the Father, or the Holy Spirit

[13] Cf. Fr. Rousselot, *Pour l'histoire du problème de l'amour au moyen âge*, Paris, 1933.

[14] There can be another love of creatures; this will be rather a "moral," Christian and supernatural love, arising therefore from justice, and through which one renders to others what is their due, in view of the basic appeal which they possess because they represent a real created perfection. But this is not the *theological* virtue of charity.

in themselves; secondarily and in a subsidiary manner, it will be preoccupied with creatures. It is impossible to explain otherwise the processes of theological action. In his study of the nature of the mixed life, Father Lemonnyer comes to the same conclusion: "Just as charity, which is primarily love of God, becomes love of neighbor by extension, so too this life made up of combined contemplation and action, is primarily contemplative, and becomes active by extension. Also, this comparison of the 'mixed' life with charity is far more than just a comparison. It is an explanation. . . . In the mixed life, as in charity itself, of which it is the perfect work, we therefore have a unique value which accomplishes its vital and homogeneous development in two phases."[15]

The predominance of *theocentrism* in the apostle's inner life is adequately explained by the fact that the theological life uses a method different from that which characterizes rational cognition. The philosopher comes to know God from His effects; he proceeds from effects to cause, from created things to God. Divine knowledge is different: it begins with God, so to speak, and in God discovers all creatures. Henceforth, if the theological life is a "deiformed" knowledge and love, we may conclude that God is known first and loved first, and creatures, one's neighbor and things, in Him, just as they appear to, and are loved by, God Himself.

The union of the theological and rational modes is unclear in the average Christian life. But in its most characteristic manifestations, particularly in the great mystics of Christianity, it is easily seen that the predominance of the theological makes itself gradually felt. The mystics say that they "rediscover" creatures, with complete spontaneity, almost naturally, because their eyes and love, like their lives, have been purified, that is, assimilated to those of God. In them, supernature permeates nature not only ontologically but even psy-

---

[15] *Somme théologique, La vie humaine, Ed. des Jeunes*, pp. 566-567.

chologically. The text quoted above from St. John of
the Cross (pp. 203-204) is witness to this, and one could
cite many others as well.

It would be extremely important to examine closely
this aspect of mystical life. We would receive many in-
sights thereby on the apostolic spirit itself in its most
basic aspects. We would be enlightened as to the meaning of the progress made by him who follows, step by
step, the path of a higher perfection.

INTERIOR LIFE — ONE AND MULTIFORM

But, one may say finally, this charity is the same
for all Christians: how could it constitute the soul of the
apostolate?

Actually, it is *fundamentally the same* for all Christians, for there is but one kind of theological virtue,
just as there is but one trinitarian life. One could even
add that all true Christian charity must, essentially, be
redemptive. This is a characteristic of Christianity.
Father Festugière writes:

"Against the backdrop of paganism, Christianity is
distinguished by three original features, particularly the
disinterested love of God. The Christian loves God not
primarily to enjoy Him, to rejoice in His presence and
sight: what he loves initially in God is the good of God,
that is, what pleases God — ultimately, what God wants.
This is so true that, in the final analysis, the love of the
Christian for God is measured by the authenticity and
completeness of his agreement with the divine plan which
is to save men. . . . It goes without saying that the natural movement of the Christian soul is to come as close
as possible to Him whom it loves. . . . But it is no less
true that its reflective movement heads in a different
direction. From the moment this soul has grasped that
to love God is to love the will of God, the plan of God,
it accepts, or rather, it desires not to see God, to suffer
this absence, if by purifying in the soul the love of
charity, the absence makes the soul love the divine plan

more, work harder for the salvation of men: 'for I desire to be separated from Christ for the sake of my
brethren.' "[16]
This observation is necessary, lest the Christian mystique, redemptive and saving, be identified with the
pagan mystique which ends with the enjoyment of the
vision of God.

However, the communication which God makes of
Himself can be diverse. In heaven, beatitude will be
different for each of the elect. Here below, too, the gift
of faith is diverse: one possesses the gift of knowledge,
another the gift of wisdom, a third the spirit of counsel.
The same can be true as regards charity. The gift of
redemptive charity is more characterized in the priest
than in the ordinary Christian. It involves a special
formality, a particular tonality, reserved to those who
are connected in the Church with the apostolate. It is,
in this sense, more complete, since the divine love is,
by nature, a redemptive and vivifying love.

Thus, the life lived by the diocesan priest, while being
fundamentally a theological life, acquires certain specific nuances: faith becomes an acute perception of the
mystery of the redemption of all men collectively in
Christ; the love of God is expressed in a saving benevolence and the desire of universal conquest. Since
there is in this life the total gift of the innermost life
of God Himself, Christ calls His priests not only servants
but also friends. Everything there is in God, He has given
them.

In the description of the interior life of the diocesan
priest, therefore, the "redemptive" aspect is essential.
It determines in part the very object of the wisdom of
faith which is present before the eyes of the apostle: the
mystery of salvation whose perspectives we described
above. It determines the particular form of pastoral
charity which, in turn, includes a permanent concern
for reconciling all things with the Father, a concern
which we find in Christ, the Apostles, and all the great
masters of the apostolate. In short, the whole climate of

[16] *L'enfant d'Agrigente*, pp. 122-123.

apostolic faith and charity is conveyed by this simple word: "redemptive."

3. SIGNIFICANCE OF MEDITATION

If this is the spirit that must animate the diocesan priest, one can see the importance for him, among other things, of the spiritual exercise called "meditation" or "mental prayer."

NECESSITY

The apostolic spirit includes the radical theocentrism of the interior life. But it is not given to everyone, nor to be sure, to all those who wish to lead an apostolic life, to bear inscribed in their hearts the sense of God, the "hunger for God," as it has been described, and the taste of the divine for its own sake. Let this be clearly understood. It is not our outer activities which must be theocentric, as in cloister life where adoration and prayer, the prayer of praise and the exercises of the contemplative life, are carried out. On the contrary, the majority of our apostolic tasks are directed toward the good of men. But the soul with which we carry on these activities must be fundamentally theocentric. Theological spirit and theocentric activities must not be confused.

On the other hand, the necessity of also loving men "according to God," in charity, demands a strong "spirit of faith" — in modern terms, what is needed is a "Christian ideology." Coming into contact with men and things, the priest must be attentive to all earthly realities; but at the same time, thanks to his intense vision of faith, he must look upon these realities *tanquam in oculo Dei*, with God's own eyes, giving them the significance, meaning, and importance which they have for God. *To see* men and things concretely, while discerning just as keenly what they signify for God, is to act in a spirit of faith. *To love* things concretely, but to esteem in them what God esteems and loves in them, that is to say, what therein is divine or deiformed, or rather, to love this creature insofar as it is deiformed: this is charity.

It is clear how necessary inner formation is to Christian ideology, how indispensable it is to know the value of created things according to faith so that, from within the priest can always correct the judgment which the perception of the senses might render incomplete or inaccurate. For the Lord, man is a "child of God," the world is an "image of God," communities are "signs of the Holy Trinity," the cosmos is the "witness of the divine immensity."

NATURE

What conclusion are we to draw from this for our daily meditation, except, first of all, that it, too, must be very *theological*. Since it is especially designed to assure the persistence throughout the day of this inner life whose necessity and fruitfulness we have seen, it is necessary that it be turned toward God, the Trinity, Christ and the Holy Spirit, and that the life of theological faith, hope, and charity predominate in it. Reflection is not excluded, nor are considerations on moral virtues and the principles of human wisdom, nor is anything which forms the substance of "meditation" in the classical sense of the term. But, if we want to give the morning exercise its real significance, we must make it a theological "mental prayer."

It would therefore not be enough for someone to say to himself: "I make my meditation every morning, and so I must have the apostolic spirit: do not the spiritual authors state that meditation is the guaranteed means of nourishing the apostolate's soul?" That could be a dangerous illusion. It takes more than just any type of meditation at all to maintain and increase in us the spirit of the true apostolate. It cannot be said that a priest who spends a half hour each day reflecting on the grandeur of the moral virtues, acquires ipso facto the sense of the mystery of salvation, personal love of our Lord, an unconquerable hope in God our Father. Daily meditation, therefore, only assures an authentic apostolic spirit if it is of the same order and type as this spirit.

It would be a good idea for those who preach priests' retreats to remind us frequently of this.

DURATION

The principle which regulates the length of morning meditation is, in brief, as follows: "How much time do I need, on the average, to ensure in my daily life the persistence and even the progress of the inner element essential to it?" The duration of the exercise of mental prayer is, therefore, essentially relative to the goal one is seeking. If living faith and love of the Lord in the midst of daily tasks can be intensified by a twenty-minute meditation, then this is enough.[17] However, it is unlikely that many priests will succeed so easily in this effort. Today more than ever, priestly life is so full of responsibilities of every kind that the mere fact of concentrating, abstracting oneself a bit, presupposes a costly effort. Because the quality of the apostolic spirit is, in general, linked to the exercise of prayer, everyone will have to reflect on this and decide for himself what his own needs are.

Prolonged mental prayer therefore finds its justification in the full exercise of our priestly life, in the need for keeping the apostolic spirit lively; it is a demand made upon us by our ideal. In introducing prolonged mental prayer into our lives, we are not trying to make ourselves into contemplatives, but to be truly apostolic in the full sense of the term.

It may, perhaps, be said that this is dangerous utilitarianism: mental prayer is not just an apostolic means, but has the value of an end. To speak thus is to forget that an exercise can be both a means and an end, so long as it is taken from a different point of view. When the priest's mental prayer can be perfectly simplified and reduced to loving our Lord, it will always put us into contact with our *end*. And thus it will be the best

---

[17] It should be clear that we are considering mental prayer purely as an exercise here. It may also be considered in itself for its own value.

means of living a "mixed" life which will include union with our Lord. There is, accordingly, no incompatibility between the role of means played by mental prayer in the organization of our apostolic lives, and the form of contact with the supreme End which it assumes in its most perfect exercise.

Perhaps these few notes will help the diocesan priest to read the ascetic authors more fruitfully, and to see in his own life the need for mental prayer, prolonged mental prayer, and the disinterested mental prayer of charity. Let us therefore remind diocesan priests that the inner life is demanded of them just so that they may become apostolic in a fuller and better way.

4. FECUNDITY OF THE INTERIOR LIFE

The apostolate as described until now, includes three elements: mission, function, and spirit. An apostle who did not possess them all would not be completely worthy of the name. A preacher who might speak against his bishop's will, even though this might lead to many conversions, could not be performing a perfectly apostolic act, since he would be lacking the necessary "mission." A priest who would devote himself to material activities unconnected to his priestly role, could not call himself, on that basis, "an Apostle of our Lord." So, too, he who does not live a profound inner life, does not possess the spirit which animated the Apostles and the models of the diocesan clergy; neither is he leading a full apostolic life. Mission, function, spirit: these are the three essential ingredients of the apostolic life. An apostolate without a "theological spirit" would be incomplete, deprived of one of its component parts. Everything which has so far been said shows the essential nature of this spirit for the apostolate.

But there is a legitimate subsidiary question: Can the apostolic and pastoral fecundity of this inner life also be described? It is in this sense that men have often spoken of the "soul of the apostolate." It is this special aspect that we wish to develop briefly in the succeeding pages.

INTERIOR LIFE AND APOSTOLIC FECUNDITY

Dom Chautard, in *The Soul of the Apostolate*, has masterfully developed advantages accruing to the apostle and the apostolate from an intense inner life.

Works, first of all, are made fruitful by the *divine virtue* inherent in the inner life[18] — "he who abides in me, and I in him, he bears much fruit" (John 15:5). The inner life, explains Dom Chautard, draws the blessings of God. It makes the apostle a sanctifier by good example; it is, in fact, incontestable that the visible influence of a priest is wielded more by the whole of his acts and words, by the general tone of his life, than by a particular work or sermon: people have intuitions about this that are unerring. Inner life also gives the apostle a highly effective supernatural radiance; one could say that the supernatural already is transfiguring him, revealing to men something of the mystery of God and divine grace: "souls perceive as if by instinct and without even clearly defining what they are experiencing, this irradiation of the supernatural."

Inner life guarantees true eloquence to the apostolic worker. It gives him the inner meaning of Christian truths and the strong conviction of an authentic faith. What a difference between the light shed by a preacher of this type and the

"ingenious or erudite applications that may be drawn therefrom by a preacher aided only by the resources of reason and a faith which is, practically speaking, remote and dead! The former shows the living truth, enveloping souls with a reality which desires not only to enlighten but also to vivify them. The latter speaks of it as of an algebraic equation — correct, to be sure, but cold and unrelated to the inner core of existence. He leaves it an abstraction and, so to speak, in the status of

[18] *L'âme de tout apostolat*, 13th ed., 1930, pp. 109-185.

a mere memorial capable at best of arousing hearts by
what is called the aesthetic character of Christianity.
'The majesty of the Scriptures astounds me; the simplicity of the Gospels speaks to my heart,' the sentimental Jean-Jacques Rousseau admitted. But what does
God in His glory care about such vague and sterile emo-
tions?"[19]

Inner life has repercussions on the ministry of worship. The priest with a deep spiritual life celebrates Holy
Mass better, conducts funeral services reverently, distributes Holy Communion with faith, baptizes in a dig-
nified manner, gives absolution to penitents while proposing some solid truth. In short, all ritual activities
derive from this interior attitude an effect that nothing
can replace — an effect which, moreover, is in no way
optional. Since some rites operate *ex opere operantis
Ecclesiae,* in order for the personal dispositions of the
faithful to insure a greater appropriation of the fruits
of Redemption through the rites, the priest must, by his
attitude, help the faithful to enter into such dispositions
and not to estrange them therefrom.

Finally, inner life has a strong influence on the action of the good shepherd. From this source he renews
his profound goodness, which is akin to the very goodness of God. There he finds patience, concern for perseverance, wisdom, and judgment. There he draws strength
and courage. And so his works are laden with divine
power; they bear something of the mysterious "energy"
which is the very definition of God; they transmit to
men a ray of the substantial Light and abiding Love.

The priest himself enjoys all the advantages secured
by the inner life. This life, Dom Chautard explains,
fortifies him against the dangers of the outer ministry,
restores his forces, unlooses his energies, multiplies his
merits, stimulates his joy, offers him legitimate solace,
defends him against discouragement, and, finally, refines
his purity of intention.[20] Filled with the strength of the

[19] *Op. cit.,* p. 152.
[20] *Op. cit.,* pp. 91-109.

Holy Spirit, the apostle is truly a sign of the presence of God in the midst of men.

VARIED AND DIVERSE INFLUENCES

The influence of the inner life on the efficacy of apostolic activity is not the same in all cases.

In the sacramental ministry, the so-called *ex opere operato* efficacy is guaranteed regardless of the inner dispositions of the priest. Though abnormal and exceptional, this fact invites us to reflect on the scope and meaning of the expression "soul of the apostolate."

In certain cases, inner life has only an indirect influence on the fruitfulness of the apostolate, from the fact that this life disposes the priest to better action or assures the apostolate itself a more perfect form. Such is the case with the priest who, when disturbing failures shake him finds in mental prayer the courage to persevere.

What are we to say about those cases where the apostle, despite his inner life, goes from failure to failure? These failures are called "trials" by all the masters of the supernatural life. Is this by way of fallacious consolation? Let us hope not! These efforts, they add, are not in vain; their supernatural efficacy has repercussions somewhere in the Church, at the pleasure of the Lord. This is unquestionably so. But is this the whole answer? Should it not be added that while apostolic success is important, it is not the final criterion of our value-judgments in this area? What has to be sought is a life which is as apostolic as possible, regardless of the results achieved *here and now*. With this understood, one may be sure that the apostolic "yield" will be that which the Lord wishes to produce by His grace in us.

Often, however, the inner life has a direct effect on zealous works, making them more perfect and, at the same time, more fruitful: this is the case in the ministry of the sacraments, the ministry of preaching, the *cura animarum.* Here the priest owes it to himself to lead an intense inner life solely in view of assuring himself an apostolate which is perfectly constituted, "technically in order," responding to any reasonable demand that can be made on it. A purely rational examination of the usual conditions for the effectiveness of the apostolate thus leads us to conclude to the strict necessity of a profound inner life.

PROPORTIONAL INFLUENCE?

Does this mean that there is a direct relationship between the value of the inner life and the efficiency of outer action? Is the one absolutely linked to the other? One would hardly reply affirmatively. To say that the inner life is a source of fecundity for works of zeal does not mean that it is their *unique* and proportional source. Also, one cannot be too careful in expressing the following equation: the apostolic spirit is to outer activities what the soul is to the body.

Would it not be a more adequate way of explaining this matter to say that Christ the Redeemer, first cause of all divine efficacy, can directly exercise His sanctifying influence on souls; nevertheless, He often uses created instruments: invisible instruments of inner sanctity, ardent charity, hidden mortification, firm hope; visible instruments of competence, ability, talents, and gifts. The priest is therefore an instrument, both visible and invisible, an instrument whose action and productiveness should be studied more closely. Still, it can be affirmed offhand, it would seem, that while these instrumentalities complement one another, nevertheless their action enjoys a relative but indisputable independence.

The study of the apostolic charisms possessed by the first disciples could be enlightening on this point. There is no proof that these charisms were supernatural in essence. Quite the opposite. A great number of them, in the opinion of exegetes, were probably natural qualities and human talents made particularly active and effective for the benefit of the apostolate. Would this not be a case of a visible and external instrumentality, also a divine and supernatural one, helping the growth of the kingdom of God?

The facts themselves seem to corroborate and confirm this point of view. It is clear that certain activities, while not possessing the theological density of a sermon by the Curé d'Ars, or the mortification potential enjoyed by a Trappist monastery, nevertheless have a real, serious, and stable influence. And the reason a priest is replaced is not always his lack of inner life; is this not a practical way on the part of the hierarchy of affirming that the human and visible instrumentality of outer works is not an empty word? In short, when one sees all the advantages the apostolate gains from the inner life, and when one realizes the undeniable contribution made thereto by natural talents and outer activity, one can only hope that diocesan priests will neglect nothing but make use of everything for the greater glory of the Lord, and for the untarnished beauty of their mother, the Church.

PART FOUR

SPIRITUALITY OF THE DIOCESAN PRIEST

CHAPTER ELEVEN

THE IDEAL OF THE APOSTOLIC LIFE

In this last part, we should like to outline some fundamental traits of what could be called the spirituality of the diocesan priest. We will recall first of all that the apostolic life of the diocesan priest must be identified with what is called "mixed" life, and not set on the plane of the active life as defined by the spiritual authors. This is the *generic* element of our spirituality and it will be the subject of the first chapter. In the second chapter we shall attempt to show within this generic type what more particularly characterizes all diocesan clergy. This will constitute the specific difference of our spirituality. Then we shall indicate the role which seems particularly incumbent upon us *today*. We shall thereupon proceed to point out, in consequence, what perfection is for us and what it is not.

A SPIRITUALITY

But is it proper to speak of a "spirituality of the diocesan clergy"? Benedictine, Dominican, Ignatian, Salesian spirituality; lay, married, single spirituality. . . . Will we not end up forgetting the wholesome Christian spirituality to be found in the Bible? One cannot deny the dangers of the centrifugal movement which at present is heading in this direction; but the diocesan clergy cannot be charged with gains too far in this regard; if anything, they have not gone far enough.

Besides, let us keep carefully in mind what we mean when we speak of the "spirituality of the diocesan clergy." "Far from planning to build up a priori an artificial theory," Msgr. E. Guerry writes, "we are asking, on the contrary, that people become aware of an existing reality, that they grasp the positive originality of the status of the diocesan clergy, in order to found, on the very nature of its particular vocation in the Church, a means of promoting its holiness and helping it to carry out more successfully, in the great life of the Church, the mission particularly reserved to it."

The generic element of our diocesan spirituality is the "apostolic life": the priest is "a contemplative in action." This is the ideal. Now let us see what the reality is.

1. THE REALITY

When one looks at diocesan priests and asks oneself whether the life they lead is truly apostolic, the answer must be "yes." Still, upon reflection, one does not dare be quite as absolute, and one begins to dilute the force of this "yes": it becomes less spontaneous, a bit hesitant. What has happened? The fact is that the initial response flowed from an overall judgment on the whole clergy and the value of its work: and there is nothing to compare with the sum of devotion, competence, disinterestedness, and grandeur involved in this work. But a more intensive consideration of the facts reveals certain gaps, here as everywhere else. What gaps? The priests certainly do not lack a "mission." Perhaps their usual occupations are not formally apostolic? It would seem not. Is the spirit of the apostolate, the "inner" element, in question? This could well be. While the priest is, with rare exceptions, unquestionably an apostle from the fact that he is "sent" authentically by his bishop and consecrates his life to tasks deriving from the mission entrusted to the ecclesiastical hierarchy, perhaps he does not always possess sufficiently that spirit which must permeate the apostolic life — his life does not unite contemplation and action.

To be sure, no one is going to meet a priest who will claim that the apostolate consists in performing purely outer actions. All recognize that the "interior life" is necessary for the pastoral ministry. But one must question them in greater detail and ask them what they mean by "inner life," what form the theological inner element of priestly action takes in them: Is it a love of the creature as such, or do they love the creature in God? Or do they love God and creation together? In the following pages, we shall have to underscore certain divergencies. They will seem all the more real because we must necessarily classify priests according to well-defined mentalities, whereas in actuality their behavior admits of many more nuances. The following sketches are therefore schematic, and do not totally represent the concrete physiognomy of priestly souls.

MORAL LOVE OF ONE'S NEIGHBOR

In certain priests, action stems from a *moral love* of the faithful. What does this mean? By moral love — as opposed to theological love — we understand here the moral virtue which stirs the priest to render to the faithful what is due them in view of the human and real goodness they represent. This love therefore is found at the heart of the virtue of justice. The man who is stirred by it considers humanity — the misery of the sinner and the sad consequences of human failings, the painful situation of families and marriages, the sins of the poor and the sins of the rich, the evils of society and the scandals of public life — and, seized by a feeling of benevolence, attempts to restore in the city and souls sound values and Christian virtues. His zeal is therefore set in motion by the human creature as such, with all its

faculties: the intellect which he hopes to conform to the
spirit of the Gospel, the will whose movements he wishes
to guarantee, the heart whose outpourings he hopes to
direct, the body whose reflexes he desires to regulate.
A wholesome and excellent love of God's creatures forces
him to action; their real goodness has become for him
the object of a legitimate attraction and interest.

This love is good. Whether one considers the object,
the end or, presumably, the circumstances, there is nothing deserving of blame. It is wholesome love because
nothing in it is disordered. It is a supernatural love
like all activities deriving from the moral virtues; just
as acts of temperance, justice and strength are authentically supernatural, the same is true of moral love of
men. It is Christian love, too, which Christ surely knew,
just as He practiced all moral virtues, His human nature
being perfectly subject to the influence of divinity. It
is fully meritorious love, like the act of every moral
virtue. It is sanctifying love thanks to which it is possible to arrive at a high degree of virtue, even to perfection (at least if this love is not considered an end in
itself), for perfection presupposes the practice of the
theological virtues. It was necessary to recall the grandeur of this Christian love of the creature *as such*, before saying that it is different from theological charity.

Of course, no priest acts exclusively out of moral
love. From the very fact that he makes an act of charity
from time to time, every priest is able to live in the
impulse of this act and, by virtue of it, elevate the rest
of his activities to the plane of the theological life itself.
This is true at least — it is well to emphasize this —
if all of this activity is truly carried out "by virtue of
the act of charity," and not merely "after an act of
charity." It is not enough, therefore, to make an act
of charity in the morning; it is also necessary that in the
course of the day no act, by its malice, shall have broken
the thread which ties our actions to the morning offering. It is nonetheless true and there is a clear difference
psychologically between him who loves creatures with

a *moral* love and him who loves them with a *theological* love.

THEOLOGICAL LOVE

Other priests live and desire to live more and more in *theological charity*. This virtue has as its characteristic feature, as its name indicates, that it makes one see things according to God and therefore like Him and in Him. The *formal* object of all theological virtues, that which in the object loved attracts us, is divinity itself. In this sense, God Himself, the Holy Trinity, will be loved above all and first of all with a theological love, and then everything which is distinct from God. This is why the great scholastics affirm that one may love with a true theological charity the angels, men, the body, and even matter.

While the formal object of theological charity is always the same, its *material* object may be divided into a *primary* material object, God Himself, and a *secondary* material object, the creature, and, particularly as far as we are concerned, man, the neighbor. The distinctions in the material object help to characterize two categories of priests who are, as a matter of fact, ruled by different psychologies: those whose "interior life" is summed up in loving their neighbor "in God" and those whose inner life consists in loving God in Himself *and* their neighbor "in God."

1. There are many priests who *love their neighbor with a theological charity*. From childhood, they have been accustomed to seeing "God in the poor," and to seeing "Jesus in the afflicted." Later, regular meditation breathed into them something of the spirit of faith which animates the great masters of the Christian spiritual life. The course in ascetical theology opened their eyes to the nature of true charity, and they set themselves generously to it. They were trained to see in their superiors official representatives of God, and

in their inferiors the "brethren" of Christ Jesus. The doctrine of the Mystical Body to which they were led, helps them to see all men in Christ, while assiduous contact with the New Testament, St. Paul in particular, has taught them to love men "in Christo," to devote themselves to them "in Christo," to reprimand them "in Christo," and to work for them "in Christo": the Christocentrism and dogma of Pauline moral theology has undoubtedly profoundly marked them. Also, thanks to these many influences, they have grown in divine wisdom, and their eyes, transformed by faith, look at men "in God."

This theological love, as we have seen, is eminently theocentric: and it should be greatly stirred up in the soul of the priest, lest it gradually become a *moral* love. Preachers and spiritual directors try to forestall this danger by insisting on the absolute necessity of meditation. The theological love of creatures is beautiful with a divine beauty because it is related to that which animates God Himself. It is supernatural in essence, because it is the love of God in which we share by the marvelous activity of the Holy Spirit: "the charity of God spread forth in our hearts by the Holy Spirit which is given to us." It is eminently Christian because Christ, the Incarnate Word, had to have it to perfection in His own humanity. It can lead directly to perfection because it is theological and divine.

2. Other priests, finally, have in their hearts the love of God *and* their neighbor. They maintain in themselves, in as actual a way as possible, the love of the "whole Christ," eager to unite themselves with the love of the Father which fired the Lord, and to prolong this love, with Christ, in the direction of the redemption of the world. They direct their predilection toward God, not to stop there in the manner of those who contemplate, but in order to live in harmony with all the movements of divine love: creation, redemption, and the glorification of the world.

This is unquestionably a rather idealistic way of

looking at things; the number of diocesan priests who accept it and live by it is not very large — and for a good reason. When young people have some facility for loving God, in Himself and for Himself, they often want to join strictly contemplative orders. On the other hand, it happens that the vocation of the diocesan priest is presented as an active vocation — "active" signifying almost exclusively exterior activity as such, even though it would seem that this does not respect the desires of our Lord and the Apostles, our true and authentic models. Moreover, those who are partisans, in principle, of the "mixed" life, do not always succeed in achieving their desires as they would like to, because the general conditions of their lives are not always adequately adapted thereto; this brings up the problem of the conditions of life of priests who teach or who do parish work in large cities. And finally, human weakness also prevents men from either accepting an ideal or from putting it into practice; this is a human problem which exists beyond the diocesan clergy too.

2. THE IDEAL

Of the three "types" of priestly inner life which we have just described: moral love, theological love of men, theological love of God and one's neighbor, the third is without doubt the only one which unreservedly deserves to be called "apostolic."

This is what the masters of the spiritual life tell us. This is what we learn from the lives of diocesan priests and secular bishops who have been canonized. This is what we see in the Apostles, who loved their Lord just as immediately, just as directly, as naturally, as their neighbor. And the God-Man, in His humanity, was united to His Father while He went about the villages of Judea doing good. "It must be said," says St. Thomas, "that not only does the active life pertain to prelates, but that they must also excel in the contemplative life. Whence Gregory says in his Pastoral, II, 1: 'Let the

Rector be outstanding in action, and above all others in contemplation.' " [1]

This passage of the Angelic Doctor brings us back to the classic distinction to which spiritual writers generally refer when they wish to determine the style or type of life adopted by a priest or a religious. Actually, we would have preferred to write these pages without making much use of such dichotomies as "action-contemplation," "active life-contemplative life," classifying, instead, diocesan priests according to the predominance in their lives of the moral love of men, the theological love of neighbor, or total theological love. This latter criterion is, for us, simpler, more intelligible and more practical; with it, we are capable of easily determining what attracts us in someone else and what animates us during action. Moreover, this criterion even seems preferable in an absolute way: by it we can better characterize the profound forces which give direction to a person's life than by determining the "operation which becomes its principal business,"[2] "the operation which, more than any other, is proper thereto, and toward which the chief inclination tends."[3] Thus, in speaking hereafter of "active life" and "contemplative life," we are thinking more of the spirit which these lives imply than of the operations which are proper to them.

THE "MIXED" LIFE

If one restricts oneself to the well-known doctrine of the "ways," one will then distinguish between active life, contemplative life and "mixed," or apostolic life, concluding, as far as the diocesan clergy is concerned, with these words of Cardinal Mercier:

"Of all the states of life, the most perfect is that of the apostolic man. Union with God through contempla-

---

[1] *Summ. theol.*, IIa IIae, q. 182, a.1, ad 1m. Though relating to bishops, this remark, with the proper distinctions, applies also to diocesan priests.

[2] *Ibid.*, IIa IIae, q. 180, a. 3, c.

[3] *Ibid.*, q. 179, a. 1, c.

tion is superior to a life absorbed in material cares;
but there is a life, says St. Thomas, still higher than
pure contemplation, and that is the mixed life of the
apostolate, in which the apostle gives to his neighbor
the superabundance of his contemplation. The life thus
understood is the most perfect of all, and it is this form
which Christ chose: 'The contemplative life is, simply
speaking, more perfect than the active life which is
occupied with corporal acts; but the active life according to which someone . . . gives to others the fruits of
contemplation, is more perfect than the life of pure
contemplation: for such a life presupposes an abundance
of contemplation: and therefore Christ chose such a
life.' Our whole effort must tend to dispose us for an
'apostolic' life thus understood."[4]

This doctrine is pure Thomism. It is found clearly
set forth in the *Summa theologica*, IIa IIae, q. 182, a.2,
c., along with the principle which explains it, charity:

"The root of merit is charity. But since charity consists in the love of God and of neighbor, to love God for
His own sake is more meritorious than to love one's
neighbor. And therefore, that which more directly pertains
to the love of God, is more meritorious by its own nature
than that which directly pertains to the love of neighbor
for the sake of God.

"The contemplative life directly and immediately pertains to the love of God: for Augustine says that the
charity of truth, that is, of divine truth, seeks holy
leisure; to this the contemplative most strongly tends,
as has been said.

"But the active life is more directly ordered to the
love of neighbor: because 'it is concerned with frequent
ministry.' And therefore, by its nature, the contemplative life is of greater merit than the active life. And
this is what Gregory says: 'The contemplative is of
greater merit than the active [life], because the latter
labors in the pursuit of the present work in which, that
is, it is necessary to come to the aid of one's neighbors;
the former however, already tastes the rest to come

[4] *Fraternité sacerdotale diocésaine*, Bruges, Desclée, De
Brouwer, 1927, pp. 106-107; the quoted text is found in *Summ.
theol.*, IIIa, q. 40, a.1, ad 2m.

with an inner savor,' namely, in the contemplation of God.

"It may nevertheless happen that someone may be more meritorious in the works of the active life than another in works of the contemplative life: for example, if on account of an abundance of divine love, so that his will may be fulfilled for His own glory, he accepts for a time to be separated . . . from the sweetness of divine contemplation. As the Apostle says: 'I desired, even I, to be anathema from Christ for the sake of my brethren,' of which Chrysostom, in his exposition, says: 'He had so saturated his whole mind with the love of Christ that what to him was desirable above all else, to be with Christ, he could condemn, because it might please Christ.' "[5]

It will be noted that the "active life" here is the one we said was animated by the theological love of neighbor, while the "mixed life" — as it is called — is the one we wanted to see animated by a total theological love whose object is primarily God and, in Him, one's neighbor. Schematically, this is the way the two classifications correspond:

1. Life animated by moral love of creatures — the active life.

2. Life animated by theological love of men — the contemplative life.

3. Life animated by total theological love — the mixed or apostolic life.

SUPERIORITY OF THE "MIXED" LIFE

At the same time, a hierarchy is set up among the different types of life. The active life is inferior to the contemplative one, but the "mixed" life is superior to it. Why is this?

St. Thomas proposes a series of reasons which show the inferiority of the active life with respect to the contemplative life. The active life, he explains, is quite taken up with external things, whereas the contemplative

─────────

[5] See also IIa IIIae, q. 188, a. 6, c.

life pertains to that which is most noble in man, the
intellect. The active life cannot last as long as the contemplative life, at least if the latter is not taken in its
extreme degree; and Mary, the figure of the contemplative life, is shown seated without moving at the feet
of the Lord. The active life involves less joy than the
contemplative one; whence this saying of St. Augustine:
"Martha worried, Mary feasted." The active life is often
ordered to something else, whereas the contemplative
one is more usually loved for its own sake. The active
life is labor and preoccupation, whereas the contemplative one is rest and tranquility. The active life remains
in the sphere of the human, the contemplative life in
that of the divine.[5a]

Still, there is a certain type of "active" life superior
to the "contemplative one," and this is the "active" life
lived in a superabundance of divine love and in view
of doing the will of God for His glory,[6] or again, the
"active" life which involves a fulness of contemplation
which is transmitted to one's neighbor.[7] It has been
called "mixed" in order better to distinguish it; it is
called "apostolic" because it was lived in a superior manner by the Apostles, and because Christ Himself chose
it for Himself.[8]

And how is this superior combination of action and
contemplation to be conceived? St. Thomas' formula,
understood in a very current way, provides an answer
to this *"contemplare et contemplata aliis tradere* — to
contemplate and give to others the things contemplated."
An excellent formula provided that it is understood
rightly. If one interprets it to mean an *alternation* of
contemplation and action — meditation in the morning
and attention to the faithful in the afternoon— one is
not taking into account all the requirements of St.
Thomas' formula; the latter speaks not of alternation,
but of communicating the "superabundance" of con-

[5a] *Summ. theol.*, IIa IIae, q. 182, a. 1, c.
[6] *Ibid.*, IIa IIae, q. 182, a.2, c.
[7] *Ibid.*, IIIa, q. 40, a.1, ad 2m.
[8] *Ibid.*, IIIa, q. 40, a.1, ad 2m.

templation. Thus, the contemplative life is always assumed to be present, the inner life is always brimming over, and it is from this overflow that one communicates. It is therefore necessary to understand that the formula is one, not of alternation, but of *synchronized union*, action and contemplation being permanently united, active, and mutually vivifying.

In other words, the "mixed" life must contain *all* the spirit of the contemplative life and *all* the spirit of the active life. The first is directly oriented toward God, whom it makes the immediate and direct object of its interest, of its faith, its love, its hope; the mixed life must possess all that also, but not only that. The second, the active life, is oriented directly toward the Christian, and makes him the immediate and direct object of its activity, its zeal, and its solicitude: the mixed life must have this spirit, but not exclusively. Thus, it is easy to understand that the third style of life is superior to the other two because it contains what constitutes them both: "when someone is called from the contemplative to the active life, this is done not as a subtraction, but as an addition."[9]

The mixed life is also superior to the contemplative one, for a number of reasons. The mixed life, first of all, is fully human, in the sense that it puts into operation all the faculties of man and not only those which are specific to him. The mixed life unites action and loving contemplation; an image of its operation might be a mother who, while looking affectionately upon her child, knits him something to wear. The mixed life unites to the interior joy of love the happiness of collaborating with Christ under the dominion of the Holy Spirit. The mixed life is loved for its own sake, because it reproduces completely the public life of the Word Incarnate. The mixed life moves both in divine and human arenas: the arms work on earth and the heart is fixed in heaven.

These are "objective" qualifications, of course, which

---

[9] *Summ. theol.*, IIa IIae, q. 182, a.1, ad 3m.

do not always work out in practice. It is, in fact, possible to live a more holy life in a less perfect way of life. Saints have lived "active lives" and there are mediocre persons in orders devoted to the mixed life. Heroism is possible in all states of life.

IMPERFECT CONCEPTIONS

We should like to distinguish from this concept of the "mixed life" three others to which we have already referred.

Let us take, first of all, the mixed life conceived exclusively as "the incarnation of the divine in earthly realities." By way of opposition to a spirituality reducing all Christian life to the "contemplative one" and the "love of God alone," men have reacted in the contrary sense by demanding that all charity be "incarnate." In other words, the sacerdotal life of the diocesan priest is seen as an "active," theological life, the priest finding God not in Himself, but in people, in works, in the functions of the temporal ministry. This is what we called the theological "active" life, loving one's neighbor in God.

It is good to have the priest's holiness thus tied to his ministry, not to occasional contemplation of doubtful value, but this reaction may be exaggerated. The priest should be asked to juxtapose the love of God and that of neighbor. He should be asked to have an "incarnate" charity, and, in addition, at the same time, a charity directed purely toward God. For while the neighbor is worthy of interest, the God of the living and the dead, who is the supreme Reality whence all others flow, is infinitely more interesting. And this interest is manifested in the contemplative life strictly so-called. This, it would seem, is the true psychology of the mixed life: the great masters of the diocesan apostolate have had their hearts directed just as directly toward God in Himself as toward their neighbor or to works considered in God.

To live a mixed life, it is not enough, either, to work and to struggle *for God*. Even though such work may be

impressive in its disinterestedness, its motive does not
raise our apostolate to the level of the theological life.
To act *for* God means that God is the raison d'être of
our activity, the basic motive-force which sets in motion
our actions, the ultimate term toward which all our
efforts tend: "everything which acts, acts for an end,"
and God is actually the end of all life. But one can work
for someone and completely forget him for days on end;
young people, when, for instance, they are carrying out
some good work, are also acting "for God," that is, in
His honor, for His glory, and for the splendor of His
Church. And yet, they do not lead a "mixed" life. The
latter implies that one is interested directly and presently
in God, like the person established in the contemplative
life. God is not only the first and last motive of actions,
but the permanent "object" of love. The great spiritual heroes did more than just work for God or for His
honor; they worked while loving Him, they loved Him
while working in the world. Witness this characteristic
passage from the life of Marie of the Incarnation: "If
I had to speak to my neighbor, my look did not leave
Him Whom I loved; after the other person answered me,
my colloquy recommenced, and the attention I gave to
what was necessary did not take away from that which
I gave to God. The same was true of my writing, where
*my attention was twofold: to my divine Object and to
the thing in question.*"[10] To be sure, it is a question in
this case of rather rare gifts; but they clearly indicate,
from this very fact, the direction in which all the graces
of the Holy Spirit tend. In the mixed life, God is therefore not the final cause of existence, but the present
object of theological love.

Finally, there is no "mixed" life either when love
of God and love of men alternate according to the
rhythm of apostolic activities themselves. When we celebrate Holy Mass, recite the Breviary and meditate, the
spirit naturally rises toward God; when we turn to

[10] D. A. Jamet, *Le témoignage de Marie de l'Incarnation*, Paris,
Beauchesne, 1932, p. 59.

men in the innumerable moral and spiritual needs of their lives, the spirit, quite naturally again, leans toward them. Accordingly, some would say that the soul is theocentric only when the professional activities are. And since most of our apostolic occupations are directed toward men, the spirit, in this hypothesis, would usually be occupied with them. This is not a mixed life. The latter is a union of theological life and ministry, and not merely an alternation.

THEOCENTRISM AND ANTHROPOCENTRISM

On this subject, it is perhaps useful to dissociate more clearly the multitude of theocentric and anthropocentric movements whose center is in the person of the priest, and which sometimes prevent him from understanding himself. Has he been ordained for the glory of God, for the salvation of his neighbor, or for his own sanctification? Must he be equally attentive to all three of these ends? Which has an authentic priority and why?

It would seem that one needs to distinguish three levels in order to unscramble the skein of these relationships. First of all, the totality of the priestly life — the person of the priest, his activities, his works, everything — has as its goal the glorification of God. This is the very finality of every *creature* as such. Nothing can escape this ultimate goal. In this sense, even the most anthropocentric activities give glory to God — if not formally, at least ontologically, as with the birds, the plants, the mountains, and the seas. Everything gives glory to God in the very measure in which it involves a perfection of being, life, intellectuality, or freedom. This is the first level at which we must place ourselves in order to judge.

On the second level there is the *personal* achievement of the priest, if one may speak thus. Through any activity whatsoever, the priest necessarily makes himself grow or diminish. Every act either advances him in the direction of his goal or makes him fall back, for the simple reason that to act is to change and to become better or worse. While it is psychologically possible to "forget oneself" in the apostolate and to "lose" oneself in God, it is impossible not to register within oneself the real contribution which every action makes to oneself. The virtue of disinterestedness necessarily makes us grow, and therefore benefits us. The priest, of necessity, is always working at his own salvation, in all of his activities; at all; he could not do otherwise, even if he always forgot himself.

Finally, on the third level, we place the special work which is reserved for priests: the apostolate. In its spirit, the apostolate is theological, and therefore basically theocentric; as to the priestly functions themselves, the majority are directed toward the good of men, whereas a lesser portion, quantitatively speaking, refer directly to God.

In distinguishing these three levels, which we should find within ourselves, it is easier to understand why spiritual authors can write that a man is a priest either for the divine glory, for his own personal salvation, or for the sanctification of souls. We need to know which of these viewpoints they are writing from, in order to grasp their thought adequately.

3. "CONTEMPLATIVE IN ACTION"

Various formulas are used to express the doctrine of the mixed life. The words which, according to Jerome Nadal, best characterized St. Ignatius — *"inactione contemplativus* — contemplative in action" — have, at least for us, some advantage perhaps over the "to contemplate and give to others the things contemplated," of St. Thomas. The first, more general formula designates less directly than the Thomistic one, a concrete and particular ideal of the doctrinal apostolate.

TWO FORMULAS

When one defines the apostolate as the "communication of the overflow of contemplation," one is always referring, explicitly or implicitly, to what St. Thomas wrote about the forms and states of human life, and in particular, to the conclusion of Article 6 of Question 188: "Among the religious orders, those hold the highest rank which are given over to teaching and preaching; they are the closest of all to the perfection of bishops. The second rank belongs to the orders dedicated to contemplation. In the third rank are the orders which devote themselves to occupations of the exterior life."[11]

St. Thomas is therefore thinking of the religious orders. He places them in a hierarchy primarily with respect to their end, secondarily according to the proper adaptation of the exercises imposed for the purpose of attaining the end.[12] Finally, he defines the "mixed life": "Contemplation ordered to action, the latter itself being wholly consecrated to the common good and expressed in certain acts which flow from it, such as the teaching of divine things, and preaching." Briefly, in the concrete manner of speaking preferred by St. Thomas, it is the ideal of the Friars Preachers which is designated. Father Lemonnyer readily acknowledges it: "St. Thomas," he writes, "is treating this question of study here in all its breadth, and in terms of the religious state in itself. It is nonetheless evident that he is thinking particularly of study as it was practiced by his own order. For the first time, it had appeared among the Preachers as both organized and collective, raised to the rank of a duty of state and placed alongside the Divine Office at the very summit of the order of means."[13] In this sense, the formula "to contemplate and give to others the things contemplated" represents, from the very outset, a definite form of the apostolic life.

When the diocesan priest gives these words a very broad, very general significance, that of a life united to God, through and in fruitful action, the Thomistic formula is an excellent one. In that event, it has been reduced, actually, to the other one: "contemplative in

[11] *Summa theologica*, "Human life," ed. des Jeunes.
[12] *Op. cit.*, p. 526.
[13] *Op. cit.*, p. 561.

action." On the other hand, for those who understand the "things contemplated" in the doctrinal implications of the phrase, as does St. Thomas himself in thinking of his Order, there could be a difficulty, that of reducing the spirit of the apostolate to the spirit of preaching, of instruction. But the "action" of the diocesan priest is as much the ministry of worship and the direction of the faithful as it is the doctrinal office. He must be united to God, *contemplativus*, in all this action.

The phrase "contemplative in action" also has this advantage, it would seem, namely that it clearly marks off the union of action and contemplation in the apostolic life. Unquestionably, "to contemplate and give to others the things contemplated," must be interpreted in the same way, and often is; nevertheless, from experience, certain people also understand it in the sense of an alternation: first, to contemplate, then to spread forth the superabundance of contemplation, and then, again, to contemplate. The "contemplative in action" makes such an interpretation very difficult.

The formula quoted by J. Nadal, finally, has the advantage of being clearly stamped: there can be doubt as to the meaning of the words: *in actione contemplativus*, whereas one may ask oneself just what is the relationship between *contemplare* and *tradere* in the Thomistic formula. Writing of the mixed life, Father Lemonnyer says:

"It is a difficult concept to define chiefly for the reason that it is in the moral and not the metaphysical order. The brief formula used to describe the 'third type of life' recognized by St. Augustine, that is, a type composed of contemplation and action, is manifestly inadequate. The relationship of contemplation and action therein has to be specified. If this relationship is one of simple juxtaposition, this 'third type of life' represents at most a classification of living beings. It does not really concern the division of human life. One must think of a positive linking of contemplation and action or vice versa, contemplation being at the service of action, or action at the service of contemplation. But, in its very generality, this formula does not really give us a new type of life. If contemplation is ordered to action, then we have nothing but an active life. If action is ordered to contemplation, all we have is a contemplative life. This connection must be studied more closely."[14]

This dualism must be resolved by theological charity: neither subordination, Father Lemonnyer concludes, nor juxtaposition, but union in twofold charity. Contemplation and action are two ends which become one, just as there is only one charity.

Besides, formulas matter little, provided that the reality itself of the mixed life, of redemptive theological charity, is lived: this is the apostolic spirit.

ATTAINMENT OF THIS IDEAL

Such an ideal, as we are well aware, is difficult to attain here below. Nor is it a full and immediate putting into operation that authors envision when they try to determine what the active or contemplative life may be. The ideal of the theological life in its total form is not attainable on a permanent basis: that would soon be paralysis unless one were graced with a charism. When a type of life is established it is intended to indicate *the definite state to which one must tend,* the goal toward which one wishes to come, the type of life one wants someday to attain, even if only in the final hours of one's existence, in order to have lived at all times in the perspectives of a full apostolate.

On this point, it seems important that priests, *from the very outset of their priestly lives,* conceive the "apostolic" life in this integral manner. They will thus be better able to orient their personal search for perfection toward a state more and more like that fixed for us by our authentic models, the holy diocesan priests and the holy bishops. If their initial apostolic ideal were limited or incomplete, what would be the goal of their existence?

[14] *Op. cit.,* p. 562.

If, for example, one believes that apostolic perfection consists in acting "for" God, how shall one concern oneself with seeing Him here and now in one's neighbor? If one believes that the priestly ideal is summed up in seeing God in the works of the ministry, how is one to make the effort to love Him also in Himself and for Himself? To the extent that priests are truly influenced by a doctrine and by the formulas which sum it up, to that same extent it is of the highest importance that the thought which is presented to them be complete and free of all error.

If a young priest, in particular, has very clearly before his eyes the apostolic ideal that has just been set forth, all his zeal will be devoted to attaining that ideal. While in the seminary, he will know what he ought to be at the age of sixty: loving God in Himself and his neighbor in God, in as actual a way as possible. He will always direct his thoughts in this sense, he will guide his mental prayer toward the acquisition of this spirit, he will organize his apostolic work according to the demands of this ideal; and so the general climate of his entire life will be dominated by the goal always dimly perceived, and his whole existence will develop under the sway of the great hope of his life: to have the real apostolic spirit, if only for a few years.

While waiting, he will select a prudent and wise regimen of life, dominated by the thought and image of the goal to be attained, but also regulated by the *present possibilities* of attainment offered him by his health, his obligations, his age, divine grace. In any event, he can be sure that if he is faithful, God who has given him to understand and to desire this life will also give him the grace to live it gradually and to establish himself in it progressively. This is a matter of time, effort and divine help: "so long as you are faithful."

Fidelity is necessary and, also, to a certain extent, *method* and *asceticism*. In order to arrive at the practice of the requirements of a "mixed" life, directed as much to God as toward men, one generally requires a substantial number of exercises of love of God in Himself, creatures quite apart. Only truly contemplative temperaments could dispense with this asceticism; but are these very numerous? To be sure that one loves God not only in His creatures but also in His reality apart from creation, it is well to spend some time with God alone. Not that one must stop eating; but the psychological effort will be, at such times, uniquely theocentric. Novices in congregations have an advantage in this matter in that they have a time set aside for this preparation, or at least a time that could be reserved for it. Seminaries start immediately with philosophical courses: spiritual and intellectual formation is carried on at the same time. It appears that in some seminaries now, a month is devoted each year to a more concentrated spiritual formation. This is perhaps the best concrete method of making possible an introduction to the "mixed" life. Unless interest in God for Himself is not underscored positively from time to time, there can be no hope of insuring it throughout the entire pastoral life. This method is, apparently, a sine qua non for those who are preparing to live, at least to some extent, according to the Gospel: "He who loses his life, will find it."

CONTEMPLATION AND ACTION

And so, diocesan priests will carry into action a highly contemplative ideal: "contemplatives in action." But let us hope that there is a desire to avoid the equivocation often included in the idea of contemplation; the latter animates *action*, rather than diminishing its intensity.

"To many pious people, the contemplative life seems to be one of simplification because, so they think, it involves a lessening of action, a 'geared down' action. This is an inadequate view. When one closely observes the behavior of the most authentic contemplatives, it is far from the case that one always finds it similar to that

of children. . . . Quite often, on the contrary, they are
vibrant, active and impressionable beings, extremely
quick in their reactions, whose very gestures reveal great
agility which when necessary carries out any action.
There is perhaps a contemplative temperament which
assumes a certain share, a certain form, of physical
calm. . . . But on the other hand and in point of fact,
there are contemplatives whom the providence of God
recruits everywhere, we might even say by preference
among personalities with strong feelings, and who are
characterized on the whole less by the apathy with which
they are commonly charged than by a certain ability
to be captured by a feeling of presence, of coming to
a halt before God."[15]
The contemplation of the apostle, therefore, does not
have the effect of rendering him inert or immobile even
exteriorly; if it is real, it must make him like God who
is "power," radiance, and love.

And if it were occasionally necessary to sacrifice one
of the objects of our charity, this would not necessarily
be our neighbor. All the saints envision the possibility
that they might need to remove themselves from contemplation and turn to the most lowly of human needs,
for the love of Christ. "One day," says St. Jeanne de
Chantal, "I asked our holy Father St. Francis de Sales
if, amidst all the matters which beset him, he had been
able to meditate. 'No,' he answered, 'but I am doing
something that is just as valuable. God indeed so loves
mankind, and wants us to love it with such solicitude
in His stead and in His name, that we are doing something agreeable to Him when we leave Him when necessary to come to the aid of our brethren.' " And therein
is found the profound reason for the superiority of the
apostolic life over the religious one, even when the latter
is contemplative. "O my Jesus," cries St. Teresa, "how
great is the love You bear the children of men! The
greatest service one can render You is to leave You
for the love of them and for their greater benefit."[16]

[15] F. Florand, "L'agitation," in *Recontres*, vol. I, *Contemplation*,
pp. 61-62.
[16] *Oeuvres*, ed. des Carmélites de Paris, vol. 5, p. 324.

THE PERFECT MODEL

In concluding this chapter, we shall turn to the God-Man. We have kept Him before our eyes in the preceding pages because He is without question the perfect model of all apostolic life. Of course, in order to make the ideas acceptable, it was necessary first of all to show that they are accepted in theory and lived in fact by certain men just like all others living in this world. But now, as we come to the end, we can set forth the pattern for the whole development: the spirit which must have animated the God-Man.

In His humanity substantially assumed by the Word, Christ at all times lived a higher life cognitively and affectively, a life made fruitful and "substantially" animated by the second Person of the Most Holy Trinity. The God-Man was eminently theocentric by nature, by His very being. He possessed in His human soul the fullness of charity, and all the modalities which can affect it: redemptive love, in particular, had the primacy. No one will ever exhaust the bottomless mystery of the holy humanity of the Savior. We shall never fully comprehend that He is our "model," in the full sense of the word. In the apostolic life, He is truly, and will always be, the "first-fruits" of all those who carry on His work.

CHAPTER TWELVE

THE APOSTOLIC LIFE OF THE DIOCESAN PRIEST

The ideal of the "mixed" life is that of the clergy; but it is not exclusive to them. We must at the outset specify what distinguishes the diocesan clergy, what is particular to them. The following pages would qualify in a special way for the designation of a "spirituality of the diocesan clergy."

SCHOOLS OF SPIRITUALITY

Unless it is possible to determine just what a spirituality is, how can one set forth the broad outlines of a spirituality of the diocesan clergy?

In a collection of articles published under the title *Les écoles de spiritualité*,[1] Morçay described the genesis of a spirituality as follows:

"All the saints must observe the commandments of God, and follow the evangelical counsels; all must imitate Christ and conform to the substantial holiness of the Father; all must pass through the various exercises of Christian asceticism. However, all do not do so in the

[1] Liége, *La pensée catholique*, 1928.

same way. The temperament of one, the environment in which another lived, their past lives, or a particular inclination, caused certain saints to insist especially on certain dogmatic truths, certain moral drives, certain ascetic practices. St. Benedict, who divides his time between work and prayer, does not resemble the charming juggler of God, Francis of Assisi, and likewise, the soldier Ignatius of Loyola, while no less a saint than the mystic Teresa, is nevertheless different from her."[2]

Still, some saints marked their times in a unique, indelible way, to the extent that numerous souls followed in their footsteps and accepted the forms of sanctity they inaugurated, finding therein the spiritual styles best suited to their own innermost desires and temperaments.

"When a saint has passed by in this world and has impressed upon the consciousness of men his way of facing up to the problem of perfection, then it is not rare for an immense number of souls whose psychology is similar to his, to move in his wake, to be inspired by his example and writings, and to constitute for him throughout the centuries, whether in the cloister or in the world, a spiritual posterity. . . . What, then, is a school of spirituality? It is the whole of the doctrines, the thoughts, the practices, the attitudes, which the holy Founder left as a heritage to the men and women who follow his luminous path and form his spiritual posterity."[3]

In short, to understand a school of spirituality, one must rediscover its historical origin, determine the dogmas which it emphasizes, select the virtues which it preaches by preference, and underline the ascetical procedures dear to it.

ELEMENTS OF A SPIRITUALITY

First of all, the *historical origin*. In a particular age, a situation demanded the creation of an order or of a congregation, and its style of spiritual life. "The Francis-

[2] *Op. cit.*, pp. 26-27.
[3] *Op. cit.*, pp. 27-28.

can Order," writes Father Pourrat, "perhaps unknown to its founder, actually responded to a need. This, in part, is what explains its extraordinary success; it is also this which will enable us to understand the characteristics of its spirituality. For the religious orders are almost always destined to tend to the needs of the age which sees them rise. Their rules and the spirit which inspires them are conditioned thereby."[4] The Church of the end of the twelfth century, he goes on, had indeed acquired immense wealth and very definite secular power. The bishops were feudal lords and temporal princes. Many monks, become too wealthy, were lax. Dante placed them in great numbers on the fourth level of the "mournful enclosure which holds the evil of the entire universe." Is it any wonder then that Francis of Assisi passionately loved Lady Poverty?

And in the sixteenth century, when humanism caused the flowers of naturalism to take root in souls, with the remembrance of ancient pagan beauty; when Protestantism, for its part, attacked Rome, the hierarchy, the visible Church, and the values of order she stood for; when the mendicant orders, which should have been poor and contemplative, were losing some of their prestige after becoming lax in spirit; there then appeared the clerks regular, and particularly the Society of Jesus, with its cultural force, its powerful organization, its special obedience to the papacy and its persevering apostolic action.

Every spirituality also has its favorite dogmas, its favorite teaching, a *dogmatic preference*. The school of St. Dominic prefers to cultivate a speculative and theological spirituality.[5] St. Francis, on the contrary, has handed down a spirit rather than a doctrine, though the thought implicit in his life is transparent: to demonstrate the folly of human wisdom, and the wisdom which resides in the folly of the Cross.[6] The "all" and the "nothing" of the works of St. John of the Cross dominate the

---

[4] *La spiritualité chrétienne.* II, *Le moyen âge*, p. 231.
[5] Pourrat, *op. cit.*, p. 179.
[6] Pourrat, *op. cit.*, p. 230.

spiritual teachings of the Carmelites. St. Ignatius unquestionably puts the emphasis on the part played by
man in apostolic activity. In the French school, the
states of the Incarnate Word are the inspiration for all
the mental prayers of the disciples of Bérulle and Con-
dren. Everywhere, a dogmatic element is put into particular relief.

Born in very specific historical circumstances, marked
by a proper doctrine, every spirituality is led of necessity to stress certain practical truths, certain virtues or *moral values*. The intense and unconditional worship of poverty and humility characterizes the sons of
St. Francis. The love of truth animates the disciples of
St. Dominic in a very special way. The virtue of religion
permeates the spirit of the French school. The spirit of
sweet and demanding charity rules the Salesian school.
Suppleness and combative vigor set off the Society destined "to the defense and propagation of the faith under
the banner of the Cross."

Whence, finally, there are certain preferred *ascetical
procedures* in each school of spirituality. The Franciscan,
especially at the beginning, found in his very depriva-
tion the best means of asceticism. In the Society of Jesus,
the spiritual exercises occupy a primary place and the
simplification of the common life is manifest. While
avoiding specialization, the Benedictine gives himself
wholeheartedly to the asceticism of liturgical life lived
to perfection. Moreover, while the cloistered religious can
abandon himself to extraordinary bodily mortifications,
which are possible in the state of life he has chosen,
the active religious must develop, above all, the abnegation of his own will, and seek in the apostolate itself
and the work which it involves, the suffering which
redeems.

There is no question here of making our spirituality
a "school of spirituality." But we can become more
enlightened regarding our own nature and the forms of
our holiness by recalling the historical moment of our
institution, as well as the dogmatic, moral, and ascetical
values which must be dear to us.

1. HISTORICAL MOMENT

When did the diocesan clergy make its appearance
in the history of the Church? It is not too difficult to
find the answer to this. Although the diocesan clergy
does not have a founder, properly speaking, at least the
reason which determined its establishment is clearly evident from the primitive history of the Christian
Churches.

DISPERSION OF THE DISCIPLES

When the disciples were dispersed and chased out of
Jerusalem, for the greater good of the diffusion of Christianity throughout the world, their first work was preaching and the establishment of a nucleus of believers, of
brethren. Philip preached in Samaria (Acts 8), Peter
went to Lydda and Joppa, (Acts 9), others reached
Phoenicia, Cyprus and Antioch (Acts 11, 19). There
were the travels of Paul throughout Asia Minor, Greece,
and Europe. And what becomes of the evangelized, these
"brethren," after the passage of the preachers and
Apostles?

Initially, and when feasible, the Apostles themselves,
it seems, used to come on the scene to find out about the
work accomplished. After Philip had evangelized Samaria, Peter and John were sent by the Twelve to see
what had come of it (Acts 8:4-17) ; when the believers
who had been driven from Jerusalem had spread the
good news to Antioch, the Apostles dispatched Barnabas
to that city so that he could report to them and carry
on the work of evangelization (Acts 11:22). In short,
as much as possible, an Apostle verified the teaching of
the new community and fortified it against the dangers
that threatened it. But this Apostle was merely in transit.

Sometimes, Paul sent select *delegates* with the mission of remaining for some time among the new "brethren." Thus, before coming to Athens, he left Silas and
Timothy in Berea (Acts 17:14-15). The Apostle of the
Gentiles often entrusted Timothy with important as-

signments: he sent him to Thessalonica to encourage the faithful and strengthen them in the faith (1 Thess. 3:2-3); to Corinth, to remind them of the apostolic teachings (1 Cor. 4:17); to Philippi, to get some news (Phil. 2:19); to Ephesus, to preserve the purity of the doctrine (1 Tim. 1:3). These were all missions of a limited duration.[7]

Quick apostolic inspections, temporary delegations, these solutions could not suffice. The new communities required *stable and permanent delegates* who would provide their needs, attend to the whole of Christian life, and remain in residence among the faithful. This altogether natural need must have become evident very early to the Apostles, and they followed it up. From their first apostolic journey, after having visited the recently founded Christian communities and having revived their fervor, Paul and Barnabas establish in each of them a council of "presbyters." "And when they had appointed presbyters for them in each church, with prayer and fasting, they commended them to the Lord" (Acts 14:22). These "presbyters" interest us greatly, for they are the first diocesan priests.[8]

INSTITUTION OF THE PRESBYTERS

The circumstances which surrounded the institution of presbyters in Asia Minor show clearly that the Apostles wished to leave to the communities a council of persons who would watch over the spiritual good, the Christian life of all the brethren, without any restriction or limitation. "Like all other societies," writes E. Jacquier, "the Christian communities had to be organized, and therefore, to be given leaders. After the departure of the missionaries, they would have remained without any bond, without any worship; their adherents were thenceforth separated from the synagogue. Moreover, they were far from any center of worship, from Jerusalem or An-

---

[7] A. Michiels, *De origine episcopatus*, Louvain, 1900, p. 249.

[8] There is no need here to reopen the debate concerning the difference between presbyters and episcopes. Cf. A. Michiels, *op. cit.*

tioch in Syria; they could expect only a visit from the
missionaries and that was a rare thing at best. The
Apostles therefore gave them leaders."[9]

Leaders with what mission? The discourse of Paul
to the "Elders" of Miletus gives us a short description
of it: "Take heed to yourselves and to the whole flock
in which the Holy Spirit has placed you as bishops,
*to rule the Church of God, which he has purchased with
his own blood*. I know that after my departure fierce
wolves will get in among you, and will not spare the
flock. And among your own selves men will rise speaking perverse things, to draw away the disciples after
them. Watch, therefore . . ." (Acts 20:28-35). Those
placed in charge of the recent communities therefore
have the task of ruling "the Church of God, which he
has purchased with his own blood"; they will be, like
the Lord during His public life, the "good shepherds."
The image is well-known; it was familiar to the writers
of the New Testament (Matt. 9:36; Luke 12:32; John
10:11; 1 Peter 5:2), it was known to the authors of the
Old Testament (Ps. 23:1; 78:13; 94:7; 99:3; Ezech.
34:5; Mich. 7:14), and it has remained a classic one in
the Church.

Grouping all the New Testament quotations pertaining to the work of the presbyters and bishops, the following picture is obtained:

"The presbyters and bishops are the shepherds of
God's flock (Acts 20:17, 28; 1 Pet. 5:1, 2); they direct
the faithful and govern the churches (1 Tim. 3:5; 5:17;
Heb. 13:7, 17, 24; 1 Pet. 5:1-5; 1 Thess. 5:12; Clem.
42, 44, 63, 1); they are the overseers of God (1 Tim.
3:5; Tit. 1:7; 1 Pet. 2:25; 5:4; Heb. 13, 17) established
by the Holy Spirit (Acts 22:28). Dignitaries of the
communities (Phil. 1:1 *et passim*), they exercise their
rule under the control and higher authority of the Apostles (Acts 15:2 f.; 20; 17 f.; 21:18; 1 Tim. 3:1 f.; 5:17-
22; Tit. 1:5). In virtue of their responsibility, they

---

[9] *Les Actes des Apôtres* (Biblical studies) in 14, 23. See also A.
Michiels, *op. cit.*, pp. 149, 232.

teach the doctrine of faith (Acts 15; 20:28-32; 21:25; 1 Tim. 3:2; 5:17; Tit. 1:9; 1 Thess. 5:12; Heb. 13:7) and offer the Eucharist (Clem. 44:4; Did. 14-15); they have a right to respect and obedience, to maintenance (1 Tim. 5:17-18); they participate in the laying on of hands (1 Tim. 4:14), but it is neither stated nor assumed that they have the power themselves of constituting other ministers; they receive their own institution from the Apostles or from their delegates or successors (Acts 14:23; 20:28; 1 Tim. 3; 5:22; Tit. 1:5; Clem. 42:44)[10]

These are the first-century predecessors of our pastors and diocesan priests.

For the sake of thoroughness, let us point out that these presbyters or bishops are often numerous; they form a kind of "council," at whose head soon will be found a chief, the *bishop*. Indeed, ecclesiastical writers speak of the presbyters, the episcopes, in the plural; they freely use expressions such as "presbyteral body,"[11] "college of priests,"[12] "presbyterate."[13] Ignatius of Antioch compares his presbyterate to the "senate of the Apostles." And who holds the authority in this council? So long as the Apostles themselves could control the direction of the Churches by visits or through messengers, they were content to establish at the head of the communities a group of presbyters whom no one ruled except the Apostles themselves or their extraordinary envoys. In Jerusalem, the πρεσβύτεροι were subject to the authority of the Apostle James; in Ephesus and in the Christian churches of Crete, Timothy and Titus are charged by Paul to watch over the maintenance of discipline and order, even among the presbyters. This state of affairs could not continue for long: several Apostles were already dead; how was their work going to be continued? This is why certain Apostles communicated the fullness of the power of orders to certain dis-

[10] Cf. A. Michiels, *op. cit.*, pp. 216-217.
[11] *Op. cit.*, p. 221.
[12] *Op. cit.*, p. 224, *et passim*.
[13] *Magn.* 6:1; also *Ephes.* 4:1; *Smyrn.* 8:1.

ciples, thereby constituting them their successors in the complete sense of the term.[14] Were these presbyters and councils of elders numerous? Did the Apostles create them everywhere? No text expresses this as such, but is it necessary to find such clear statements? Luke does not consider it opportune to note the institution of presbyters each time it took place: he speaks to us about the presbyters of Jerusalem and Ephesus without preamble or explanation, as if he were dealing with an accepted institution (Acts 15:20). "The Acts," writes A. Michiels, "which name the presbyters of Jerusalem, also report (14:22) that Paul and Barnabas, at the time of their first voyage, established and ordained presbyters in the communities founded by them. This institution established for the benefit of the faithful could have had no other end than to guide the disciples in the ways of the Gospel, to assure them the service of the divine Word and the other means of salvation. This fact is brought out only for the first voyage; but there is no reason to doubt that Paul always acted thus."[15]

THROUGH THE AGES

Someone may say, but what about *teachers,* do they no longer count? Of course they do, and their activity is also explained, in the last analysis, by the desire of the Church to feed the flock of the Lord. The presbyters and the episcopes had to provide for all the needs of their flocks, and especially for the purity of doctrine. The rise of humanistic education based on values admirable in many ways but non-Christian, has challenged the Christian conception of the world and of life. Thus, it is incumbent upon the Church to open schools and so to guarantee the persistence of thought inspired by Christianity. Often under the direction of religious, this work may also be carried on by diocesan priests.

[14] A. Michiels, *op. cit.,* pp. 221-222.
[15] A. Michiels, *op. cit.,* p. 149. Cf. also p. 167: "No text either states or implies that certain churches had no presbyters at their head."

Thus it is clear that if diocesan priests become teachers, it is not formally for the purpose of promoting human culture or profane education, no matter how elevated they may be, but primarily to insure, throughout this cultural and authentic intellectual growth, the continuance of a Christian conception of man, the world, and life. Here, it would seem, is the specific reason for the presence of priests in teaching.

The same is also true in the field of "social" work. Here priestly intervention does not have as its formal purpose participation in reforms of the secular order; but the priest, as such, works for the improvement of institutions because he has realized that the latter have strong repercussions on the citizen's religious life. He knows that wanting this religious life without providing adequate material conditions for it is often illusory. This concept of the participation of the clergy in the task of social renovation is not a recent one; it antedates Catholic Action and the Young Christian Workers movement in particular. This is the meaning which the work of the Abbé de Tourville, who continued the activities of Le Play, had at the end of the last century. F. Klein writes of the Abbé:

"As interesting as these [social] studies were in his eyes, it was not for their sake that he had applied his powerful mind thereto. A priest above all, he had felt himself drawn to searching for the true social laws only when he had perceived in them conditions necessary for the proper functioning of religious life. It was what he heard in the confessional at St. Augustine's, that made him decide to go to St. Sulpice Square to the office of Frederick Le Play; it was for the purpose of accomplishing the divine work that he used to come to ask the human help of the author of *European Working-men* and *Social Reform*. He already realized that grace acts that much more readily on man when it finds in him a more perfect nature and, around him, worldly influences more in conformity with the higher destinies assigned to us by God."[16]

[16] *Lumière et vie*, Paris, 1929, pp. IX-X.

Although to this cultural and social activity directly demanded by its more formal mission, the Church may add certain manifestations of intellectual or material benevolence, she still remains in the footsteps of Christ who moved about on earth doing good, healing the sick, consoling the afflicted. Pastoral charity is always the ultimate explanation for such activity.

2. DOGMATIC PREFERENCE

It would seem that the dogma which dominates the spirituality of the diocesan clergy is that of a mediating and especially redemptive instrumentality, considered however in its visible form, in its diverse manifestations, and linked with a group of faithful. It is the very image of the Word Incarnate in His public life.

INSTRUMENTS OF CHRIST

The diocesan priest is an *instrument* of the living Christ who desires to prolong His work of mediation. Thus, his whole concern will consist in achieving perfectly in himself all that is required of a good instrument.

An instrument is "an efficient cause raised up by a principal agent in such a way as to produce an effect more noble and more perfect than itself. Two essential traits distinguish it from the principal cause: it attains an effect greater than its own native energies, it operates by means of a foreign influence communicated thereto."[17]

This definition holds, in the main outlines, for the redemptive instrumentality of the clergy. The latter must, consequently, have the sense of *collaboration in the work of Christ* very vividly in their hearts: this feeling is essential to instrumentality: συνεργοί, said Paul. This collaboration leads the priest to accomplish acts which go beyond the bounds of his native energies, even his voluntary and intellectual energies: such is the in-

[17] E. Hugon, O.P., *La causalité instrumentale dans l'ordre surnaturel*, Paris, Téqui, 1924, pp. 31-32.

comparable ennoblement which affects him, the sublime elevation to which he is led, his prime claim to glory. Does the priest always appreciate this instrumentality? Do we not meet priests who appreciate in their colleagues only that which is not strictly sacerdotal? But the priest also finds in this attitude a specific reason for maintaining the sense of profound dependence with respect to God, of great humility in the action he is undertaking; indeed, all the divine energies which come through him do not come *from* him. He operates by means of a foreign influence which is communicated to him from on High.

The instrument also carries out an action which is *proper* to it; it has its proper virtue. To cut, a piece of metal must undergo certain transformations; it is not enough to give it just as is to someone. Now, the priest is the instrument of the Lord in the world; his task, as we shall show, is multiform and changing; he must tend to all the needs of the Christian community. The instrumentality he is supposed to have must therefore be of exceptional richness, in great abundance, of unmatched fullness.

Still, the order of salvation is not identical at every point with the temporal order. In the latter, the work to be carried out depends mainly on the quality of the instrument. No one believes that it is possible to paint with the help of a billiard ball, or that one can cut down a tree with the help of a ball of yarn. In the supernatural order, the same law holds true in principle; and the Church does all she can to see that priests are as well formed as possible both from the natural and from the supernatural point of view.

Having stated this principle, let us add first of all that the possibilities for progress and perfection do not seem the same in the two orders, the natural and the supernatural. Natural gifts and talents cannot be multiplied at will: today, as formerly in the Church of Corinth, "not many wise . . . not many mighty, not many noble" (1 Cor. 1:26). The intensity of union with Christ, however, does not of itself appear to be restricted by earthly factors; history demonstrates that heroic virtues flourish in persons whose situations are in every respect different.

Besides, it has been noted that while supernatural qualities can sometimes compensate for the poverty of natural gifts, it is less evident that natural gifts can just as effectively replace strong supernatural virtues. Such seems to be the order of redemption. Superior moral qualities can overshadow physical defects; bodily and psychological qualities less readily replace inner life, at least when one looks at it from the point of view of the redemptive instrumentality, which is our viewpoint. "The foolish things of the world has God chosen to put to shame the 'wise,' and the weak things of the world has God chosen to put to shame the strong, and the base things of the world and the despised has God chosen, and the things that are not, to bring to naught the things that are" (1 Cor. 1:27-28). It is nonetheless true that the ideal is to possess both types of qualities intensely in order to realize within oneself the fullness of the visible and invisible instrumentality of apostolic life.

For the perfection of the instrument consists in being adequately proportionate to its end: "Because an instrument is not sought for its own sake, but for the sake of the end, something is not made better the greater is the instrument, but the more proportionate it is to the end."[18] This perfect adaptation to Christian redemption imposes on the diocesan priest the possession of all the natural or supernatural qualities necessary for the accomplishment of the task entrusted to him by the bishop.

VISIBLE MINISTRY

Nevertheless, the diocesan clergy assumes a particular form of co-redemption: it ensures the *visible and multiform ministry of a determinate group of the faithful.* The redemptive instrumentality proper to it is therefore not similar to that of the Carmelites or the Carthu-

---

[18] St. Thomas *Summa Theol.*, IIa IIae, q. 188, a. 7, ad 1m.

sians: it is "visible" in a very special way, while of course not excluding the invisible radiance of inner charity; it is "multiform" in its earthly expressions, but without betraying any of its spiritual unity; it is "linked to a group of the faithful," without in any way renouncing the work of the universal Church.

The apostolate of the diocesan priest is *visible* in a very particular way. Let us look at the life of the holy Curé d'Ars, St. Francis de Sales, St. Ignatius of Antioch, or that of the holy priests with whom we rub elbows daily. They do not bury themselves in a cloister, nor do they retire from the world. It was not with that intention in mind that Paul and the Apostles used to create councils of presbyters. Their role is to "rule the Church of the Lord," that is, to give to the faithful the supernatural nourishment of the sacraments, to offer with them the Eucharistic Supper, to break for them the bread of sound and fruitful doctrine, to entrust them to the benevolent care of God, to maintain the fervor of the best and to recall the strayed ones to order. That is the work expected of the diocesan priest — a work of doctrine as well as worship; a work directed toward God as well as men, but always with and for the community; a work of preservation or conversion, always according to the concrete needs of the faithful. The talents of the diocesan priest must be many.

The spirit of the cloistered religious should also be present to the diocesan priest. Paul demands that episcopal ministry be without reproach, and that the bishop himself be "holy and just" (Tit. 1:8). Worship is not a mere ceremonial function, but a religious act to be accomplished "worthily, attentively, devotedly" and which calls for personal commitment. While there is a "work accomplished," every sacrament also includes ceremonies, rites, and prayers which will come into play only if the priest piously fulfills his sacred ministry and in a holy manner: for instance, in the manner of baptizing, with the strong impression which adults sometimes derive from it; or in the manner of distributing the eucharistic Christ; or in the manner of genuflecting, or of conducting Benediction, etc. Likewise, the teaching of Christian doctrine profits enormously from the inner holiness of the priest who is preaching: so much has been said about the accents of profound conviction with which the Curé d'Ars used to preach, "seeing the invisible realities of which he spoke." What does this mean except that the intensity of his faith and the fervor of his charity increased tenfold the natural eloquence and influence of his spoken words of life. And in activities, what a difference can be noted between the priest who is a perfect organizer, but only that, and the one who, through his talents, lets his soul shine through!

MULTIFORM APOSTOLATE

The activity of the diocesan priest is also *multiform* in its earthly expressions: this is another of its characteristics. When the Apostles established presbyters in the infant communities, it was so that these men could tend to all the concrete, daily needs of these communities. In fact, in the description of the activities entrusted to the presbyters, nothing is missing: service of worship, service of the word and truth, direction and spiritual supervision, authority and administration in the Christian life, presiding in the exercises of prayer and the celebration of the Last Supper, care for all the sheep of a specific region, to adoring God in their name and asking for His blessings. The principle is clear: *all* the concrete and daily necessities. This requires an extraordinary flexibility on the part of diocesan priests: pastors of their flocks, they must always adapt themselves for the defense of the flock and its perfection, like a strategist in wartime. When schools and universities are opened, when specialized chaplaincies are created, it will not be out of a desire for "novelty," but in order better to respond to the wish of the apostle: "tend the flock of the Lord"; do all that is necessary for the total Christian life of all the faithful who are entrusted to you.

LINKED TO A GROUP OF THE FAITHFUL

Finally, the redemptive instrumentality of the diocesan priest is *linked to a specific group of the faithful.* When the Apostles named presbyters, it was for Berea, Lystra, Iconium, Ephesus, and not for the universal Church. Not for the Berea or the Iconium of all the centuries, but for these cities as they existed in their own time; whence the concrete and contemporary character which the activity of the diocesan clergy will of necessity acquire. The Sunday Mass will be "Mass for the People" while also being the sacrifice offered "for the salvation of the whole world." The Divine Office will be recited in the name of the whole Church; but who is to prevent the pastor of the parish from recommending especially to the Lord those whom the Holy Church herself has entrusted to him? His teaching is that of the universal Church, but he will adapt it to his hearers, for he knows their qualities and shortcomings. The works which he will develop will be those judiciously chosen to make Christ shine forth in this particular group of believers.

The group we speak of is not always or necessarily the parish. There are military chaplains, directors of religious communities, each having a portion of Christians toward whom he exercises a true priestly fatherhood, from the fact that the circumstances and organization of life prevent these faithful from coming to the parish altar with the other parishioners. There are also educational institutions, hospitals, and various groups which have their own chaplains or instructors: the work of pastoral charity carried out on behalf of these faithful is necessarily more specialized.

In the cases mentioned above, the faithful are grouped not according to geography — the parish or diocese — but according to logic: the army, students, the sick, etc. To be more rationally performed and therefore more perfect, pastoral charity must be carried out in accordance with the concrete needs of the faithful, and correspond adequately thereto. The Church has never hesitated to give specialized training to certain priests in order to enable them to be of more rational and therefore more perfect service to specific groups of the faithful. This is why, when we speak of "a group of the faithful," we cannot think only of the parish community.

This specialized apostolate was very well known at the beginning of the Church. We can point to the existence of "apostles" who were not the Twelve but missionaries, impelled by the Spirit and abandoning everything to go forth and found new Christian communities in pagan territory. There were also "prophets," who edified, consoled and exhorted; "doctors" who instructed and taught; "evangelists," who strengthened the young communities recently established by the Apostles; "hospitalers" who assisted the unfortunate; "almsgivers" who distributed aid to the poor and indigent: all, by profession, reproduced an aspect of the highly varied ministry which Christ carried on during His public life. Today, many of these functions useful to the Christian community are assumed by the diocesan clergy and carried on by them.

PUBLIC LIFE OF THE INCARNATE WORD

Also, to those who might inquire which dogma should be especially important to diocesan priests, this reply should be made: generally speaking, that of the mediative and redemptive instrumentality which they assume as an extension of that of the Lord. More particularly, the dogma of the Incarnate Word in His public life.

In His public life, as a matter of fact, Christ conducted an especially visible and tangible activity: He is seen, His voice is heard, He is followed, step by step: He is always visibly present. His activity is also many-sided: He preaches and reprimands, He teaches men to pray and call upon God, He inaugurates the worship of the Eucharist and Baptism, He forgives sins and invites men to penance, He helps the good people who follow Him and He looks for the lost sheep. Finally, the activity of Christ is presented as connected with a particular group of men: the Lord comes to Palestine, speaks especially to the Jews, His examples are taken from their environment, the errors He attacks are their errors, the vices He stigmatizes are theirs, His enemies are the men of His own time.

Let us also add that, in His public life, the Lord clearly manifests His *humanity:* He eats and drinks, He walks over the countryside, He sits on the edge of the well of Jacob, He is invited to dinner. The transfiguration on Mount Tabor is an exception. Thus it is with the diocesan priest: he seems very much tied to earthly realities, very much involved in temporal things, very little like St. John of the Cross in ecstasy. But this picture must not confuse us. In His public life, Christ was the Word and lived, just as on Tabor, the Trinitarian life. So, too, the diocesan priest, in the midst of his earthly activities, will be united, heart and mind, with God, just as the Incarnate Word was here below. Then and only then will he exercise perfectly the pastoral charity of which Christ gave a unique example: "Greater love than this no man has that he should lay down his life for his friends."

3. MORAL VALUES

PASTORAL CHARITY

The virtue that must predominate in the diocesan priest is to be found in the logic of his origins and his doctrinal preferences: it is *pastoral charity:* "to tend to the Church of the Lord."

This is the way the inspired writings understand the matter. The presbyter or episcope is the pastor of the local Church, the father of all those who are children of God. The activities entrusted to the clergy are all a matter of spiritual or temporal charity. The often repeated counsels of the Apostles all tend to perfect this pastoral charity and make it holy, prudent, wise, modest, and active.

Moreover, the priest is, above all, the *bishop's helper:* "cooperator ordinis nostri," the Pontifical says. "It is a remarkable fact that the ancient prayers in the Pontifical for the consecration of the priest and the deacon, at the time when the imposition of hands originally took place, do not speak of the Eucharistic powers (for the deacons there is a simple allusion to the altar; for the priests, nothing whatever is said), but strongly emphasize their quality as *subordinate auxiliaries of the bishop.* This is their great title to glory, their definition: they are charged, by virtue of their intimate dependence upon the bishop, together with and under his direction, to extend the Redemption (including the Eucharist) throughout the world by the exercise of apostolic charity."[19] It is the latter which characterizes episcopal activity; it is the virtue which must shine forth in the bishop. St. Thomas states it thus: "It pertains to the perfection of the episcopal state to exhibit zeal for the salvation of one's neighbor," and "the perfection of the episcopal state consists in this that a man, out of divine love, obligates himself to that which tends unto the salvation of his neighbor."[20] We must, then, find the same state of soul, the same apostolic virtues expected of every bishop, in the diocesan priest.

It is therefore more out of pastoral charity that the priest will teach, than out of a love of truth as such; it is more out of pastoral charity that he will celebrate the redemptive sacrifice and the acts of Christian worship, than out of a desire of performing an act of perfect religion as such. It is out of pastoral charity that he will direct men and activities, and not for the pleasure of administering well or directing wisely. Out of pastoral charity he will help them to sanctify themselves, elevating some, seeking out others. Thus, all the virtues assume in the soul of the diocesan priest, a particular aspect.

[19] E. Masure, *Parish Priest*, pp. 67-68.
[20] *Summa theol.*, IIa IIae, q. 185, a.4.

PASTORAL ASPECT OF ALL THE VIRTUES

Priestly *poverty* is not simply desired for its own sake. The priest who loves his flock sees their concrete, pressing needs; he gives them what he is, what he has, and what he can. He becomes poor, out of pastoral charity; he knows that when one has given all, one can demand much. This is a poverty not of disappropriation but of pastoral charity.

For its part, *chastity* is, at least under one aspect, freedom of spirit, availability as regards the apostolate, worship and the "care of souls." The asceticism required by continence is permeated with pastoral charity and the life of celibacy led by the clergy is demanded by it.

Even religion, in its most liturgical aspect, assumes a particular appearance for the shepherd of souls. The latter celebrates Sunday Mass for his people. The diocesan priest must have the sense of the individual Church over which he presides and which he authentically represents in the presence of the Divine Majesty. He prays for his people, makes requests in their name, adores in their stead, implores with them, cries out like them. The Mass, therefore, has a more concrete, a more earthy aspect, if one may say so, with all of the drawbacks but also all the advantages that this can involve.

This special physiognomy of the virtues in the apostle has been so well described by M. Daniélou that there seems to be no need to repeat the same thing less effectively. The virtues formed in us by the Master are always the same ones: humility, simplicity, detachment, the spirit of understanding, obedience. But

"these fundamental virtues take on different nuances in the contemplative and in the apostle. The humility of the apostle is formed not so much from a deliberate search for humiliation as from a great abandon, a practical disdain of himself which causes him to place little stock in his own effort and honor, and to have no complacency, no turning back on himself. He has no pref-

erence for the hidden life or lowly labors, nor does he
fear nor desire great responsibilities. His form of humility makes him absolutely available and prepared for
everything.

"The same holds true for poverty. For him, it consists less in the use of simple objects, the privation of
everything which is not strictly necessary, than in a
great inner liberty which allows him, according to St.
Paul's thought, to be now in poverty and now in abundance, using all the goods of this world, both material
and spiritual, only with a great purity of intention in
the degree necessary for the glory of God. This degree
is sometimes very difficult to find, for example in what
pertains to the preservation of health and physical
strength, the maintenance of a certain mental equilibrium, the development of personality, studies, contacts
to be maintained with the world, with relatives: the
apostle must, for all this, depend on the continual assistance of the Holy Spirit, and rely on the judgment
of truly objective and spiritual persons. . . .

"In the matter of charity, we may note that in
monasteries one is, above all, asked to judge and interpret nothing, to accept everything with the same
gentleness without taking into account natural sym-
pathies or antipathies. The apostle, on the other hand,
must judge those whom he is charged with raising,
forming, and directing; he will habitually take his stand
on the ground of truth, for otherwise nothing solid can
be established. Charity for him will not consist in not
seeing real deficiencies, even serious defects, but in having toward his brethren the sentiments of Christ: patience, respect for souls . . . a wholly spiritual zeal."[21]

Obedience, too, acquires an original power. A member
of a diocese, united to the *presbyterium* and to the bishop, the priest must be in his place, fulfill his role, carry
out the share of work assigned to him. In obeying,
he knows that he is participating in a great redemptive
action which is carried out step by step under the aegis
of the King of Kings. He is also performing a work of

---

[21] *Action et inspiration,* Paris, 1938, pp. 189-191.

understanding, solidarity, and common direction. The climate of our obedience is, above all, that of pastoral charity.

PRIESTLY PATERNITY

This is why it has often been said that the diocesan priest, sent among a group of the faithful to dispense all the spiritual blessings during long years, exercises toward them a veritable "paternity." For is not paternity the normal result of love?

But let us properly understand this. Paternity does not only mean that the priest, in the midst of the flock he has known for a long time and who come to him in all their needs, always shows himself to be good, kind, patient, indulgent, and cordial, as must a good father of a family. The father of the parish family must, above all, regulate the future of the Christian community, just as the father of a family who is worthy of the name is truly the enlightened head of the household. The priest is also the teacher of his people; like the competent father of a family, he takes in hand or verifies the instruction and education of his children, and does not content himself with a careless glance at their lessons and distractions. The priest is truly the pontiff who intercedes for his people, like the father of a family who goes to church in the morning to commend to God his wife and children, thereby carrying out a work of mediation in which some ancient peoples saw an authentic priesthood. The paternity of the priest is therefore directive, doctrinal, and religious, as well as benevolent and conciliatory.

The diocesan clergy may lay claim to this spiritual paternity on a very special basis: for it is to them that the ministry of the divine life — Baptism, Penance, Matrimony and Extreme Unction — is reserved in principle. While present law leaves the faithful completely free to approach anyone at all with respect to the care of their souls, the principle of the authority of the diocesan priest, the priest of the place, in these matters, remains clearly formulated in the canonical tradition.

Moreover, since the diocesan priest is, by definition, linked to a specific group of people for a considerable length of time, there necessarily arise between the shepherd and his flock sentiments of affectionate respect; bonds of a community of life are forged. The faithful have "their" pastor, who is like their possession, property, and wealth. The factor of time plays the major role here. Quite different is the priest who comes by to preach a mission, to hear confessions, to help with the Sunday Masses; the transitory nature of his ministry cannot engender the intimate relationships which a long stay insures and cements. And the faithful spontaneously recognize this state of affairs when they speak, favorably or not, of *their* pastor. Truly, "the order of bishops pertains above all to the raising up of *fathers*."[22]

4. ASCETICAL PRACTICES
IN AND THROUGH THE APOSTOLATE

What has been said of the origin of the diocesan clergy, of the doctrines which are important to it, and of the virtues which must animate it, is sufficient demonstration of the fact that its personal perfection must be sought, on the whole, in the multiple charitable activities of its redemptive mission. In other words, the priest must sanctify himself above all *in and through* his priestly and apostolic duties of state. The latter, if it proceeds from pastoral charity, is also an excellent formula of asceticism. The priestly state, E. Masure writes, is "capable by itself of furnishing its members with means of perfection through and in the exercise of the duties which it imposes on them, for these duties are acts of charity, and therefore acts of perfection. A diocesan priest who has a true understanding of his state, that is, of its relations with the state of life of his bishop,

---

[22] St. Epiphanius, *Contra haer.*, LXXV, 4; *P.G.*, vol. XLII, c. 507.

and who acts accordingly, is perpetually training himself in charity, and therefore training himself in holiness."[23]

The fact is, as Thomas puts it so well, that every state of life has its own special difficulty, its *particular heroism:* "If indeed one looks into the difficulty of leading a good life in religion and in an office having the care of souls, it is more difficult to lead a good life with the care of souls on account of external dangers, although the life of a religious is more difficult as to the nature itself of the work, because of the strictness of regular observance."[24] The Breviary, despite its restful beauty, can become a heavy responsibility; it must often be distributed otherwise than one would wish because of urgent needs, unexpected visits, and unfortunate delays. The life of worship, sublime in its essence, knows inevitable limitations: eternal new beginnings, routine confessions, Communions distributed by the thousand, the monotony of classes and catechism lessons, unbearable people, halfhearted Mass participation, etc. One is reminded of the list of dangers faced by the Apostle of the Gentiles in the course of his ministry. The priest is pressed from all sides, by God and by men, by worship and activities, by the temporal and the spiritual, by expansive charity and the duty of personal sanctification. He must possess all things while remaining poor, obey without losing his sense of bold initiative, show himself everywhere without losing his prestige, speak without tiring, reprove without offending.

Apostolic activities, while they do have their mortifying aspect, also and above all have a value of union with God that deserves to be stressed. Is there anything in the world more suitable for maintaining us in redemptive charity than the daily celebration of Holy Mass? Is there any prayer more suitable for bringing us close to God than that of the Divine Office? The psalms, a poetic and religious work par excellence, put us into direct con-

[23] *Op. cit.*, p. 106.
[24] IIa IIae, q. 184, a.8, c.

tact with God. Is it possible not to be united with God
and neighbor in the administration of the sacraments,
when we are instruments of Christ living on behalf of
men to give them the life of grace, to renew it, to sanctify their family life, or to assure their stability in
the faith? In communicating the Divine Revelation —
preaching, explaining of the Gospel, talking with people
— are we not a kind of imperfect though real echo of
the great Divine Voice, the Word of God? When we help
men approach God, are we not repeating the actions of
the Good Shepherd? In themselves, through their primary and obvious significance, apostolic activities make
us rediscover the soul of Christ.

Dom Chautard, who is surely not suspect in this
matter, has strongly proclaimed that works can and
must be a *means of sanctification*. And his syllogism is
clearly formulated:

"Our Lord demands in a formal way from those of
His creatures Whom He associates with His apostolate,
not only that they *preserve* themselves in virtue, but also
that they *make progress* in it. . . . Moreover, as we have
established from the outset, works are desired by God.
Therefore, to see in works, taken in themselves, an
obstacle to sanctification, and to affirm that, even though
they *emanate from the divine will* they will *necessarily*
slow down our progress toward perfection, would be an
insult, a blasphemy directed at the divine Wisdom,
Goodness and Providence. . . . The apostolate, regardless
of the form in which it presents itself, if it is *willed*
by God, not only does not have in itself the effect of
altering the atmosphere of solid virtue in which a soul
concerned for its salvation and spiritual progress must
abide, but even constitutes at all times for the apostle a
means of sanctification, if it is carried out *under the
requisite conditions*."[25]

We must be grateful to Masure for having reminded
us forcefully that sanctification must be sought in one's
duties of state. He has pointed out everything that is

[25] *L'âme de tout apostolat*, 13th ed., 1930, pp. 70-71.

sanctifying in the exercise of pastoral charity; everything that is mortifying in the pastoral ministry which is well carried out, and everything that is unifying in zeal based on theological charity. He warns us:

"In the search for the means of perfection, there is an ever-present danger. It is the danger of identifying two states of life whose principles are very different, and of forgetting that the true inward law of the diocesan priesthood is apostolic charity, that this charity is, in principle sanctifying of its very self, that it is identified with perfection, and that in the exercise or even in the acquiring of the strictly priestly virtues, of pastoral and missionary virtues in particular, lies a seed of holiness that no ascesis will ever completely replace. In any case, to fail to distinguish between two vocations and two states of life is to risk doing injustice to both."[26]

IN AND THROUGH THE MINISTRY

It would therefore be indispensable for the diocesan priest to relearn to esteem pastoral charity at its true value. When theologians, following St. Thomas, compare the state of perfection of the religious and that of the bishop, they conclude to the superiority of the latter, because it involves the continuous exercise of pastoral charity, whereas the former state is a search for personal perfection. "But in the category of perfection, the bishops are considered perfectors, religious, on the other hand, as perfect. One of them pertains to action, the other to passivity. Whence it is clear that the state of perfection is greater in bishops than in the religious."[27] And later on, the Holy Doctor adds: "And therefore whenever anyone is able to be useful to the salvation of others he who has obligated himself to that which can procure not only his own salvation but also that of others, would be retrogressing if he wished to transfer to the state of religion in order to attend to his own salvation

---

[26] *Op. cit.*, pp. 147-148.
[27] IIa IIae, q. 184, a.7, c.

only."[28] From these passages, about which much could be written, we only wish to retain the reason why pastoral charity is superior to the search for personal sanctification alone.

In fact, the diocesan priest does not sufficiently appreciate the beauty of the work which is his. Priests sometimes admire the young novice sweeping out the monastery as a sign of humility, the monk asking his abbot for some permission, the community assembled in Church and beautifully chanting the Office. And rightly so. But many of the same priests find it quite ordinary and unexciting to care for the altars of their own churches; they can see no heroism in teaching the catechism for the thousandth time and in consoling the same unfortunate for the hundredth time; they find it annoying to be called at any time to the church or homes, there to rejoice or weep, without regard either for their time, their personal concerns, their comfort, or anything else. Indeed, the priest does not appreciate sufficiently all these charitable activities, and only rarely sees in them highly superior means of perfection.

In addition, it has happened, especially in former times, that religious, taking as the absolute ideal the one they represent, have judged the value of certain priestly lives from this point of view. In that case, the diocesan priest is evaluated to the extent that his life and occupations resemble the type of existence proper to this or that order or congregation. Cardinal Mercier writes:

"As a matter of fact, religious in large numbers are quite imbued with the idea that perfection is in the monasteries. They prize their vocation very highly and are legitimately proud of it; their pride maintains in them an esprit de corps, which for them is a strength and a blessing. But it sometimes happens that they fall into the bias to which, in the field of science, the specialists are exposed: over-specialization leads to exclusiveness and an occasional loss from sight of the

[28] IIa IIae, q. 185, a.4.

grandeur of the whole. . . . Religious enamoured of their order do not always appreciate with full justice either the other orders or the place occupied by the 'secular' clergy in the ecclesiastical hierarchy. A venerable priest used to say to me: 'They have for us more compassion than they do esteem.' That we sometimes in fact justify their compassion, I do not gainsay. But they will certainly agree that by right, we are in a position to claim their esteem."[29]

Here is a small indication of this kind of lack of understanding. During World War II, a young priest from one of the orders was put to work in a parish. He began the work, he told me later, with a rather unfavorable idea of the diocesan clergy. "But," he said, "after living this life for three years, I realized how much heroism it took simply to hang on, despite everything and everybody, from the first of January to the thirty-first of December." This young priest probably had looked about among diocesan priests for an ideal of perfection for the faithful and had been disappointed. But he undoubtedly did not know that there are other ways of practicing the *same virtues*, and, in any case, *other* ways of achieving a high degree of charity — which is what everyone must desire, for charity alone is the measure of sanctity. And if, before his parish experience, this priest had had to preach a retreat to the diocesan clergy, would he not have been inclined to demand of them that they come as close as possible to religious perfection, instead of insisting, as he would today, on the ascetic and unifying value of the apostolate itself?

"THEOLOGICAL" PASTORAL CHARITY

Having said this, let us immediately admit that this pastoral charity, of which Masure speaks with such praise and which is a synonym for perfection, is "theological" charity with all that this involves of the *theo-*

---

[29] *Vie intérieure*, Entretien IV.

centric and *supernatural.* One should therefore not be content with just any zeal, just any activity. So that the priestly ministry, as such, may be truly sanctifying, it must truly be an act of theological charity. St. Thomas writes of the bishop: "The very fact that bishops are concerned about those things which pertain to the love of the neighbor, comes from the abundance of the divine love . . . for this is the sign of greater love, that a man for the sake of a friend should serve another, even if he wishes to serve his friend only."[30] What is true of the bishop must be true also of those whose whole grandeur is to be his co-workers.

Now experience proves that the priestly functions do not lead *automatically* to theological life and perfection. To say Holy Mass often does not necessarily imply an increase of union with Christ the Priest. It is possible to recite the Breviary with such lassitude that a layman would have difficulty recognizing it as a prayer: "elevation of the mind to God." Neighborly service is not always an act of the good shepherd, and, in preaching, it is not always an echo of God's eternal word that one hears.

It is understood, then, that to guarantee the genuineness of his pastoral ministry, to assure pastoral charity its authentically divine nature, the diocesan priest draws from the treasury of the *general* means of sanctification that the Church places at the disposal of *all* the faithful — laymen, religious, priests. Such means are the mental prayer which is preparatory to a conscious life with God, extraordinary mortification recalling the principle of habitual austerity, prayers and devotions suitable for reviving union with God, acute faith, lively hope. These general means of sanctification therefore interest the priest, and especially him, as the sine qua non for a fully theological pastoral charity. To the ministry itself, which is our duty of state, these means have a relationship of means to end which cannot

[30] IIa IIae, q. 184, a.7, ad 2m.

be lost sight of without great damage to their efficacy. We assume them for a purpose and according to specific norms: the *purpose* is the authentication of our pastoral ministry, as well as the practice of Christian asceticism; the *norms* are the potentialities of the concrete apostolic life which we must lead, as well as the development of the virtues and the life of a baptized person.[31]

---

[31] Regarding the place of the different general means of perfection in the apostolic life, see chapter XIV below.

CHAPTER THIRTEEN

THE DIOCESAN PRIEST TODAY

After having defined the spirituality of the diocesan clergy in its general and specific aspects, there remains one last step — to underscore what this spirituality involves *now*. Of course, a diocesan priest is always the same kind of priest, just as the Roman Catholic Church is always the same, throughout the course of centuries. And this is why we have just determined, in the last two chapters, the essential and permanent elements of his spirituality.

Nevertheless, history shows that mankind evolves, progresses, retreats or stands still. It shows the philosophical and religious transformations which affect minds and hearts. It makes us the witnesses of political and social changes which have profound repercussions on morals. It stresses the industrial and technological progress which sometimes revolutionizes entire sections of human activity. So, too, the eternal work of mediation of the Spouse of Christ must assume various forms at each age of the world. And the unchanging message of the Lord must be presented differently in each of these ages. In short, at each of its steps, mankind expects from the Church a message appropriate to the evil from which it suffers, a specific remedy for the wound which has been inflicted on it.

What could be more natural? Does not the physician, the "redeemer of health," seek to establish for each patient and for each phase of the same ailment, as precise a diagnosis as possible, in order to be able to prescribe a topical medication and not some all-purpose treatment? And must not the priest directing a soul, find the counsel which is demanded by the person according to the latter's present dispositions? And so, the entire Catholic priesthood must make a diagnosis of the present world: to look for the topical remedy, perhaps renew certain forms of mediation, find the real and doctrinal response to the needs of the moment. In that sense, the Catholic priesthood must enjoy a healthy "modernity," a wise "up-to-date" quality.

1. THE WISE MODERNITY OF THE CHURCH

CONCERN FOR ADAPTATION

The example of this type of modernity has always been given in the Christian Church by the hierarchy. Christ Himself adapted His message to His Jewish hearers and presupposed in them the errors of their race. Paul replied to the Judaizers of his time and to the newcomers from Hellenistic paganism; the best of his doctrinal work is often encased in polemic or pastoral frameworks. The Fathers and Doctors of the Church, our contemporary popes and the hierarchy, have frankly undertaken the struggle against the errors of their times and have created the institutions which seemed indispensable to the work of salvation. The era of basilicas and churches succeeded that of the catacombs. To the inspired writings, the twelfth century added theological science, and the sixteenth saw the diffusion of catechisms. The episcopal and palace schools changed, during the Renaissance, into colleges for the humanities. Seminaries as we know them date from the sixteenth century. Military chaplains are of a more recent time, as are the Code of Canon Law and the sacramentals which bring to airplanes and automobiles the blessing of the Church. Thus, the living and perpetual testimony of the ecclesiastical magisterium, of the supreme ministry, of Rome and the papacy unquestionably reveals a profound desire: that of carrying out a contemporary mediation. The diocesan priest, who personifies the Catholic priesthood for his generation, would not have the authentic "ecclesiastical" spirit if he refused this wise modernity: "to think with the Church" is also to have the concern for the present shown by the papacy and the hierarchy.

The history of Christianity proves therefore that the leaders of the Church have regularly requested their immediate co-workers to insist upon certain doctrines, stress certain virtues, attend to the development of certain institutions, remedy certain specific evils and forestall certain imminent dangers. Paul made urgent recommendations to Timothy and Titus; and Paul VI continues this series of solemn demands, adapting them to present conditions. "And here now, Venerable Brethren," wrote Pius XI in *Ubi Arcano*, "is what We are asking you to tell your priests. The Pope, witness and not long ago, collaborator, of the works of every kind which they have courageously undertaken for the flock of Christ, has always appreciated and continues to appreciate very highly the admirable zeal they have shown in the accomplishment of their task, as also their ingenuity in discovering *ever-new methods* for facing the new situations created by the evolution of the times."

INTELLIGENT MODERNITY

The acquisition of this "ecclesiastical" modernity can be more or less favored by the temperament of each man, and by the formation given to future diocesan priests.

First, *temperament*. Professional job counsellors advise young people to stay away from this or that trade because "it does not suit them." Paul was reluctant to have John Mark accompany him; the latter, to all appearances, seemed to Paul not to be daring enough (cf. Acts 13:13; 15:38). Among candidates for the priesthood, some are more suited for, say, teaching than for administrative work. If therefore personal dispositions can be favorable to certain tasks, they can also, in particular, predispose future priests to respond to the evils from which their generation is suffering. Likewise, certain natural shortcomings can be particularly regrettable. The priest who likes to isolate himself from lay life to ensure his own serenity would seem less suitable today, for the world expects a mediator.

And then *formation*. We know that the principles which guide educational institutions are not the same everywhere, and that we have "good" schools and "backward" schools. The apostolic formation of the clergy can also be adapted more or less successfully to the demands of an age. This is why Pius XI, shortly after his election as pope, wrote to Cardinal Bisleti, Prefect of the Sacred Congregation of Seminaries and Universities: " ... contemporary needs will be carefully taken into account. The course of events has introduced into the ways of the Christian people many usages unknown to our fathers; the priest must today be perfectly up to date regarding these innovations, in order to draw from the strength of Christ the new remedies for new evils, and to make the salutary influence of religion penetrate into all the fibers of human society."[1] This means that deficiencies can exist in the preparation of priests for the contemporary apostolate. Not to stress in their formation contemporary problems, not to drill them in the virtues which are especially necessary, constitutes a doubly damaging failure. The priest who does not possess very perfectly that which his people specifically need is like the physician who would be ignorant of precisely the remedy needed for the ailment he has just discovered in his patient.

Moreover, the old adage expresses the desirable ideal quite well "these things ought to be done, and those not omitted"; that is, unite the strong traditional virtues to a wise contemporary orientation. Both one and the

<hr />

[1] *Actes de Pie XI*, Paris, Bonne Presse, vol. 1, pp. 93-94.

other, not one without the other. No complete apostolate without a contemporary orientation; no wise modernity without a serious foundation in tradition. The good and holy priest has them both, in his own way perhaps, but unquestionably. It would be false to set the tendencies in opposition: they must be combined and complement one another: *nova et vetera*. This is the very face of the Catholic Church; this is indeed the permanent witness given by the papacy.

PERMANENT TIMELINESS

What does this *modernity* involve? Again let us consider the hierarchy. How, for example, is the present-day papacy different from the Twelve? In essence, it is not different at all. Christian thought, ecclesiastical society and sacred rites are essentially the same: and this is what constitutes the very substance of what the priest must possess. Nevertheless, a modern papal encyclical is not altogether like the Epistle to the Galatians! The fact is that a certain number of points have been further studied and further developed, whereas others have remained in the background.

Like a spiritual director who must take into account the particular circumstances of a person he is trying to help become a better Christian, the parish priest, to help his people, must be aware that they, too, have a history, which he must know. It is up to him to enlighten men regarding the questions which cause them difficulty; it is up to him to encourage them in those areas where they are especially weak; it is up to him to adapt his whole pastoral action in terms of the general characteristics of a group of people. A collective ill demands a collective remedy.

To determine this ultimate aspect of the spirituality of the diocesan priest is to set the doctrinal and religious climate, the social and cultural status, in which he dwells. And to "situate" a man — this exactly presupposes a *philosophy of history*. Only those who manage to find their place in the network of currents and tendencies of an age truly know whence they come, where they are, and where they are going. They alone are adults; they alone can become wise men and leaders. Actually, every age finds itself crisscrossed by philosophical, religious, social and cultural tendencies each of which has its own point of departure and direction. Man locates himself at some point in their crossings, he is formed by them; he is permeated with them without knowing it, without willing it. It is for the priest to learn what is going on among others and in himself, in order to be able to carry out, with full vigor and complete lucidity, an effective mediation. What must be kept is kept; what is mistaken will be rejected; what has gone awry he will straighten out. "Cleanse what is soiled, bend what is rigid, guide what is astray." It is necessary to know what is wounded or amiss; it is also necessary to have the qualities implied in the act of correction and healing. And every age has its wounds, its deviations, its errors, and its miseries. To determine what is incumbent here and now upon the sacerdotal "mediator," given his "situation" in the movement of history, is to write the third chapter of the spirituality of the diocesan clergy.

We cannot undertake this work, which would take years to complete and which would have to be timely enough to be contemporary and broad enough to encompass a whole generation. In a general way, however, one may say that it seems that our work of mediation has been limited too exclusively to indvidual formation. Today, the papacy demands of the clergy that it be also concerned with institutions and the unbelieving masses, to bring them both back to Christ the Lord. Whence the necessity of working for the new harmony which must bring together the World and God, the masses and the Lord Jesus.

2. THE WORLD AND GOD

CONTEMPORARY DUALISM

It has become commonplace to say that since the Renaissance there exists a Gospel-world *dualism,* particularly in the area of institutions. By Gospel, one understands all the fundamental supernatural realities such as Christ, religion and morality. "The world" symbolizes temporal values: the family, the state, businesses and professions, sciences, arts, culture.

This ailment is perhaps the most profound of all those which affect the temporal life of the Church; it is inscribed at the heart of almost all of the ideological movements which direct events today. For some, religion is a matter of conscience: all outer activities are therefore independent of it. Socialism proclaims that religion is a private affair; public life cannot therefore receive the slightest impulse, the least regulation, from it. Totalitarianisms, such as Nazism and Fascism yesterday and Communism today, accept religion only to the extent that it is inoffensive to the life of their societies, so long as it does not cause the dough to rise.

This divorce is very pronounced; it is manifest in all sectors of life. Doctrines, for example, are infested with it: there exists a philosophy of Christian inspiration and a separate, closed, philosophy; some economists hark back to Christian principles, while others neatly reject every normative value; dissertations in law most often appeal to juridical positivism, nowadays so widespread; over against works of Christian sociology, one could range entire libraries of atheistic and materialistic writings; a rationalist pedagogy stands opposed to the pedagogy of Christian inspiration; history open to the influence of God is extremely rare, if one considers the amount of historical work hermetically sealed off from supernatural values.

Let us, however, acknowledge that this problem has sometimes received an unhappy solution — clericalism. It is certain that Christian thought must be applied to all earthly relations. It is also certain that the evangelical ferment must leaven the dough of temporal values, that is, that the family, the state, the professions, culture, philosophy, must be ennobled, transfigured, sublimated, in all their component parts, by Christianity. God desires that His will be done on earth as it is in heaven: the Church,

therefore, shall have the duty of using all her resources
to bring this about. In so doing, she is also rendering
to the world an outstanding service, for she is connect-
ing it to the sources of authentic life, which alone can
assure its growth and prosperity. But if the ecclesiastics
were to seize the reins of power, if they were to "lay
their hands" on institutions instead of insistently requiring them to become cleansed, if they were to wish
to run politics instead of demanding that civil society
be raised to the level of the men and the Christians who
dwell in it, if they were content to group the baptized
physically instead of teaching them to live anywhere in
a Christian manner, if they reserved to themselves a
monopoly on divine grace instead of announcing that
Christ also gives Himself outside of church walls and
without sacramental rites, they would be betraying the
witness of Christ which is presence and not possession,
spirit and not matter, service and not domination.

ELIMINATING THIS DUALISM

The priest needs to be "a man of his times," and he
will be if he understands the situation in which he finds
himself; many, however, lacking the minimum philosophy
of history required for this purpose, are unaware of the
times to which they belong, and are incapable of locat-
ing themselves in the great human movement which is
going on. Priests must grasp this situation, perceive the
basic dualism which is manifested in it, experience the
painful divisions which afflict the whole world, and
finally note that there is here an immense field open to
the work of mediation, the latter being a force for
reconciliation, an effort at union, a will to insert the
created into Christ. To ignore this basic condition of
the world through lassitude or a refusal to look at reality,
is to condemn oneself to sterility and betray the mission
which the Lord has confided to us.

Eliminating this kind of dualism in oneself and in
individuals and environments of life, is an immense and
burdensome task, but how needed it is! It is immense,

because this dualism profoundly permeates societies, culture and the most diverse institutions. Burdensome, because nothing is more difficult and painful than to undertake a struggle against the basic failing of an era. This effort demands of the priest many intellectual and moral qualities: knowledge of the Christian concept of life, the world, thought, and institutions; a tenacious will to plant the cross in the midst of worldly values jealous of their false autonomy; the daily courage to resume work while some are continuously bent on undermining its foundations. The long series of perils which Paul experienced could be repeated at this point. The most serious of these dangers is hidden in the psychology of many Catholics, priests as well as laymen, who profess and unconsciously live a "liberal" Christianity and who deny, without noticing it, the universal domain of God over all created reality, and the universal kingship of Jesus over every worldly value.

In short, the priest will make every effort to be present everywhere, to establish and make grow a new harmony between God and the World. But in what direction is he to orient his activity?

INCARNATE SPIRITUALITY

The fundamental law of human history is one of progressive spiritualization. Man's development is dominated by this process, and all asceticism, natural or Christian, has as its goal the mastery of mind over matter, not by exclusion but by transfiguration. Now man is neither sterile nor isolated. He extends himself in innumerable cultural or social forms which, proceeding from him, sometimes detach themselves from his person, in some way faithfully multiplying his image: a treatise by Aristotle still reveals to men the thought of its author. Man is also surrounded by worldly realities which others have helped to bring into existence and stabilize. Now, these temporal values which serve humanity must be adapted to its needs and evolution. And just as man's development is regulated by the law of spirituality and the growth which flows therefrom, the realities which are at man's service or which emanate from him, must participate in the same evolution and follow the same lines of growth.

This was true, writes Father Malevez, for the Adamic economy: grace "called for, gave to itself at least in germ, a state of the universe, even the material universe, marvelously favorable to the development of natural man. The dogma of origins invites us to think that, normally, for its own well-being, grace desires a transformation of the body itself and its environment."[2]

What would have been true in the Adamic dispensation is unquestionably true in the historical Christian economy. Through Revelation, we know that God became man so that man might become deiform — Θεοποίησις, the formula of the Greek Fathers is clear — and so that the world itself, His image, might acquire through redemption a likeness akin to adoptive filiation (Rom. 8:19). And since God is Spirit, deiformity cannot be other than a progress of authentic spiritualization. Moreover, since the Christian economy really had its beginning with Christ, since grace is a real beginning of glory, since the Spirit has already been given to the world (let us recall the cosmic perspectives of the captivity Epistles), one may believe that the work of spiritualization is everywhere carried on, at least in a hidden way, in the image of the hidden and invisible glory which ennobled the human nature of Christ before His resurrection.[3]

Unfortunately, the effort of the priesthood toward a better spirituality is hampered, particularly, by a misunderstanding of past centuries. The sense of the term "spirituality" has been poorly grasped. Instead of interpreting it according to the πνευματικός of Paul — a notion whose contents are linked to those of the Πνεῦμα — men have slid toward an abstract idea of spirit. There has been a cleavage between spirit and life. Whence the

[2] "La philosophie chrétienne du progrès," in *Nouv. revue théol.,* 1937, p. 377.

[3] Cf. *Summa theologica,* IIIa, q. 19, a.1, ad 2m.

disincarnate spirituality of thought, the religious formalism, the moral Jansenism turning into laxism in deed, and the abstract ideology that we have inherited. Man in the flesh, the family, the community and the nation, professional life, even ecclesiastical life, have too often been forgotten. Today, there is a healthy reaction in favor of "incarnation": the rediscovery of man, the family, the nation, the religious community. The priest cannot but rejoice at this return to greater human sanity, and he will participate therein wholeheartedly.

But if he keeps present in his mind the final perspectives of his faith, he will soon see that the present movement of "incarnation" cannot terminate in itself. One re-establishes contact with the fundamental realities not only for the sake of this contact, but for the work of transfiguration which must be accomplished therein. It is necessary to become incarnate, but in order to spiritualize. God became man so that mankind might become like unto God. A break in the cable isolated the tractor from the trailer which ran wild; the tractor comes back toward the trailer but in order to lead it to the end of the trip. Here especially, is manifest the importance of the priest. More than anyone else, he must be able in principle to determine what in the Pauline sense of the word, the work of "spiritualization" involves, because he is the accredited bearer of the revealed message. His ministry of real and concrete mediation finds therefore a vast area of application today; it calls for solid theological positions, a Christian conception of the world, an alert sense of the potentialities for progress, a permanent grasp of the goal so that there will be no deviation, for the temporal domain is slippery. In these times when those who direct nations are searching for the general conditions of international human equilibrium, diocesan priests must keep those fundamental intuitions pure ("to become incarnate in order to spiritualize") which the civil authorities will try to express in appropriate techniques. Those priests who grasp the greatness of this work and who participate in it, unquestionably enjoy a sound modernity; they are of their times. But exactly what do we understand by spirituality?

WHAT IS "SPIRITUALIZATION"?

In the manner of the Apostle, spirituality refers to all that is under the fruitful influence of the Holy Spirit; and this Spirit is sanctity, unity, and universality.

It is *sanctity*. Is He not called the *Holy* Spirit so many times in the New Testament? And this holiness, far from remaining purely ontological, is translated temporally into wisdom (Eph. 1:17), into truth (John 14:17; 15:26), into charity (Rom. 5:5). The fruits of the Spirit are charity, joy, peace, patience, meekness, goodness, fidelity, kindness, temperance (Gal. 5:22-23). Are these fruits to remain purely inward gifts? That would be to remove their most tangible effectiveness. On the contrary. They will be translated in this world by all that favors its ennobling: the beautifying of the home and family, the improvement of professional life and working environment, purity of civil society and the economic world, elevation of the forms of recreation and the use of leisure time, progress in human and industrial technology, refinement of the arts and humanist values, culture and sciences, the rule of essential religious values. The true apostle keeps deep within himself an ardent desire for the expansion of all these values, because, directly or indirectly, they outline the renovation of the face of the earth by impressing thereon, already, certain traits of the future City glorified in the Spirit: "Send forth thy Spirit and they shall be created and thou shalt renew the face of the earth."

The Spirit is *unity*. Let us reread the list of the fruits of the Spirit. For the most part, these are the indispensable conditions of unity in the common life of families, cities and human societies: charity, peace, patience, meekness, fidelity and kindness — what seeds of unity for the life of men! The faithful are one through the Spirit (1 Cor. 12:13). And they must strive to "preserve the unity which the Spirit produces in souls, so that all their wills may be linked, like a bundle, by peace. Paul enumerates the elements of this unity which must be preserved. The Christians form a single body, a visible society, animated and vivified by one same Spirit."[4] Are we to imagine that this unity will not have any repercussions on temporal and daily life? All Christian morality proves otherwise: the whole life of the Christian must be permeated with the unity willed inwardly by the Spirit: an organic unity, without uniformity, anarchic chaos or opposition of classes; unity really incarnate in this world, prefiguring the unity of the City of God.

The Spirit is *universality*. Christian unity necessarily calls for universality. "For in one Spirit," writes Paul to the Corinthians, "we were all baptized into one body, whether Jews or Gentiles, slaves or free; and we were all given to drink of one Spirit" (1 Cor. 12:13). This is the breath of universality unleashed in the Christian world since Peter baptized the centurion Cornelius (Acts 10), since Paul evangelized the Gentiles (Gal. 2:8), since the Apostles left Palestine for the ends of the earth. Something of this spirit goes out from Christians and marks their worldly actions. They have read in the Apocalypse, that the heavenly Jerusalem has "three gates on the east, and on the north three gates, and on the south three gates, and on the west three gates": a symbol of catholicity. And they know that the Earthly City, although temporal, must also be the prelude to the heavenly Jerusalem.

Caution is needed in exploring the temporal implications of this spirit, but it is an exploration which must be undertaken. The Church which is one, holy and catholic, because she is apostolic, favors initiatives which are of the same order as her traditional characteristics. Priests should imitate her.

---

[4] J. Huby, *Les épîtres de la captivité*, p. 196.

3. THE MASSES AND CHRIST

Contemporary human history, it seems, gravitates around this fact: the emancipation of the masses. As the Renaissance gave rise to the awakening of the laity, as the French Revolution sanctioned the triumph of the middle class, so the twentieth century is witnessing the emancipation of the worker, the "deproletarianization" of the masses. While too schematic, what follows does not, in our opinion, falsify fundamental historical truth.

THE MIDDLE AGES

The Middle Ages were the era of the "clerics" — *clerici*. They held a monopoly on science, letters, thought, and religion, to the point that the word "clerk" became the synonym for an educated man.

The Renaissance marked the gradual preponderance of the laity. H. Pirenne writes:

"Until the Renaissance, the intellectual history of Europe is only a chapter in the history of the Church. There was so little lay thought that even those who fight against the Church are entirely dominated by her and think only of transforming her. With the Renaissance, the mastery of the Church over thought is questioned. The cleric loses his monopoly of knowledge. Spiritual life in turn becomes laicized, philosophy ceases to be the handmaiden of theology, and art, like literature, breaks away from the tutelage imposed on it since the eighth century. For the ascetical ideal, a purely human ideal is substituted, and this ideal finds its highest expression in antiquity. The humanist replaces the cleric, just as virtue (*virtù*) replaces piety. There is no doubt that while it can be said that the Renaissance substitutes man for the Christian, it is not anti-religious."[5]

If the Renaissance helped man to attain maturity and achieve emancipation, it must also be remembered that the man envisioned here is the humanist. In the six-

---

[5] *Histoire de l'Europe*, p. 393.

teenth century, "man" signified "humanist" — the well-
born man who had natural beauty and culture. Representing "civilization," he opposed the barbarism of
science conceived as the whole range of intellectual and
mechanical processes which dispensed man from thinking for himself, as well as the barbarism of ignorance
which refused knowledge and culture because these
things painfully complicated life. The humanist in all
things contributed artistic taste: he was concerned about
proportions, about elegance, he had a desire for light
and order, with a touch of uplift, of dignity. He was
open to human affections: *De amicitia* had taught him
the beauty of friendship and he cultivated it. Nothing
human was foreign to him. Also, he was fully aware of
the entire "human species"; but he was even more proud
of his own worth and readily set himself apart from the
ignorant masses who were but numbers: *nos numerus
sumus!* Finally, the humanist had faith in life: he tasted
it and loved it; he accepted it unreservedly. Basically he
was an optimist.[6]

MODERN TIMES

Still, the humanist repeated too often that every man
is an absolute, that each soul has its price and its value:
once reduced to the human level, these affirmations lost
their humanistic value. Society and nobility first of all
appropriated the discovery of man made by the Renaissance. There are a number of reasons which help us to
understand why this was so: this society could be cultivated, civilized and optimistic in its view of life. The
rest of men were, in fact, ignorant and generally illiterate.

Then, the bourgeoisie became aware of itself. Of
course, even during the Middle Ages, rulers had to take
into account the great urban middle classes. During the
sixteenth century, an economic upsurge brought wealth
to the bourgeoisie and with it power, sometimes culture,

• F. Strowski, *La sagesse française*, pp. 35-38.

often independence. Still, it must be acknowledged that it was in the eighteenth century, with the French Revolution, that the middle classes made their own personality triumph and had their rights definitively recognized everywhere, even in political structures. In August, 1830, Louis-Philippe I was proclaimed, not King of France, but King of the French: the July Monarchy crowned the emancipation of the bourgeoisie.

Thus, the same movement of emancipation and coming to adulthood has reached the world of the worker. This is the phenomenon through which we are living today — the deproletarianization of the masses. The principle set forth by the humanists has merely developed its potentialities. Between the "social revolution" of the present period and the Renaissance, there is no opposition, but a fundamental continuity. And since this discovery is being made in an "existentialist" period and through the masses, one can imagine the violence and incoercible nature of the movement it will launch.

THE PAPACY

The attitude of the papacy in the face of this state of things is admirable. First of all, it invites the entire clergy to devote a goodly share of its forces to activities aimed at bringing the working masses back to the Gospel and Christ. Is it possible, really, to be more explicit, to show more anguish, than Pius XI in *Divini Redemptoris?* He writes there that:

"every other activity no matter how excellent, must yield before the vital necessity of saving the very basis of the faith and Christian civilization. Let the priests in the parishes, therefore, without prejudice, to be sure, to that which is required for the ordinary care of the faithful, reserve the greatest and best part of their forces and activity in order to win back the working masses to Christ and Church, and to cause the Christian spirit to penetrate those circles from which it is the most estranged. They will find in the popular masses a willingness to listen, an abundance of unexpected fruit, that

will reward them for the difficult labor of the initial
ground-breaking."

Moreover, the papacy has given an unprecedented
example of boldness. Though the masses have not yet
received the consecration of their social and political
"emancipation," the Church has officially recognized
that in the field of the Christian apostolate, the workers
have reached their "majority." It is to them that the
papacy entrusts the apostolic mission of "reconquering"
the workers and working-class environments, making
them participate authentically in the mediative work reserved to the hierarchy, with an official mandate, religious objectives, ecclesiastical responsibility. This fact,
a turning point in the history of the Christian apostolate,
cannot be overemphasized.

MISSION OF THE CLERGY

Of priests, the popes ask first of all that they prepare themselves doctrinally: "A very delicate task,"
wrote Pius XI in *Quadragesimo Anno,* "imposes itself
on priests. Let all those who are growing up for the
service of the Church prepare themselves by a serious
study of the principles which regulate the social order."
It has often been noted, indeed, that the great contemporary errors are concerned either with fundamental
dogma or with social morality: the high proportion of
pontifical encyclicals devoted to this latter topic is vivid
testimony of this fact. We must expect a serious initia-
tion to these areas which are intimately linked to family,
civic, and professional life, and which are the object of
much discussion.

Priests are also asked to reconsider their teachings,
their sacred functions, to see if the masses can find
nourishment therein, just as easily as do more cultivated persons. Can the *doctrine* we teach be understood
by all? What are the sources of the expressions and
vocabulary we use? Where do we get the examples we
propose? What is the public we have more or less un-

consciously before our eyes? Do we remember that our whole formation itself is linked with a specific social structure with its own tastes, habits, reflexes, interests, expectations, fears and its loves?

By whom can the *liturgy*, with its offices and rites, be understood, followed, and appreciated? Who can really be associated with daily Mass, with the Holy Week services, with First Friday devotions, etc.? What way of life and which occupations make it possible to be a "model parishioner"? Do our services encourage participation by all?

Whom can *morality* itself truly enlighten and guide? Could industrialists and workers say that, by listening to all their pastor's sermons, they know how to be directed in their daily lives? Is morality unconsciously preached for those who are withdrawn from life in the world? Do we think of everybody? Have we done all we can to orient toward God and to baptize everything that exists, everything new that makes its appearance?

It would thus be a good idea to review all our professional priestly activities, and to ask ourselves if we are "all things to all men," free, above divisions of any kind, detached from every special interest, in order to complete the work of the incarnation of the divine in humanity's midst — humanity poised on the horizon of a greater, emancipated world.

Finally, priests have the obligation of showing people that *sanctification* can be the heritage of all those who respond to grace. Today more than ever it is necessary to state this very clearly. If Christianity cannot be attached to a particular form of government, it is no more fitting for it to be chained to a particular economic system, a particular phase of mankind's social history. At a time when we are witnessing the accession of the masses to maturity, it does not behoove the Church to appear to reserve herself to the privileged classes, no more than she had the right to reserve herself to the nobility when the middle classes were approaching their own emancipation. If the economic organization can adapt itself to the masses, if social frameworks can take into account the coming to adult status of the workers, it must not happen that a delay in the religious and spiritual order should cause these human riches to be lost to Christ. Either this coming to age of the masses will remain part of an atheistic system — as is the case with Communism — or the Church, become all things to all men, will take unto herself these magnificent resources, this ample material for sanctification. If we are there, the growth which today affects "mankind" will reveal the internal power of Christianity; if we miss, all of mankind as it grows will pass over our heads, for centuries to come.

Actually, and almost of necessity, even the "presentation" of unchanging Christianity is partially linked to the economic and social structures of the age: this is an unconscious assimilation. But we must be able to withdraw therefrom at the very moment social and economic structures are transformed. Since the Middle Ages the history of the idea of sanctification demonstrates especially well the direction in which we must orient ourselves.

SANCTITY PRESENTED TO ALL

The Middle Ages seem to *reserve* sanctification — or the fullness of Christian life — to convents and to regular clerks. To become holy one leaves the "world," one shelters oneself from vulgarity and ignorance and consecrates oneself to God: perfection is quite definitely identified with the state of religion. The secular clergy, which by definition lives in the world, is, in principle, in a perilous situation: it can hardly be holy, and heaven is praised when it is simply moral.

This mentality leads to a certain *clericalism*, about which very little has been said as yet: monastic clericalism. This ties sanctification to presence in a favored place, and does not even raise the question of holiness "in" the world and lay life. Moreover, it links the means of sanctification to presence in a place of recollection and prayer, and practically forgets that Christ also acts in an invisible way, outside places of worship, in every meritorious act. This mentality can be pinpointed in the reply that many Christians still make: "Oh, sanctity is for the monks!" A true statement, to a certain degree, but one which has the earmarks of the worst kind of pessimism.

St. Francis de Sales showed himself genial to the Renaissance: he baptized the fundamental principle of humanism. The Humanists had said: every man can develop in his own humanity; the Bishop of Geneva wrote: every man transfigured by grace can develop in this transfigured humanity. Thus he represents in ascetic thought what Erasmus and the Humanists signify for thought itself. In his *Introduction to the Devout Life*,[7] under the title: "devotion is suitable in every sort of vocation and profession," he writes these guideposts for Christian asceticism:

"It is an error, a heresy, to wish to ban the devout life from the company of soldiers, the workshops of artisans, the court of princes, the home of married people. It is true that purely contemplative, monastic, and religious devotion cannot be practiced in those vocations; but, besides these three kinds of devotion, there are many others which are proper for perfecting those who live in wordly states. . . . St. Joseph, Lydia, and St. Crispin were perfectly devout in their shops; St. Anne, St. Martha, St. Monica, Aquila, and Priscilla, in their homes; Cornelius, St. Sebastian, St. Maurice, in the Army; Constantine, Helen, St. Louis, Blessed Amé, and St. Edward, on their thrones. It has even happened that many have lost perfection in solitude — which is nevertheless so desirable for perfection — and have preserved it amid the crowds, which seem so little favorable to perfection."

Like the Humanists who speak of "man" while thinking concretely only of "humanists," St. Francis de Sales is sure that perfection is possible for every man *in every occupation*, but in fact he has in mind only the people of a certain social milieu: the ladies of the high society

[7] Book I, ch. 3.

of the period, personified by Mme. de Charmoisy. H.
Bordeaux, in presenting the *Introduction*, makes the
point:

"Originally written for Mme. de Charmoisy, the *Introduction* seems to envision, though on an enlarged scale,
one individual case. Mme. de Charmoisy loved her hus-
band and was loved by him; she was wealthy and did
not know want; she had a balanced spirit, without exaltation. Can the counsels given her be utilized by others?
To be sure, marriage is treated at length in the *Introduction*, but it is a marriage of love. Of course, there is
a consideration of the false sentiments in which our
hearts are wrongly entangled, but these are all sad passions, puppy-loves and friendships, and not those passions which tend to carry the soul away like a bit of
straw on the sea. To be sure, there is question of serving
the poor, but not of bearing with poverty oneself, when
one must hide it from all eyes like a stain."[8]

In short, the *Introduction* was written by someone
who was actually thinking of a specific Philothea, a lady
of high society, of a cultivated and well-to-do family background, wealthy and unacquainted with want, of moderate passions, carefully educated and enjoying a great
deal of leisure.

Sanctification is possible only in the convents, said
the Middle Ages; it is possible in high society, people
thought in the sixteenth and seventeenth centuries. The
possibility of sanctifying oneself in the world will henceforth be admitted for ever larger groups of human
beings. After high society, it will be the bourgeoisie.
However, in this case, it will be noted that the fruitful
Salesian principle has not been thoroughly rethought.
The middle classes which envision perfection as a possibility are those which resemble somewhat the society
of yesteryear and are able to live somewhat in the fashion
of Philothea or Mme. de Charmoisy. But the industrialist,
the financier, the physician and the lawyer, the politician
and the economist have hardly learned how they could

[8] Ed. Nelson, pp. 8-9.

envision sanctification in and through *their professional and daily lives*. They also repeat that sanctification is not for them. And some of them, by their wishes, call for a new Francis de Sales.

And now the worker himself is becoming aware of his greatness as a man, of his potentialities, of his power; he aspires to grow, to develop, and to expand. He, too, will therefore have to learn that supernatural growth is possible for him, that the power and beauty of grace can flourish in him, and that, as a child of God, he can also hope for limitless development according to the extent of the gift granted by Christ. In addition, the preaching of a working-class layman's holiness is urgent and indispensable.

4. "MISSIONARY" APOSTOLATE

The vigorous mediation effort undertaken by the papacy and the hierarchy at the present time in the world, as well as the concern for bringing the working masses back to Christ, have put the spotlight on the missionary ideal, the zeal of the pioneers of Christianity. The term "missionary" is wielded like a symbol, a program, an appeal. It is addressed to the laity, who are told that while they are the Church taught, they are not the Church passive. It is addressed to priests, to remind them that in addition to a ministry of preservation, a work of "conquest" has been reserved for them by their duties of state: "the parish priest, ex officio, is bound to exercise the care of souls on behalf of *all* his parishioners" (c. 464).

THE MISSIONARY IDEAL

It is quite clear that if we hold to the accepted breakdown — and what reason would there be not to? — there is a "missionary" and a "stationary" clergy. The former has as its field of apostolate those regions that have not as yet been hierarchically organized, while the latter are sent into areas which already have the bene-

fit of regular ecclesiastical organization. From this point
of view, it is quite certain that the diocesan priest, by
hypothesis, is part of the "stationary" clergy and not the
"missionary" one. No one, I believe, would deny this.

How is it then, that some apply so assiduously to
the sedentary clergy the term which juridically must
characterize the missionaries?

The explanation is given that it is written in the
Gospels that the disciple of our Lord must, if he is a
good shepherd, abandon for a time the ninety-nine faithful and peaceable sheep, to go and look for the lost sheep
until he finds it; then, joyously, he will take it up on
his shoulders and bring it back to the fold. And there
shall be more joy over one sheep found again than for
the ninety-nine others. Of course, that is a parable, but
one may nevertheless conclude that the Lord desires
His own to have a very universal zeal.

As a matter of fact, it is said, the most diverse circumstances have brought it about that the diocesan
clergy, at least in the great cities, is no longer equal to
the task entrusted to it. The nucleus of practicing
Catholics already takes up almost all of the priest's time.
He spends it saying Mass, administering the sacraments,
giving catechism lessons, counseling parish groups, visiting the sick, etc. Those Catholics the priest does not
meet in these circumstances, he can know, at best, only
by sight — whence disaffection, estrangement, forgetfulness, ignorance, indifference. Add to this the influence of the secular press, the weaknesses of the baptized, the deficiencies of the clergy itself, and it is un-
derstandable that sheep leave the fold, stray away, and
are lost. And it has even been noted that the baptized
in our own lands can become less religious than the
pagans in mission countries, who always retain in their
hearts a kind of fear of divinity, which is closer to religious sentiment than the rationalism and indifference
of our civilized people.

To remind priests of the scope of their apostolic task,
the word "missionary" has been used. This means that

the apostolate of the diocesan priest must be universal and not limited. He must aim to bring into the fold all the baptized, not just a few. He must regain for Christ the lost sheep, and not merely hold on timidly to those who have not strayed. If necessary he must use missionary techniques in so-called Christian countries, where the baptized are sometimes in a condition worse than that of natives in mission lands. We have to take an interest in all our sheep, to conquer or to protect them as the case may be, and use whatever methods are necessary according to the situation.

It is nothing more, after all, than acting as would a good father of a family. Such a man is interested in all of his children and treats each one according to his own temperament and needs. If one of the children leaves the paternal house, will not the love of that father become conquering, missionary? Will he not try to approach the child in ways which would not make sense for the children who have remained at home? This father is, therefore, universal in his affections. He is a preserver or a conqueror depending on whether his children are faithful or not. In this way, he conducts himself as a good family man.

What is more, if several of his children had defected, the father of the family would spend much more time looking for them than in conversing with those who have remained at home. And it is certain that he would urgently invite the latter to help him bring their brothers back home. Thus, the diocesan priest will spend much of his time bringing the strayed ones back, and will even invite the best among the faithful to this task of "conquest." The popes insist on the collaboration of the laity in the work of the hierarchy. And their insistence is readily understood when we think of what a good father would do. And is not every diocesan priest the father of the community over which he presides?

Is this not what St. Paul expected of the episcopes and presbyters he placed at the head of the Christian communities he had just created? Before leaving, con-

cerned for the future of the faithful who had heard the
word of the Spirit, he would confide to them the care
of the new-born Christian community; this required
growth as well as its preservation, the care of the hesitant as well as solicitude for the convinced, the conquest
of those not yet baptized as well as the service of the
Last Supper for those who have received the baptismal
purification and the laying on of hands.

THE MISSIONARY SPIRIT

One cannot guarantee that all diocesan priests have
this spirit. And those who do have it often find it practically impossible to put their desires into execution:
there is not enough time, no matter what they do. What
then? Perhaps the example of the father of the family would help us once more. If the father and mother
stay at home with a child, while several older brothers
have decided to leave, no doubt the father will say to
his wife someday: "You take care of this one, get help
if necessary from competent and devoted people; in the
meantime, I will take the necessary steps to bring back
the others. Afterward, when we are all reunited, we will
resume our quiet life at home." Likewise, perhaps, it
would be good to specialize the tasks of the clergy, because educating a faithful soul supernaturally and seeking out a strayed sheep imply quite different talents,
efforts, and procedures. Perhaps the work of perfecting the faithful could be entrusted more particularly
to certain priests, and others could be prepared to bring
the unfaithful back to the fold. When the baptized have
all returned, then all priests can joyfully and serenely
resume the normal community life.

The idea of specializing diocesan priests for certain
tasks and for a certain time is far from new. What are
the clerical teachers in our schools if not priests trained
for a teaching magisterium linked to humanism and
education? What are military chaplains except diocesan
priests to whom a group of the baptized has been en-

trusted? There is specialization of personnel and of tasks, and even a specialization of rites — in each new edition of the Roman Ritual, new sacramentals for new aspects of life, manifest the authentic will of the Church to retain at all costs her cultual universality and to lose sight of no temporal reality.

Here again, the lesson taught to priests by the history of the Church is an important one. The future will tell how well they learn it.

CHAPTER FOURTEEN

SANCTITY AND THE DIOCESAN APOSTOLATE

Spiritual works strongly insist on the difference between perfection itself and the means of perfection, or the spiritual systems which favor it. We should now like to trace the outlines of the ideal of sanctity proper to the diocesan clergy, first in itself, then in its relation to the means and state of perfection.

1. THE DIOCESAN PRIEST'S IDEAL OF SANCTITY

The ideal of sanctity proper to the diocesan clergy involves the fervent, even heroic, execution of all that his spirituality requires: "mixed" or apostolic life, the qualities of a diocesan priest, a healthy modernity. Add to that the personal vocation, that is, the very concrete form of apostolic life that Providence expects of each man in view of the natural gifts It has distributed to him and the role which the bishop has reserved for him in the diocese.

Sanctity involves each of these four elements. A priest who does not live a "mixed" life to any appreciable degree will never be a diocesan priest such as the Apostles intended. A priest who lacks the profound desire to be a "shepherd" as described above, will never be a perfect diocesan priest. A priest who would disdain the doctrinal and psychological requirements of a healthy modernity would not be "perfect." And a priest who could not manage to group all these values within the framework of his own natural gifts and the concrete attributions given him by his superiors — in the sense indicated in the section devoted to the *mission* — would not be living the diocesan pastorate to the full.

It would therefore be inexact to state that the sanctity of the apostolic life of the diocesan priest is summed up in perfectly carrying out the *duties of his state,* if by duties of state we understand the actual and personal professional activities, distinct from the spirit that must animate them. It would be equally inaccurate to affirm that the perfection of the diocesan priesthood consists in theological charity, unless one includes therein the perfection of the action which translates temporally, presently, and personally, the inner movement of the loving soul toward Christ.

SACERDOTAL PERFECTION

A being is perfect, *per-fectum,* when it corresponds exactly to what God expects of it, when it fully carries out the design formed by Providence for it. The work of perfection is not comparable to a long journey during which every step will bring us closer to the goal to be reached: man must respond perfectly at every moment to the will of God for him and also "reach the goal," coincide with his End, "fulfill himself." Thus, to be perfect, for us, is to be wholly "diocesan priests."

This perfection is therefore, by nature, unquestionably quite complex. Every man represents a bundle of values all of which must find their perfect fulfillment in him. Every man possesses a body, an intellect, a will, a heart, a temporal function, and, presumably, the state of grace: sanctity implies that each of these powers is to be led to its fullest development.

IN ACTIVITIES

This work of perfection will bear, first of all, on the "matter" of the apostolate, that is, on the activities of religious mediation — the communication of life and truth, the direction of the Christian people — whose continuous improvement must be assured.

These activities can be, always, more intense, better regulated, better prepared, more perfectly carried out, more precisely understood, more beautiful and more permeated with supernatural meaning, more numerous or more judiciously chosen. The communication of life calls for constant progress in the preparation for the sacraments and in their administration, a better understanding of the rites, more attention with regard to the ministry of worship, more interest in its fruitfulness, more religious sense in its performance. The communication of the truth always implies more perfection in preaching, more care in diction and delivery, more polish in the preparation, a more supernatural atmosphere in the transmitting of the word of God, a continuous knowledge of contemporary thought, a more intimate perception of the doctrinal and moral deficiencies of the faithful. Finally, the direction of the Christian people demands greater breadth of overall vision, more reflectiveness and realism in the examination of concrete situations, more imagination and boldness in apostolic enterprises, greater wisdom in the organization of the Christian community, more perseverance in initiative, more paternal goodness in personal contacts.

All this must be done without forgetting that these efforts must be stamped with a *healthy up-to-date quality*. We will concern ourselves with those sacred activities best suited for returning to worldly values their Christian significance. We will make an effort to give more help to the less cultured faithful in associating themselves with the Eucharistic Sacrifice and the sacraments. We will readily recall the doctrinal themes which express God's sway over the whole earth, and especially the universal Kingship of Christ, the universal fruitfulness of the Gospel. We will always try more and more to adapt the preaching to the people; the latter will be taught the art of becoming holy. In the direction of souls, we will root out in particular the latent dualism between conscience and life. Finally, we shall intensify the sense of conquest and multiply those activities which can benefit the latter.

This enumeration should be extended at length in order to make it an ideal picture of all that is involved in a perfect conception of apostolic activities. Too often, we are content with good will without imagination, and that man is called "excellent" who does not work excellently in the Lord's field. To be prepared to become perfect is not enough: one must have before one's eyes and appropriate to oneself in actual fact the concrete marks of improvement. The fullest possible description of all the desired or desirable forms of progress would constitute a work of utmost importance for the spiritual advancement of the diocesan clergy.

At any rate, the possibilities of perfection are, in this area, ultimately limited. First of all, because they concern the visible and earthly occupations to which a priest can only devote a certain number of hours per day; then, because every priest finds himself inevitably limited by his talents, his capacities, his person itself. Though it cannot be minimized, progress in this area is subject to the laws of quantity, of space, and of time.

IN THE THEOLOGICAL SPIRIT

It is different with those advances which can develop the other component of the apostolate, its "spirit." This time, we are in the domain of quality, we go beyond the limitations of time and space, we move constantly forward into the immense depths of the divine charity. Nothing can stop spiritual improvement.

Faith can be ever more intense, more profound in its intuitions and broader in its vision of the Christian mystery. Hope can be ever more expectant, more rooted in God and more fixed in our hearts, more sure and more decisive, younger and more vibrant, more dynamic and more audacious. Charity, finally, can be stronger, more total, more universal, and more intense, better ordered and better expressed, more theocentric without forgetting man, purer and more transcendant. The whole domain of the inner life of the priest is in question here, with its most refined forms and its most subtly different phases. A description of this life should bear not only on the apostolic theological life at the beginning of its development in the young cleric entering the royal path of the Lord; it should also translate the rich experience of those who have traveled the various stages of the spiritual life, in order that those who are still on the way might better know the direction, the obstacles, the helps, the goal.

IN HIS PERSONAL VOCATION

For all, there will remain a very personal task to be done; for every priest has a special vocation that God has made known to him both through his natural talents and through the ministry which the bishop entrusts him. God does not ask philosophers to have muscles as highly developed as those of athletes; He does not require the Poor Clare to acquire the erudition of a professor of comparative history of literature or of religions: their personal vocation does not demand this. This vocation, let us point out to avoid confusion, does not replace the man; it does not prevent him from developing his body, his intellect, his will and his heart; but it does fix and determine how man's constituent elements may find, together and in harmony, not the individual perfection of their nature taken separately, but their concrete perfection in the whole man. This is why the diocesan priest also should develop himself physically, intellectually, supernaturally, according to the needs of his earthly vocation; he should develop his body, nourish his spirit, strengthen his will, enrich his memory, activate his interior charity and intensify his hope, according to the concrete indications given him by the imperatives of his own nature and of the mission he must fulfill here below.

The ideal common to every diocesan priest will therefore find in each one an original realization, in view of his natural vocation and his individual function in the world. Regarding the apostolic perfection proper to each priest one may write, *mutatis mutandis,* what has been said of Humanism:

"Every Christian can tend toward a certain personal realization of Humanism. Of all, a *minimum* of human development is even required so that they can be fully men and Christians. Nevertheless, Humanism is indispensable to the Church as such, and the concrete participation of her members will necessarily be quite diverse depending on the states of life proper to each of them. Functions and tasks are manifold in the body of Christ. And the degree of human development and culture will also be profoundly varied. The priest, the Carmelite nun, the physician, or the worker will not achieve it identically. In no case will the Christian be able to think that he is dispensed from making his natural faculties, under the grace of the Spirit and a most intense faithfulness to His impulses, deliver what God has a right to see them give. If He has permitted and raised up saints less balanced, humanly speaking, than others in whom genius and sanctity were combined, that is a matter of predestination. It is up to each soul to be faithful to its calling and to seek its own human perfection in the way God asks of it. The circumstances in which it will find itself will indicate this."[1]

IN THE MOTIVE

Let us add, for the sake of completeness, that the motive which calls forth and justifies this effort at progress must itself also be essentially apostolic. The profound reason which leads us to undertake the road which ascends to the Carmel is the mission entrusted to us by the Lord. This is the ministry of the altar, obviously,

[1] R. Robert, O.P., "Principes théologiques de l'humanisme chrétien," in *Orientations,* February 1939, pp. 367-368.

since the priest happens to be the sacrificer of the New
Law; also, let us repeat one last time the words which
St. Thomas has written on this subject: "through holy
orders a man is assigned to the most holy mysteries . . .
for which greater interior sanctity is required than even
the religious state demands." There is the ministry of
souls, too; the "cura animarum" which requires pastoral
charity akin to that which constitutes the bishop in a
state of perfection superior to that of the religious as
such. Thus there is a twofold basis, essentially apostolic.

And this is a basis more exacting than that which the
commitment to the religious life entails. In the order of
religious mediation that may be entrusted to mankind,
nothing surpasses the honor of becoming the minister
of the unique sacrifice, the eternal and perfect sacrifice
of the New Covenant; and nothing can, of itself, call
for more ardent inner dispositions than the fact of
being chosen as priest of the sacrifice. On the other hand,
in the realm of charity, nothing surpasses the way of life
of him who gives himself entirely, talents and life, for
the spiritual good of men: "Greater love than this no
man has, that a man lays down his life for his friend,"
and nothing, therefore, can arouse us to greater fervor
than the fact of having been called to collaborate directly in the redemption of the world. Whether one considers the work of the diocesan priest as relating to
the Eucharistic Body of the Lord, or whether one envi-
sions his activity as on behalf of the Mystical Body of
Christ, the need for sanctity in both instances appears
to be maximal . . . at least if the *sancta sancte tractare*
and the *sanctissima sanctissime tractare* have any meaning.

The diocesan apostolate is therefore our basis for
the search for perfection. This consideration is very
strongly evident in *Vie Intérieure* by Cardinal Mercier:
"The regular priest, like the 'secular' priests, draws
from his priesthood, from the sublimity of the functions
to which the priestly character assigns the one who receives them, from the ministry of the souls with which

his bishop or the Supreme Pontiff associates him, the highest reasons for his obligation to be holy. Both before and after his monastic profession, the priest who becomes a religious must always look to his priesthood for the most profound and most decisive motive for his call to religion and to sanctity."[2] Certainly, no one will claim anything different nowadays; but it was proper to reaffirm it clearly, particularly for the benefit of the faithful.

APOSTOLATE AND MEANS OF PERFECTION

We said above that the apostolic activities of the diocesan priest — his duties of state — could be an excellent source of perfection and sanctity, provided they are animated by the apostolic spirit, by redemptive theological charity. And, we added, to guarantee the genuineness of these activities, that the priest must draw from the treasury of general and traditional means of perfection which the Church offers to all her children. The faithful only make use of one or another of these means, according to their own tastes and to their generosity. On the other hand, the religious have methodically organized their use of these means to their own advantage, thus forming a true system of means of perfection, a system authentically recognized by the Church, a system which places them in a canonical "state" of perfection.

This being the case, certain ascetical writers have simply proposed that diocesan priests take up for their own good the *religious life* in its entirety or only in part. They juxtapose the religious and the pastoral life and seem to link apostolic perfection to this condition.

There has been strong reaction to this position. Fearful that the search for perfection through appropriating the religious life might get the diocesan priest out of the habit of seeking and finding in his apostolate itself the means of increasing his pastoral charity and sanc-

<hr/>

[2] *Op. cit.*, pp. 197-198.

tity, some authors reject all that constitutes the spiritual regime of the religious — including, even, at times the means of sanctification which the Church places at the disposal of all the faithful — and wish to find diocesan perfection only in those occupations which specifically arise from the ministry: sacraments, Breviary, preaching, direction of souls. The diocesan priest, they explain, must find his sanctification solely in his duties of state, that is, "in" and "through" the apostolate; sanctity is not to be sought elsewhere than in the punctual fulfillment of one's duties of state.

This reaction, far too vigorous in some, had some fortunate consequences. Diocesan priests saw more clearly that their "professional" occupations must be their means of perfection; they reminded themselves that they must find God in the course of sometimes painful counseling, during occasionally fatiguing catechism classes, when they are supervising the parish groups, etc.

However, one cannot forget that all the means brought to bear by the religious to sanctify themselves are not means which necessarily belong exclusively to the religious life. Religious meditate regularly: is this a reason for us to refrain from doing so? Some of them make a special practice of mortification: is this a reason for neglecting it? They live according to the evangelical counsels: must we therefore lose interest in the counsels ourselves? They sanction their gift of self by vows: is this sufficient reason for us to be opposed to every form of vow?

That would be to act in a rather puerile fashion, all the more so as these means are, after all, offered by the Church to *all* the faithful without distinction, to the simple baptized person as well as to the religious. If they are found applied especially in religious life, it is not because they belong exclusively to the "regulars," but quite simply because the latter have chosen certain means and have organized and grouped them into a stable and public formula. Per se, nothing prevents the diocesan priest, therefore, from employing them in turn. In so doing, he will not be taking anything from the religious life as such — he will be using means which are offered by the Church to *all*. It should even be pointed out to diocesan priests that they have an even stricter obligation to have recourse to these means because of the fact that it is more urgent for them to guarantee the genuineness of their apostolic activity.

Besides, these distinctions found a striking argument in the creation in 1947 of the secular institutes. These institutes, a new state of perfection in the Church, include the same general and traditional means of perfection as do the religious orders, such as meditation, the evangelical counsels, etc. And yet they are radically different from the latter because of their "secular" nature, in which is found "their whole reason for existence and which must appear in everything," according to the Motu Proprio *Primo Feliciter*. In this case, the "apostolic" life has become the decisive and adequate norm of the organization of these means of perfection. In the same way, diocesan priests will, even without being part of a secular institute, be able to form by and for themselves, a "grouping" of means of perfection chosen with regard for the nature of their concrete apostolic task.

But the more a priest wishes to appropriate certain general means of perfection, the more he will need to remind himself that the latter remain varied, subsidiary, and free. The *unity of the clergy* is basically rooted in the common spirit of pastoral charity: this virtue must continue to be for all priests the primary factor of unity and fraternity. Recourse to the counsels, to vows, to mental prayer, to certain penitential practices, far from causing divisions or shocks in the clergy, should intensify pastoral charity and thereby cause an increase in unity in the great sacerdotal family. When he undertakes certain means of perfection, the priest will recall that sanctity is measured solely by the fervor of his charity toward God and his neighbor, regardless of the nature, the number, and the form of the means he uses to achieve it.

2. SANCTITY, COUNSELS AND VOWS

The religious life, theologians write, is an excellent means of perfection, but is not identical with sanctity: "The perfection of charity is itself the end of the religious state; but the state of religion is a certain discipline or exercise for achieving perfection" (IIa IIae, q. 186, a. 2, c.). Acknowledging this evidence, it is easy for us to repeat, after so many others, that sanctity is not identical with the counsels, or with the vows, but that it does find in these "means" an excellent source of help.

SANCTITY AND COUNSELS

Sanctity consists in being in perfect harmony with God, in loving nothing more than Him, despite Him, or as much as Him (IIa IIae, q. 184, a. 3, ad 3m): this is charity. It is the object of a precept: every man is obliged to love God with his whole heart, with his whole soul, and with all his strength. The perfection of charity does not automatically fall directly under the precept, but each man is bound to exercise an adequate minimum of authentic "charity." Additional explanations on this score can be found in the standard authors.

The counsels are means or instruments of sanctity: this is the most certain and the most traditional teaching of theology. "Some authors have concluded that Christian life consists in the observance of the precepts, and perfection in the observance of the counsels," writes Tanquerey. "That is a rather simplistic view which, if taken amiss, could lead to dangerous consequences. In reality, sanctity demands first of all the fulfillment of the precepts, and secondarily, the observance of a certain number of counsels. This, indeed, is the teaching of St. Thomas."[3] The latter writes: "Among the precepts, there are some which are principal, and rank as ends with respect to the other precepts and to the counsels: these are the precepts pertaining to charity. The

---

[3] *Précis de théologie ascétique et mystique*, no. 336.

counsels are ordered to them; not that they cannot be observed without practicing the counsels, but in the sense that they are means of guaranteeing their more perfect observance" (IIa IIae, q. 189, a. 1, ad 5m). And Suarez, three centuries later, noted in his turn that: "the counsels and their observance do not contain formal perfection, but are instruments for acquiring the latter; *it is possible to find perfection without them; and therefore it is also possible to have without them a state which requires a perfect man and demands perfect works:* this pertains to the state of exercising perfection."[4] This last statement is extremely important for the diocesan clergy.

What, therefore, is the precise place of the counsels in the economy of Christian sanctity, especially in relation to precepts? The Angelic Doctor replies: "it is necessary therefore that the precepts of the New Law be understood to have been given concerning those things which are necessary to attain the end of eternal beatitude, to which the New Law is an immediate introduction; but the counsels should be understood to be about those things by which man can attain the above-mentioned goal *better* and more expeditiously" (Ia IIae, q. 108, a. 4, c.). Therefore, it in no way diminishes the grandeur of the counsels to repeat that they do not contain perfection, but that they are excellent instruments in the hands of whoever aspires to self-improvement. "Perfection is found principally in the love of God," concludes Fr. Garrigou-Lagrange, using St. Thomas' own terms, "and secondarily in the love of neighbor; these are the objects of the main precepts of the divine law; it exists only accidentally in the means or instruments of perfection which are indicated to us by the evangelical counsels."[5]

Whence it flows, first of all, that the counsels are not the *only* means of perfection. In replying to the question: "Are all religious bound to observe the coun-

---

[4] *De statu religionis,* bk. 1, I, c. xv, in *Opera,* vol. xv; cf. *Vie intérieure,* pp. 199-200.

[5] *Op. cit.,* vol. 1, p. 163.

sels?" St. Thomas notes, judiciously, that there are numerous instruments of perfection: "some things pertain to perfection instrumentally and by way of a disposition, as poverty and continence and abstinence and *other things of this type*" (IIa IIae, q. 186, a. 2, c.). The bishop, for example, is in a state of perfection without officially committing himself to all the counsels, but rather to the full exercise of pastoral charity. And the saints who lived in the married state arrived at a perfect charity without the help of the vow of continence.

Moreover, among the different instruments of perfection, the counsels are not necessarily *the best*. This is clear from the fact that the theologians who compare the state of perfection of religious to that of the bishop conclude that the latter is objectively superior because it is based on pastoral charity and the work of the redemption of men: "In the category of perfection however the bishops are considered as perfectors, religious as the perfected. . . . Whence it is clear that the state of perfection is greater in the bishops than in the religious" (IIa IIae, q. 184, a. 7, c.)."

On the other hand, the principle itself of the counsels is universal. All those who want to follow Christ to the end owe it to themselves to adopt them at least in spirit. "Let him who can understand, understand," is not addressed only to religious; clerics, faithful laymen, have understood and accepted the full message of the Lord. Holy laymen have unquestionably practiced the counsels — except, sometimes, that of virginity — without being part of any religious community, without being in a canonical "state" of perfection. Diocesan priests and canonized bishops have found the perfection of charity in the private practice of the counsels, particularly of those which were required by the life of perfect pastoral charity.

DIOCESAN PRIESTS AND COUNSELS

And this brings us back to the diocesan priest. To what extent does he practice the evangelical counsels?

Of course, at least in the West, he observes the counsel of continence; this is what led St. Thomas to the conclusion, as we shall see later, that the diocesan priest possesses something of what constitutes the religious in a "state" of perfection. Also, by virtue of his ordination and of jurisdiction, he also practices obedience. Of course, it is not, in theory, the obedience of the religious. It might even be demonstrated that religious obedience has a different significance than the subjection of the diocesan priest with respect to his bishop, but that would lead us too far afield. And finally, the matter of the counsel of obedience varies greatly in the different religious congregations. The same is true of poverty. "The vow of poverty has greater or less scope, and imposes obligations that are more or less strict according to the diversity of the religious orders. And it is not always a matter of greater or less fervor which sets up these differences; they may be called for by a difference in goals, in ministries, etc. . . ."[6]

One would like to stress that last line, for it explains the attitude of the diocesan priest and sheds light on the spirit which animates his search for sanctity. For, in his case, the best and the prime means of perfection is an entire and total participation in the pastoral charity of the bishop, a portion of whose ministry he receives as his share. Everything is subordinated to this charity, including the practice or nonpractice of the counsels, regardless of their nature. Accordingly, the diocesan priest can in no way be reproached for not accepting the counsels in a form which could perhaps hinder the normal development of diocesan pastoral charity: this would be a falsification of his perspectives.

But, having said that, it is well also to remind diocesan priests that since their apostolate demands a very high sanctity, they might and perhaps should at times ask themselves whether certain counsels whose practice harmonizes quite well with the conditions of their lives, should not be the object of their choice. In

[6] P. Cotel, *Catéchisme des voeux*, 1939, no. 43.

this sense, the counsels can be very well received in the life of the diocesan clergy.

SANCTITY AND VOWS

Whenever one speaks of the sanctification of the diocesan clergy, the question of vows is also often raised, as if a certain tendency to sanctity were indissolubly tied to the pronouncing of vows, and more particularly the vows of religion; for it is of these that one thinks, concretely. Is this really the case? Or must we repeat that the vows are not "sanctity" and that, on the other hand, they are not the exclusive property of religious life?

The vows are not "sanctity." A promise made to God of something possible and better, the vow does not guarantee the practice of every virtue through the intermediary of some sacred mechanism. Man can be unfaithful to a vow as easily as to the virtue which embellishes it, he can be deficient in religious fidelity as well as to the other obligations of his profession. The facts exist to demonstrate this. Some persons remain imperfect, even though they have made vows of religion. Certain laymen make a temporary vow of chastity, for example, only in order to manage not to violate the major precepts: this is still not sanctity.

On the other hand, the vow is not a good reserved properly and exclusively to the religious. In this sense, Tanquerey's *Précis de théologie ascétique et mystique* could be quite misleading if one can believe the index of the work, vows are only discussed in terms of religious, under nos. 367-372. But the economy of the vows embraces more than that. *All* the faithful — lay, religious or clerical — recognize full well that they will not be able to perfect themselves or be sanctified in the duties of their state without calling on certain means which will enable them to guarantee the vigor and fervor of their daily activity.

To respond to these needs, the Church proposes to *all* various means such as meditation, mortification, seclusion, if only temporarily, and also the vows. The latter can certainly be conceived of as special acts of religion. But, from our point of view, they mean more than that. A person may judge that the recitation of the rosary is very useful to him, because this exercise of piety gives his life a certain religious atmosphere: in this case, no one will find it unusual to see this person make a vow to recite his rosary every day. Why this vow? To assure in a more firm and stable manner the religious practice whose blessings for his life he so clearly appreciates. When the religious desires to grow in charity, and, to this end, practices the counsels of poverty, obedience, and chastity, what is he doing except to guarantee his decision by the pronouncing of vows pertaining to this threefold objective? So, too, the diocesan priest may judge that this or that particular means of perfection is indispensable to him to ensure the intensity of his pastoral charity; why could he not also guarantee the stability of these means by taking vows?

DIOCESAN PRIESTS AND VOWS

If the matter is so simple, then, whence comes the fact that the question of vows is truly a source of difficulty and of conflict among authors interested in the spirituality of the clergy? The answer seems to be this: as a matter of fact, many people confuse the principle of the vow with an application of this principle such as is made in the organization of the religious life. As soon as there is question of "vows" for the diocesan priest, the image of the "regular" life seems to arise. One can, therefore, understand the objection formulated by many priests: the sacramental priesthood, they say, must fully suffice, since the requirements that flow from it are greater than those which derive from mere vows: *major sanctitas*. What would one want with vows! The solemnity of the ordination to the priesthood is certainly equivalent to that of the pronouncing of vows. The psychological influence of the ceremonies surrounding the transmitting of the priesthood is surely equal to that left in the soul by the gift of the vows. The religious meaning of ordination is every bit as authentic as that deriving from the vows.

All of this must of course be readily conceded, though it must be regretted that the profound value of the priesthood is not put into greater relief for us as well as sometimes for the religious. Among the latter, there are many who claim even today that the obligation of gradual improvement comes to them primarily from the vows, and secondarily, in a subsidiary manner, from their priesthood. What can be expected of those who, in this frame of mind, come to preach retreats to priests who will never be anything "but" priests, without making any vows? Is there not something to be corrected there, both in the regulars and the seculars?

But the objection itself, which we formulated above, derives from the undeserved identification which is made between "vows" and "the vows" of the religious. There is, it would seem, a more precise way of considering the relationships which exist between the diocesan priesthood and the vows. For the priesthood demands a high degree of charity, chastity, obedience, temperance, poverty and of other virtues as well. What reason would there be to prevent certain priests from stabilizing by vow a certain manner of obedience, poverty, chastity or even of other virtues, just as certain religious commit themselves to three or four vows whose matter is spelled out in their Rules?

Religious, it has been written, from the point of view of the vows only, are like baptized persons who, aware of the fundamental obligations of their Baptism, wish to use all the means at their disposal to lead their lives and their Christian ideal perfectly. Their vows, signs of total submission to the Lord, arrange themselves harmoniously around their baptismal regeneration which thereby acquires a very special luster and value.[7] In this sense, religious face two demands for perfection: one, basic and primordial, has been deposited

[7] Cf. G. Morin, O.S.B., *L'idéal monastique*, Maredsous, 1944, pp. 92 ff.

in them by the sacrament of Baptism, and the other, secondary and in the order of means, derives from their religious profession. This dualism, quite relative, indeed does not seem to confuse matters: it seems to be neither irreducible nor disadvantageous. Religious, it is said in substance, are, from the point of view of the vows, baptized persons who wish to live in the fullest measure the ideal of their regeneration: this is the unity of their lives.

Could we not argue similarly for priests, the "ordained"? Could they not guarantee the complete development of their apostolic priesthood by the practice of virtues whose matter would become that of a corresponding vow? These vows would range themselves around the priestly life; they would become richer because of its finality, they would be molded along the lines of the requirements of its practice, and would be limited to its domain. These vows, therefore, would not be introducing artificially some part of religious life into that of the diocesan priest, as if the obligations of the priesthood were insufficient, any more than the vows taken by religious harm the fundamental consecration of themselves which is included in their Baptism. They would not be establishing in us a kind of dualism, "vows of religion" being superimposed on sacerdotal obligations, since they would simply be stabilizing these obligations themselves and conferring on them a new value. They would not suspend the priest between the tendencies to the apostolate and to personal sanctification, since they would be designed to give value to the apostolate itself, so that it might, in fact, be carried out supernaturally and therefore be sanctifying.

Of course, priests are tempted to make vows in those *same matters* which have always been the privilege of the religious: chastity, obedience, poverty. Nor are the reasons for acting in this way hard to find: these matters are recognized by the whole tradition of the Church, as particularly important and "synthesizing." But this material identity should not lead us to the conclusion that the meaning of the "apostolic" vows is the same as that of the vows of "religion"; on the contrary, they differ as to their end, their object, their limits. If until now, only the vows of "religion" constitute a stable formula, canonically recorded and commonly received in the Church, there is nothing to prevent some "apostolic" vows from someday constituting another stable formula, authentically accepted by the Church, entirely original because fully adapted to the diocesan priesthood. When that day comes, there would be in the Church two great forms of vows, and two collective applications of the general principle which consists in "vowing" to God certain better and possible actions.

On this point, the situation has been greatly clarified by the creation in 1947 of the secular institutes. These institutes propose and impose on their members certain "commitments" aimed at "secular and apostolic" sanctity, which are just as demanding as the traditional vows of religion. Here, then, is the very principle of the vow being implemented according to a new and specifically apostolic formula. Diocesan priests may profit greatly from the spirit of the secular institutes to establish for themselves a group of means of perfection entirely adapted to their state of life, and without injecting a kind of dualism into their existence.

SEMINARIANS AND VOWS

We have attempted to show that vows, in themselves, are not a monopoly of the religious, that they are not identical with sanctity, and that they can very easily be used in the diocesan apostolate. However, it would not do for seminarians, after reading these pages, to want to move immediately into the practice stage.

Before coming to a final decision about anything at all in this domain, it is well to have gone beyond the time of generous but juvenile enthusiasms for everything that is beautiful and noble in itself. Of course, the Church herself imposes celibacy from the seminary on, thereby showing that she already presupposes a certain maturity in her clerics before they have been thrown into life. But, as regards poverty, obedience, or other vows, it seems that only a certain amount of *real contact with the ministry* can indicate concretely to each individual whether any decisions in this matter will be of any real use, any serious effectiveness, in his case.

In the meantime, those who have a reasoned and well-founded esteem for these means of perfection should concern themselves with developing the spirit thereof and living them psychologically; they will turn their attention to the austere practice of the virtues which correspond to the vows, as well as to the nobility of the counsels which are definitively stamped in the soul by the vows. And those who prefer to insure the fervor of their charity in other ways, will show, by their comprehensive attitude, that their spiritual life even though it does not involve vows, is no less effective. Thus, once more, unity will retain its primacy.

3. SANCTITY, MENTAL PRAYER AND PENANCE

From the lips of preachers one can garner syllogisms similar to this one: "apostolic perfection can only be the perfection of charity; but the perfection of charity is expressed in the highest form in contemplation. Therefore, apostolic perfection is attained above all in contemplation."

Witness this statement by Father Garrigou-Lagrange, concerning the errors relating to the essence of perfection:

"Some Christians might be led to say: perfection consists chiefly in *contemplation*, which derives from the gift of wisdom, and to prove it, they invoke St. Paul's words: 'In malice be children and in mind mature' (1 Cor. 14:20); 'Wisdom, however, we speak among those who are mature . . . the spiritual man judges all things . . . but we have the mind of Christ' (1 Cor. 2:6, 15, 16). Reading these inspired texts too naturally and too hastily, certain persons might perhaps think they could attain perfection rapidly by reading the great mystics, without concerning themselves enough

about practicing the virtues these authors recommend, and without being sufficiently mindful of the fact that true contemplation must be thoroughly saturated with supernatural charity and forgetfulness of self."[8]
We must, then, recall briefly the place of contemplation in the overall picture of the Christian life.

Examining the question closely, one discovers that neither the theologians nor the spiritual authors make contemplation the *absolute norm* of the acts which sanctify us. While restating that the work of Mary is, in itself, superior to that of Martha, they concede that it is sometimes better to leave "Rachel for Lia," that is, "the heights of the contemplation of God," in order to serve Him in one of His humblest faithful people. So, too, the Christian is judged according to the way in which he fulfills his duties of state, his professional, family, and civic obligations: and no one will believe in the sanctity of someone who would be negligent in this area, though he were to claim that he enjoyed an intense contemplative life. Those are some of the restrictions applied to the value of contemplation.

MYSTICISM AND SANCTITY

These limitations apply obviously to contemplation taken in the sense of the θεωρία of Hellenism, regardless of how religious it might be. This θεωρία, as a matter of fact, is a contemplative activity reserved to a few people privileged by nature, by which they manage to resemble the gods to a certain degree, thus guaranteeing immortality for themselves. A very high ideal, to be sure, but one which is neither religious, nor Christian. It is not religious but philosophical, explains Father Festugière, because it is the man himself who, contemplating the Idea by virtue of a moral and intellectual exercise, finally participates in Its eternity and divinity: it is man himself who becomes equal to the gods and saves himself. But in every religion, the gift of divine life is granted by God Himself, who thereby

[8] *Perfection chrétienne et contemplation*, vol. 1, p. 153.

descends toward men in order to raise them up to Him. The two paths are quite opposite.[9]

Nor is this ideal Christian: Father Festugière's excellent studies give us the reason here, too. Comparing the pagan mystique to the Christian mystique, he notes that the former tends entirely toward the knowledge of mysteries. To illustrate his statement, he tells the story of a Greek priest who, visiting the monk Olympios, asks him the characteristic question: "With this way of life, do you not obtain a vision from your God?" And, after a negative response from the Christian monk: "We, however, when we offer sacrifices to our god, find that he hides nothing from us but reveals his mysteries to us."[10] This anecdote, the author continues, brings to light the contrast between the Hellenic mystique and Christianity. On the one hand, the desire to know; on the other. . . . Permit us to quote once more:

"I am only offering here the simple testimony of an historian, but one whose rule has always been not to dissociate study from life. Now, upon contrasting in this way, with an experience, the Pauline texts on the one hand, and the mystical writings of the Greek religion on the other, it seems to me that the most truly distinctive trait of Christianity was indeed the one I just mentioned: in the face of religious movements whose primary and essential purpose is the mystical state, that is, 'the intuition of God present,' Christianity is distinguished by a different end, charity. To see God or, in some way to feel, to experience, God, is the goal of the 'carnal men' of Corinth, the Gnostics and theopaths of all sects, of the pagan host of the monks of Scete. But the spiritual Christian, according to St. Paul, sets an entirely different goal before himself: to work in cooperation with God, θεοῦ γάρ ἐσμεν συνεργοί (1 Cor. 3:9). The Christian revolution is summed up in this contrast."[11]

The antithesis is great, although one should not conclude that the synergy of Christ and the Christian includes no

9 *L'idéal religieux des grecs et l'Evangile*, Paris, 1932, pp. 40-41.
10 *L'enfant d'Agrigente*, Paris, 1941, p. 121.
11 *Op. cit.*, p. 124.

experience of God. But it is preferable, above all, to stress that the soul of Christianity is charity.

THEOLOGICAL LIFE AND SANCTITY

Does what holds for the θεωρία apply to the act of contemplation which is identical with the theological life? Can there be any act more perfect than that which puts us into conscious and formal contact with our final End and our absolute Good?

Yes and no. Every perfect apostolic act must, obviously, be ordered to our final end; otherwise, it would be neither sanctifying nor even honest. But the act of "contemplation," which in itself involves a direct ordering to God, could be carried out under such circumstances that it would lose this ordering and would only be an illusory act of charity. A human act, indeed, has three sources of morality: the purpose, the object and the circumstances — those well-known circumstances: "quis, quid, quando, quomodo, quibus auxiliis. . . ." And, while contemplation understood as exercise or prayer involves a direct ordering to God by reason of the object, *ratione objecti*, it may sometimes be entirely displaced *ratione circumstantiae*, by reason of the circumstances. The person who, from his or her sanctuary, would see a man drowning and would not abandon contemplation to bring help and attempt to save him would sin gravely, *ratione circumstantiae*, against charity. Likewise, the diocesan priest, who has chosen a life involving a number of external and social priestly activities, must at times abandon solitary meditation in order to go after souls or to conquer them. Nothing could be clearer.

It is also possible to prove in another way that it is sometimes necessary to abandon meditation or mental prayer to help people. At first glance, indeed, it would seem that the act of charity performed in mental prayer is perfectly self-sufficient and can be considered as an absolute. But for man, a corporal and social being inserted into spatio-temporal relationships, it is not possible to be ordered to the ultimate end without at the same time passing through a whole range of intermediary ends, and it is only in being ordered to these intermediate ends that one may consider himself ordered *also* to the final end: "there can be no proper relation of anything to its final end except through the intermediary of the end which depends on its own nature."

Here, too, an example will help us to understand. The purest act of charity by a Carmelite nun will find its temporal expression in this decision: "I shall stay in my convent." The purest act of charity by a missionary will find its temporal expression in this decision: "I am leaving my own country and going to pagan lands." Why these different decisions, whose origin is an identical act of charity, if not because this charity is truly complete only if it is accompanied by a visible and temporal transposition? In the diocesan priest, an act of charity nourished in meditation or mental prayer, in order to be true, demands that, at the moment when a person has urgent need of his spiritual assistance, the priest go to his flock and render the religious service expected of him: he is leaving Rachel for Lia, in order to grow in true charity.

In all the foregoing, it may have been noted that the contemplation one is abandoning for action is not the theological life — the spirit of the apostolate — but the *exercise* of mental prayer which is incumbent upon every priest who desires to preserve this spirit in the course of the day. It is not mental prayer-*spirit* that one may leave behind, but mental prayer-*exercise*. And this shows that the term contemplation, as used in the action-contemplation dichotomy, is ambiguous. When one speaks of leaving aside contemplation for action, one understands mental prayer-exercise, meditation preparatory to the apostolic life, the means. When one speaks of *contemplare et contemplata aliis tradere,* one means mental prayer-spirit, the integrating and constituent element of the apostolate: this element, to the extent possible, cannot be abandoned.

SANCTITY AND MORTIFICATION

Is it necessary, finally, to dissociate sanctity from the practice of penance? There can be no hesitation here. Of course, certain religious orders make a deep impression by the rigorous austerity of their lives, by their continuous and definitive privations. On the other hand, hagiographies take pleasure in stressing the numerous and difficult mortifications performed by the saints, even by those who are considered imitable: while not similar to the prowess of a Stylites, the mortifications of a St. Thérèse of the Child Jesus are no less extreme.

And there is certainly no question of eliminating mortifications and penances from the lives of the diocesan clergy: it would take a whole chapter to determine their indisputable supernatural effectiveness. Our only point here is to recall that their goal is to intensify charity. Is austerity really unifying, a sign and expression of love? It would seem so. When a mother devotes herself, wears herself out in caring for her child, is she not experiencing the most beautiful hours of maternal love? The act of charity pushed to the extreme always involves, at that level, physical or moral suffering. Devotion carried to its limit necessarily involves the pain of fecundity. The authentic witness generally terminates in a kind of martyrdom.

Also, *all heroism* in any vocation or profession whatsoever, necessarily flourishes in austerity and labor. Certain religious have organized a regimen of life which includes very specific forms of mortification, and it is wise to proceed in this way when a human collectivity is involved; but the best monks among them would unquestionably come to it by themselves, provided their fervor were maintained. So, too, a heroic mother, a heroic pastor, come to lead a truly loving, and therefore difficult, life.

However, the *manner* in which austerity is expressed differs according to the vocation of each person. The monk, in his life of charity, seeks a thousand and one ways of giving evidence to God of his ardent love, and he multiplies acts of reparation. The diocesan priest, in his apostolic life, at every moment meets persons and situations, difficulties and reverses, which are a very heavy cross. But since extraordinary monastic mortifications are often considered a mark of supreme generosity, and since there is perhaps not enough appreciation of the perpetual renunciation which affects the shepherd of souls in his simple and ordinary life, people often finally believe that the religious have a monopoly on austerity.

Now, as St. John Chrysostom explained, the virtue of the monk is very great and worthy of admiration: he mortifies himself completely by fasts, privations, harassing labors, vigils. Nevertheless, the perfection demanded of the priest can be just as real and just as complete, because of the fact that he is in far less favorable circumstances than the monk. Then, there follows a significant comparison:

"If one admires this manner of remaining in oneself and fleeing from association with people, I would also say that this is a proof of energy, not, however, an adequate testimony of the presence in the soul of all the virility of virtue. The man who is seated at the helm inside a harbor has not as yet given a very vigorous proof of his ability; but if he manages to save his ship on the open sea during a storm, no one will deny that he is an excellent captain. There is no need, therefore, for us to admire the monk too enthusiastically, because, remaining within himself, he is not troubled, nor does he commit many and grave sins: nothing arouses, nothing awakens his soul. But he who, thrown into the midst of the crowds and forced to put up with the sins of the people, could remain just as upright and firm in the storm as in the calm weather, that man would deserve to be applauded and admired, for he has furnished adequate proof of personal virtue."[12]

---

[12] *De sacerdotio*, VI, 5-7.

APOSTOLATE AND PENANCE

The example of Christ shows us clearly how one can find mortification and penance in the apostolate, how one can stamp his work with expiation and reparation. Reading the life of the Lord, and especially, following the phases of the public activity which was to lead Him finally to the tragic apotheosis — *hora mea* — one finds hardly any reference to means of expiation which since that time have been called extraordinary. And yet, who would dare deny that the suffering of Christ was immense: it is of Him that the author of the Epistle to the Hebrews wrote these mysterious and anguished words: "In the days of his earthly life, with a loud cry and tears [Jesus], offered up prayers and supplications to him who was able to save him from death" (5:7). And He found it essentially *in* His apostolate, or as we would say today, in the fulfilment of His mission. The "witness" He wished to give was delayed, rejected, misunderstood, fought against, until He who offered it was put to death. Incomprehension on the part of men, lack of understanding in the disciples, opposition of the priests and doctors, fury of the Sadducees, perfidy of the Sanhedrin, nothing was spared the Lord and "Apostle" of our faith (Heb. 3:1). Must we not expect, therefore, to see the disciple treated even more poorly than the Master? Is it not in their apostolic life that the true disciples of the Savior will find, above all, the suffering which expiates and makes reparation?

Need we recall the death of the deacon Stephen? The anguish of Peter and John? The trials of Paul? "In all things we suffer tribulation," he writes, "we are sore pressed, but we are not destitute; we endure persecution, but we are not forsaken; we are cast down, but we do not perish; always bearing about in our body the dying of Jesus, so that the life also of Jesus may be made manifest in our bodily frame" (2 Cor. 4:8-10). How often, in this Second Epistle to the Corinthians, the Apostle refers to this multitude of tribulations which beset him on every side, in the midst of which, however, he radiates joy. There is no need to press the point: ever since apostolic times and down to our own day, the glorious record of Christianity bears witness to this truth. And the Greek term for "witness" has become, accordingly, suitable for designated martyrdom: μάρτυς. Everywhere, expiatory suffering, expiatory death itself, is included in the exercise of the apostolate.

At least, this is so if the apostle is *like Christ* and like all those who have given Him a supreme testimony, or in other words, if he is ardent either in an intense inner life or with a truly Pauline zeal. If Christ had not borne a specific and clear witness, if Stephen had not spoken words which truly committed him, if the martyrs had been willing to betray a little that which had been intrusted to them in the domain of the truth or of life, they would not have suffered in the course of their ministry. And history, besides the glorious record, also reveals a rather sorry record of the line of mediocre, lazy, and opportunistic souls whose witness, under the guise of "common sense" and "prudence," lacks the vigor of authentic Christianity. They bear witness, but for themselves, or for other values. And the world, in whose eyes they are inoffensive, does not make them suffer either visibly or even hiddenly.

Nor is this empty theory: every zealous priest can testify to the contrary. Those who are truly "apostles," and therefore preoccupied with the reign of the Lord, desirous of saving men and of re-establishing the world in Christ, determined to defend the authentic evangelical truth, soon run into opposition, obstacles, difficulties, refusals, intrigues. They soon realize that they will find in their apostolic life, both preventive mortification and expiatory penance. For the devil, and the men he uses, come on stage without delay to destroy, undermine and end the work of grace. Concretely, it will be, for example, the way in which one is received by the Christians one is visiting, the ability of cultivated people to render one inoffensive, the obstacles raised by malevolent persons against young priests, inevitable misunderstanding among people; the constant need to reorganize one's time in terms of visits received at both opportune and inopportune times; the inconceivable egocentrism of visitors who think only of themselves; the hardening of hearts captured by impurity; the opacity of minds deformed by error or lies; unjust interpretations placed on our undertakings, etc. The more one is really an apostle, the more he will have experienced thousands of similar situations which bind him to the true pattern of the disciples of Jesus Christ. Those who are without suffering are often apostles in name only, for the apostolate presupposes an immense love, and love always changes into suffering.

4. SANCTITY AND STATE OF PERFECTION

Without wishing to, merely following a line of thought, one is finally brought back to an ancient dispute: perfection and state of perfection. It is in a very irenic spirit that we shall bring out a few phases of it here, since, nowadays, everyone is in agreement on the essential point: there are persons who are perfect in the eyes of God, without, however, being in a "state" of perfection; there are less perfect persons who are in a "state" of perfection.

In theory, the existence of various states of perfection is recognized, and particularly, that of the bishop and the religious. The state of perfection, explains St. Thomas, requires the perpetual obligation of binding oneself to all that pertains to perfection, and this, "with a certain solemnity." Now, these conditions are verified in the case of both the religious and bishops. The religious commit themselves by vow to abstain from certain secular values they were permitted to use, in order to attend more freely to the things of God; and the commitment they make is accompanied by the solemnity of the profession and the blessing. As to bishops, they likewise commit themselves to all that has to do with perfection when they assume the pastoral office, with the obligation of giving their life for their sheep; this profession is accompanied by a solemn consecration.[13]

DIOCESAN PRIEST AND STATE OF PERFECTION

Without wishing to provoke any discussion among canon lawyers, or to defend any thesis, one may point out that ordination constitutes the diocesan priest in a way of life which does bear some resemblance to a "state" of life. A state of perfection, we were saying, requires, in principle, that one obligate himself on a perpetual basis with respect to that which leads to perfection, and do so with a certain solemnity. The solemnity of ordination is incontrovertibly sufficient. The perpetual obligation of taking on that which leads to perfection also exists. Actually, in what does this consist in the bishop's case? St. Thomas replies: "Bishops obligate themselves to those things which pertain to perfection, taking on the pastoral office to which it pertains that the pastor gives his life for his sheep" (IIa IIae, q. 184, a. 5, c.). And he completes his thought a bit further on: "The perfection of the episcopal state consists in the fact that someone, out of divine love, obligates himself to that which pertains to the salvation of the neighbor. And therefore so long as he is obligated to that which has to do with pastoral care, so long is he able to profit the subjects under him unto salvation . . . which indeed he should not neglect either on account of the peace of divine contemplation . . . or again for the sake of avoiding any adverse thing or of acquiring wealth; because, as John says, the good shepherd lays down his life for his sheep" (IIa IIae, q. 185, a. 4). Would a layman not conversant with canonical definitions recognize in this description his own pastor as easily as his bishop?

It is said that the diocesan priest is not in a state of perfection because he does not have personal stability explicitly professed and visibly authenticated by the Church. The conferring of a pastorate or of an ecclesias-

---

[13] St. Thomas, *Summa Theologica*, IIa IIae, q. 184, a.5, c.

tical responsibility, explains St. Thomas in his commentary on St. Matthew, chapter 19, does not take on these characteristics. Also, "they can have perfection according to their acts, but not according to their state, because the state is conferred only with solemnity." Some have pointed out, however, that even here, the difference between bishops and priests is not absolute. Bishops, in certain countries, may change dioceses several times during their lives, so that the bonds which unite them to a diocese do not, in fact, seem much tighter than those which bind a pastor to his parish. On the contrary, pastors and curates are sometimes more "diocesan," if one may say so, than their bishop.[14]

Nowadays, the state of perfection represented by the religious life also involves the common life: "In any religious order the common life is to be carefully observed by all even in those things which pertain to food, clothing, and shelter" (C.J.C., c. 594). But it is a well-known fact that the state of religion admits of many exceptions, and that some religious can live away from their convents, even for several months of the year, without ceasing to be in a "state" of perfection.

Add to that the fact that the subdiaconate, to the extent that it is accompanied by a vow, permits the diocesan priest to verify in part what is required of him who lives in a state of perfection. St. Thomas writes: "Those who receive orders are not thereby obligated to those things which have to do with perfection except insofar as, in the Western Church, a vow of continence, which is one of the things which pertain to perfection, is pronounced in the reception of holy Orders" (IIa IIae, q. 184, a. 6, c.). And, for his part, the clear response of the new priest to the question: "Do you promise, to me and my successors, respect and obedience?" establishes him in a condition of life which requires on a permanent basis both respect and obedience, even though by reason of fidelity and not strictly by virtue of religion.

[14] Cf. Card. Mercier, *La vie intérieure*, pp. 194-195.

It is in consideration of all this, no doubt, that Suarez, the theologian par excellence of *De Religione,* has acknowledged for priests a certain *inchoative* "state of perfection": "I believe that priests, by virtue of their ordination, have a higher and more holy state which demands of them many works of perfection; because of this obligation they can be said to be in some way, at least inchoatively, in a state of perfection."[15]

And, more recently, Fr. M.-J. Nicolas wrote: "In reality, the condition of priests has changed considerably since St. Thomas' time. Since they are ordained in the name of their dioceses, it is difficult not to see in the bond which unites them to the bishop, whose co-workers they are, a link strong enough to constitute them in a state of life. . . . Perhaps, therefore, it is accurate to speak of the *state* of the diocesan priest, noting, however, that this state . . . finds its determining elements in the promise of obedience to the bishop, in the 'title of service of the diocese,' and in the vow of chastity."[16]

These things are mentioned not to wring an admission that the diocesan priest is also in a "state of perfection," but to warn those who are too rigid in opposing "those who are in a state of perfection" and "mere secular priests," to make proper distinctions.

STATE OF PERFECTION AND REQUIREMENT OF SANCTITY

From the fact that the diocesan priest is not in a canonical "state" of perfection, one should not draw conclusions which greatly exceed the premises.

First of all, to be in a state of perfection does not mean that one is held necessarily to greater sanctity than every person not constituted in that state. The diocesan priest, for example, finds in his sacred ministry a more imperious call to sanctity than that which is in-

[15] *De virtute et statu religionis,* bk. 1, chap. XVII, in *Opera,* vol. XV.
[16] "Sacerdoce diocésain et vie religieuse," in *Revue thomiste,* 1946, p. 181.

cluded in the religious life as such, and the state of perfection of the "regular" as such. The fact is, that the higher "state of perfection" and the higher basis of demand for sanctity, are two different things. To confuse the two would have the unfortunate result of minimizing both among the "regulars" as well as among the "seculars," the cult of their sacerdotal ministry and the intrinsic dignity of their redemptive work. It would be foolhardy to guarantee that such an equivocation does not exist in both groups now: among the "seculars," when they believe that perfection is the business of the "regulars"; among the "regulars," when they seek in their religious life strictly so-called, rather than in their priesthood, a basis for seeking perfection and spiritual progress.

Whence those passages in books of spirituality which we always read with a certain regret. Here is an example. In a book devoted to the manner of hearing confessions, Father Salsmans, S.J., invites the priest to help as follows a young man who is thinking about his future: "The spiritual director will first draw the young man's attention to the different states of life. To be logical, the choice must first of all be made between life in the world and the religious state: is he going to make to God the total offering of himself by means of the evangelical counsels, perhaps in far-off countries as a missionary, or is he going to remain in the world, either as a secular priest, or as a layman, single or married?"[17] Accordingly, we have this quite unexpected schema: religious state (missionary) — life in the world (priest or layman, married or single).

STATE OF PERFECTION AND SANCTITY

On the other hand, to be in a canonical state of perfection does not necessarily signify that one possesses the interior perfection of sanctity. Sanctity and "state" of perfection are realities of a different order altogether. The juridical and canonical state of perfection

[17] *Biecht-hooren*, Louvain, 1944, no. 86, p. 117.

is one thing; real sanctity possessed in fact by someone who enjoys perfect theological charity, is another.

From the point of view of the canonical state of perfection, "it is certain that the religious state is more perfect than the nonreligious one, that the religious priest is in a more perfect state than the secular one: for the religious state presupposes that one makes a vow to observe the evangelical counsels which Jesus offered as means of perfection. This does not mean that a particular religious is more perfect than a particular priest; and that is the whole of it, for perfection does not consist in the state one embraces, but in the life one leads therein and in the acts of virtue that are performed. One must therefore consider things concretely."[18] In other words, it is not the habit which makes the monk, and the real perfection of a man is that which he has in the eyes of God. In the correspondence of Cardinal Pierre de Bérulle, there is a letter sent by him toward the end of the month of December, 1620, to the subprioress of the Carmel of Orleans, Theresa of Jesus, who had manifested a desire to have her nuns directed by some Fathers of their Order in preference to secular priests. This is what he replied to her: "Your new superiors have worked so hard for you; does that not entitle them to be revered by you as your Fathers, since even though they are not Carmelites by habit, they are so in fact by zeal and by the piety of Elias? How many Carmelites may there be in the world who have only received the mantle of Elias and not his spirit twice over, and how many secular priests who, without the mantle, have received his spirit? How many Teresians without the habit, and how many Teresians without the spirit of Mother Teresa?"[19]

And this, too, is quite Thomistic: "Nothing prevents some who are not in the state of perfection from being perfect, and some in the state of perfection from not

---

[18] Card. J. E. van Roey, *Au service de l'Eglise*, vol. 1, p. 173.
[19] J. Dagens, *Correspondance du Cardinal Pierre de Bérulle*, vol. II, p. 185.

being perfect" (IIa IIae, q. 184, a. 4, c.). Nothing could be clearer.

SANCTITY AND MEANS OF PERFECTION

Having made these points, here is the way it seems to us that the question can be approached.

Perfection, for man, is identical with *charity*, not with sentiments of human philanthropy, or some sentimental love of Christ or the Father. When we say charity, we mean conscious love of and effective focusing of the whole man — body and soul, higher and lower faculties — on God, the final end proposed to us by revelation. Charity is, therefore, "order to an end."

This basic moral rectitude adapts itself to every state of life, and the Church is careful to propose to her faithful authentic saints who lived in the most diverse temporal situations: popes and monks, kings and citizens, married and single persons, rich and poor, learned and illiterate. Perfection in charity, that is to say, sanctity itself, is therefore possible in all states and in all professions, as St. Francis de Sales so clearly states.[20] Also, when we hear St. Thomas recall that the sacred ministry with which the priest is invested calls for eminent interior holiness, we will conclude, first of all, that he is bound to a greater degree of theological charity than that expected of him if he were to enter a state of perfection.

Shall the concrete means which the priest is to put into operation be of an entirely different type than those which are the heritage of the states of perfection?

Of course, the *general means* of perfection are the same for all men, in all states of life. To be perfect, for the pope, the monk, and the layman alike, is to live by divine grace, dwell under the dominion of the same Spirit, resemble the same Christ, conform to the essential holiness of the same Father. To be perfect, for everyone here below, necessarily demands a certain life of

[20] *Introduction to the Devout Life*, Bk. I, ch. 3; cf. also L. De Blois, *Institutio spiritualis*, chap. V.

prayer, a certain amount of mortification, the consci-
entious performance of the duties of state. In this area,
too, at the level of the general means of perfection,
there can be no question of introducing any neat distinctions.

But these general means of perfection have been
variously combined among themselves, in such a way as
to secure for mankind typical "spiritual systems."

For the majority of men, the spiritual regimen is the
family, the ownership of goods, a profession or a trade,
freedom of action in the world and the disposition of
their own vital services. Most men can seek and find
in this regimen, in these conditions of existence, in this
"state" of things, the concrete means that will enable
them to live an ardent Christian life, and to sanctify
themselves. The examples given by St. Francis de Sales
are sufficient illustration.

Some, having heard the divine call, choose a spiritual
system more favorable in itself to the development of
their baptismal regeneration: practice of the evangelical
counsels, religious stability of the vows and common life,
in short, the life of a state of perfection as organized
by the Church. It is in this ensemble of means, in this
"state of life," that they will strive to attain their full
supernatural destiny, their sanctity. The end remains
the same, but the whole range of means employed, as
revelation demonstrates, is unquestionably superior.

Others of the faithful, instead of choosing a spiritual
regimen directly ordered to their own sanctification, offer
themselves to the Church in order to extend, in the very
forms chosen by the Apostles, the work of redemption
undertaken by the Lord. By itself, this co-redeemer's
life is not ordered to personal sanctification; but it involves activities which, in themselves, are highly sanctifying and, moreover, include a higher requirement for
perfection, says St. Thomas, than that which has its
source in the vows of religion. This is the priestly
apostolic life and, in particular, that of the diocesan
priest.

Comparing the perfection of the diocesan priest to that of the religious, Cardinal Mercier wrote:

"In this blessed ascent toward the perfection of charity, the means of the religious and those of the cleric offer different modalities, but these are secondary. For everyone the goal is the same: perfect charity. The essential means are the same: grace and cooperation with grace in the state of life in which Providence has placed us. The subsidiary means vary from state to state, from individual to individual; it would be a mistake to impose on or to counsel indiscriminately for clerics, for priests, means proper to the special state of the religious, just as it would be wrong to impose on or to counsel for religious all the practical means of charity which the minister of the altar and the pastor of souls find in the accomplishment of their ecclesiastical and pastoral functions.

"Charity is one thing, a particular method favorable to the exercise of charity is another. Charity is a theological virtue; chastity, poverty, obedience, religion, are moral virtues. From the necessity of the former, one cannot logically conclude the necessity of any particular form of exercise of the latter."[21]

[21] *Vie intérieure,* pp. 174-175.

CONCLUSION

What we have tried to do, on behalf of all our colleagues, is to show the beauty and grandeur of the diocesan apostolic priesthood. These priests, as a matter of fact, sometimes lack this force of union which gives all life its vigor and impetus, because of the fact that the very conditions of the apostolate isolate them, psychologically and morally. Too often, they do not envision their vocation with sufficient confidence and pride, because the greatness of their ideal does not rise before their eyes with all the desirable clarity and vigor. Too often, finally, they allow their first fervor to diminish, because they do not see clearly enough that the pastoral ministry, in its eucharistic work and "cura animarum" is, in itself, a secure foundation and a supreme call for towering perfection.

To raise our ideal very high is in no way to minimize or to lower that of the orders or congregations. Today when apostolic collaboration is becoming intense, when "regulars" and "seculars" unite ever more fraternally to insure the growth of the Kingdom of the Lord, it would be regrettable to provoke any shocks, to cause needless debate. It would not be good, for instance, for the diocesan clergy to feel affronted in its honor each time the Jesuits, the Dominicans, or the Franciscans exalt their holy founder or their glorious vocation: why

leave in the dark that which constitutes the grandeur
of the Church and the moral support of the religious
themselves? On the other hand, it would be unfortunate
if the religious did not properly interpret those rare
books which remind the diocesan clergy of the nobility
of its origins, the greatness of its ideal, the importance
of its worldly work: the Church, again, can but find
therein a cause for spiritual joy, and the priests themselves have an immense need for such works.

The more diocesan priests, like the regular clergy
and together with them, feel themselves constrained to
make progress in sanctity because of their vocation itself,
the more the universal apostolate will be guaranteed a
brilliant future. From heaven, the glorified Lord and
the Church triumphant will see an intensified growth
of divine love in this world, and, in Rome, the Successor
of Peter and the Vicar of Jesus Christ, considering all
those who labor on this earth for the holy Church, will
smile with paternal joy and give comfort to all her
sons of predilection.

ANNEXED DOCUMENTS

We are publishing under this heading excerpts of books or articles concerning the doctrine of the diocesan clergy and its spirituality which, for various reasons, might not be otherwise easily accessible.

I. *THE DIOCESAN VOCATION AND GENEROSITY*

DIOCESAN CLERGY AND GENEROSITY

In a letter dated July 13, 1952, the Sacred Congregation for Extraordinary Ecclesiastical Affairs transmitted to us through the Apostolic Nunciature in Brussels, a detailed note from His Holiness in reply to some requests for clarification that had been made from various quarters to the Holy See.

✠ ANDRE-MARIE
Bishop of Namur

Namur, September 3, 1952.

* * * *

1. When it is stated that a priest who wants to tend to perfection must become a religious, or at least become a member of a secular institute; and if a young man who is hesitating between the secular priesthood and entry into religion is told that it is a matter of generosity; when it is affirmed that whoever chooses the secular

clergy thereby proves that he is not generous enough to give himself entirely to the service of God; if one does not consider himself able to counsel a young man thus hesitating to enter the Seminary instead of the religious state; if some even go so far as to say that the Church "tolerates" the secular Clergy as a last resort, though the ideal thing would be for all priests to be religious: — that is a false understanding and an erroneous application of the Allocution of the Holy Father of December 8, 1950 (Acta Apostolicae Sedis, 43, 1951, pp. 26-36). The Bishops are within their rights if they are opposed to recruiting campaigns for religious societies which have inaccurate theoretical bases liable to lead into error, which are in practice the least bit disloyal, and if they set just and firm limits to such campaigns by administrative edict.

2. The above-mentioned Allocution of the Holy Father was intended above all to clarify and emphasize three questions:

a. What is the position of the regular clergy (clerus religiosus) with respect to the secular clergy (clerus saecularis) in the constitution given by Christ to His Church (pp. 27-29)? The answer was:

"If one keeps in mind the order established by Christ, neither of the two special forms of clergy has the prerogative of divine law, since that law neither places one above the other nor deplaces either one" (p. 28).

b. What is the relationship of the "cleric" and the "religious" with respect to the "state of perfection" as the state of the evangelical counsels (p. 29)? The reply to that was:

"The cleric . . . is not bound by divine law to the evangelical counsels of poverty, chastity, and obedience; and he is especially not bound in the same way and for the same reason — the fact that this obligation arises out of vows taken publicly in embracing the religious state. This, however, does not prevent the cleric from taking on these bonds of his own free will, privately. . . . But the regular cleric, not insofar as he is a cleric, but insofar as he is a religious, professes the condition and state of evangelical perfection" (p. 29). For the rest, it was expressly affirmed that even the "Instituta Saecularia" (Secular Institutes) carry out the essence of the "state of perfection," "because of the fact that their members are in some way bound to observe the evangelical counsels" (p. 29). If "clerics" come together in such an "Institutum Saeculare," then they too are in the state of acquiring perfection, not as clerics, but as members of the Secular Institute" (p. 30).

c. What are the objective motives for embracing the religious state (p. 30) ? That which is stated in the pontifical allocution concerning the religious state considered in itself, as a state of perfection, must not be identified with the vocation of the individual to personal perfection, whether in the "state of perfection" or outside it, as happens in the case of certain religious societies in their methods of recruiting, about which there have been complaints.

The three foregoing clarifications are not immediately concerned with the individual person, but the state, its legal position, and its inner nature. They do not therefore touch upon the vocation of the individual to a specific state in the Church, nor upon the vocation of the individual to personal perfection in his state, nor upon the perfection actually attained by the individual in his state or vocation.

The discussion is accordingly not about the personal perfection of the individual. This perfection is measured by the degree of love, of "theological charity" found in the individual. The criterion of the intensity and purity of love is, according to the Master's own words, the doing of the will of God. The individual is, therefore, in the eyes of God, more and more perfect the more perfectly he fulfills the divine will. In this regard, it matters very little in which state he is, whether lay or ecclesiastic, and, for the priest, whether he is secular or regular.

It follows that it would not be correct to say that the secular priest, in regard to his personal holiness, is less clearly called to perfection than the regular priest, or that the decision of a young man to choose the vocation of the secular priesthood is a determination to a lesser personal holiness than if he had chosen priesthood in the religious state. It may actually be the case. It may also be the case that the choice by a particular individual of a state other than that of perfection proceeds from a greater love of God and a higher spirit of sacrifice than the choice of the religious state by someone else.

As far as the priest is concerned, and the candidate for the priesthood as well, it is not difficult to see that by reason of the dignity and the duties of the priestly function, he too is called in a very special way to personal perfection. This is true even in the case where the man invested with sacerdotal perfection lives lawfully in the "married state," as in the Eastern Rites.

In conclusion, it must be said that the vocation of the individual to holiness or to personal perfection, the adoption and permanent practice of the latter, cannot be confused with the question of the "state of perfection" in the juridical sense of the term. The state of perfection is called, and actually is such, because by means of the three evangelical counsels, it turns aside the principal obstacles to the effort of personal sanctity, or, more accurately, because it is, by its very nature, designed to keep these obstacles at bay. But it does not follow from the mere fact of embracing the state of perfection that this state will achieve its purposes in the life of the individual religious, that it will actually lead to holiness; that all depends on the effort of the subject, on the degree to which, in cooperation with divine grace, he puts the evangelical counsels into operation in his life.

II. *THE DIOCESAN CLERGY FACE TO FACE WITH ITS PRESENT EVANGELIZING MISSION*

Among the most valuable and significant documents to be entered in the file of this discussion, we must cite a book prepared at the same time as ours, *The Diocesan Clergy Face to Face with its Present Evangelizing Mission* (French title: *Le clergé diocésain en face de sa mission actuelle d'évangélisation*) with the sub-titles: *Its Spirituality, Its Formation in the Major Seminaries, Its Scheme of Life*). Published in manuscript form in 1945.

This book reproduces the general report of the inquiry conducted by the *Assembly of French Cardinals and Archbishops* on the diocesan clergy. Msgr. Guerry, Coadjutor Archbishop to His Excellency the Archbishop of Cambrai, arranged it for publication. Eighty-two French dioceses participated in the study, submitting a total of 148 reports which together constitute a file of some 1200 pages.

It is impossible to summarize a work of this dimension. Its chief interest lies in the general agreement of reports coming in from all corners of the country. We will present some characteristic excerpts taken either from the replies to the inquiry or from the eminent editor who synthesized them.

THE FACTS

Among priests . . .

"The most evident fact is the isolated life which the ministry imposes on almost all parish priests. The best priests suffer from not being able to move more often in a fraternal milieu, in a priestly environment; this is for them at times a kind of lassitude, of anguish, about which they complain" (p. 5).

"The regrets of supernatural priests, very frequently heard, concern the lack of cordial, deep and steady contacts with authority. . . . They have the impression that they are not really known and understood personally in the different circumstances of life, the impression therefore of being treated 'impersonally,' more like pawns on a chessboard than as human beings" (p. 6).

Among young people . . .

They fear "not developing themselves fully in the diocesan priesthood or to be operating below their capacity therein. Religious superiors are thought to know their subordinates better, to utilize their abilities better, to ask of them only what they are able to give" (p. 11).

"Many of us admit that we are profoundly disturbed by certain defections and, perhaps even more, by contact with certain mediocre priests who seem no longer to believe in the nobility of their mission, nor in the efficacy of their ministry" (p. 11).

The voice of families . . .

"I note that the majority of aristocratic and middle-class families do not want their children to be 'parish priests.' They accept with joy when they enter the religious orders: the Jesuits, the Dominicans, the Benedictines. Why? The ordinary sacerdotal functions do not seem to have enough 'value.' There seems to be a turnabout developing as a result of a vigorous campaign" (p. 13).

THE CAUSES

Material situation of the clergy . . .

"The material situation of the country priest contributes to a lower esteem of his mission. A poorly kept rectory because the pastor cannot afford a servant. The need for the priest to obtain his food supplies like a common housewife. And, above all, the need to beg for money for the maintenance of the pastor; this gives the peasants the impression that the priest has to beg in order to live, a disastrous impression in many rural environments" (p. 21).

"But one must neither generalize nor dramatize. . . . Too often the reader retains only this: priests are an unhappy sort. My son will become a teacher rather than a parish priest, and he may even remain a peasant" (p. 23).

Defects in recruiting . . .

"On the outside, public opinion seizes upon certain admissions to the major seminary to give credit to the paradox that an imbecile always can find a cassock to put on, while inside, the seminarians suffer from a particularly serious inferiority complex. In spite of all the dangers to which it is headed, pell-mell, obsession with numbers seems ineradicable" (p. 25).

Lack of bearing of certain priests . . .

"This lack of dignity and of upbringing seems to be growing among young priests, both in their persons and the way they wear their ecclesiastical clothes, and also in their conversation and relations with the world. . . . It seems that there is a great let-down here, because of a forgetting of the human virtues, in the French clergy. . . . And we are speaking only of bearing and courtesy. If we were to go into the matter of justice and simple honesty, regular business matters, payment of debts, fidelity to contracts or to the given word, there would be much to say: in this regard a courageous book should be cited, *Regards sur le ministère sacerdotal* (Reflections on the sacerdotal ministry), by Msgr. Dubourg" (pp. 26-27).

Deficiencies in the intellectual order . . .

"Here, too, the clergy has gradually lost the choice position it formerly occupied. Especially in the cities, the intellectual mediocrity of priests does considerable harm to the prestige of the calling. The weakness of certain sermons, the inability on the part of certain priests to sustain an intelligent and documented conversation, the ignorance of many with regard to the great currents of contemporary thought . . . the concerns of their times . . . all these deficiencies are gradually creating a chasm between the clergy and certain circles" (p. 27).

Deficiencies of the spiritual and apostolic order . . .

"He is increasingly absorbed in material tasks: attendance at burials and marriages, bookkeeping, material responsibility for activities, which leads him to lose sight of the essentially supernatural goal of his apostolate" (p. 30).

Deficiencies of diocesan organization . . .

"We must go one step further and ask ourselves whether, in individual priestly failings, there is not a share of responsibility which falls on our diocesan organization itself. Here we are broaching the subject of the deficiencies of a general nature in the way of life of our diocesan clergy. There are three main ones:

1. Lack of a framework of formation and spiritual support in the first years of the ministry;

2. Inadequacy of the means of spiritual and intellectual formation furnished by the diocese to priests engaged in the ministry;

3. The non-existence of the diocesan community as a way of life for the diocesan clergy" (p. 31).

Here, for each of the points cited by Msgr. Guerry, is an excerpt from the replies:

1. "During the first years of priesthood, priests are left too much to themselves. We are persuaded that their priestly orientation largely depends on the first meetings, the first contacts they have had with other priests, with their pastors especially, in the case of young curates. Certain pastors make no effort to form them" (p. 31).

2. "In sum, the institutions established by the Church in her Canon Law, continue to operate as in the past, but in practice, everyone agrees in recognizing that they no longer play a sufficiently useful role and do not 'hit home' enough in the real life of priests, their intellectual or spiritual life, to fortify or sustain it" (p. 37).

3. "When, in answer to these complaints, one mentions the coming of the bishop for Confirmation, or the relative ease of a visit to the bishop's residence . . . one hears replies like these: 'True, the bishop does come every four or five years, but he administers Confirmation quickly (*sic*), he does not inform himself at all, or so little, or in such a general way, about the state of the parish, that there is neither time nor desire to speak to him with an open heart. And so, one keeps one's

problems to oneself, one suffers, sometimes one cries. And, beset by moral sufferings like this, one slides into discouragement' " (p. 39).

THE REMEDIES

1. A spirit

"The composite of the replies underscores powerfully the need for a spiritual doctrine to shed full light on the grandeur and the proper characteristics of the diocesan clergy in its union with the bishop. An urgent reform . . . a major problem: a mystique of the diocesan clergy must be created. . . . This is the most important problem of the inquiry . . . " (pp. 47-48).

Then follow several pages on the general features of this spirituality of the diocesan clergy: a communitarian and conquering spirituality, but one essentially of the Church.

2. The major seminaries

Msgr. Guerry himself, at the outset, frames the question in all its breadth:

"We are aware of the whole admirable job that our seminaries have done in France since the 17th century. At no time did it occur to those making the inquiry to throw upon the seminaries the responsibility for the clergy's deficiencies. But, at a time when problems of extreme seriousness are being posed for the episcopate, the latter has the right and duty to inquire whether it has taken all the steps it can to insure that the seminaries will be able to fulfill the formative mission entrusted to them. We must face the evidence: our country is profoundly de-Christianized . . . ; but our seminaries were established in a Christian society; they have retained the frames of reference, the customs, the spirit, the mark of their times. It is not a question of not recognizing the good they accomplished in the past; it is a question of asking ourselves whether they are equipped for the new tasks of the apostolate in the 20th century" (pp. 56-57).

The teaching of theology

"It is all the more necessary to affirm the need for a truly scientific study of theology, in view of the fact that today's young people do not, generally, have a taste for intellectual work and show themselves impatient to act, eager for ready-made formulas and technical processes that would, so they think, dispense them from a study too 'cut off from reality.' These expressions, which circulate like slogans in the circles of our young priests, must be forcefully denounced" (p. 60).

Among the practical means of making theology "live," the inquiry cites: a wise utilization of the sources of revelation, a truly synthesizing instruction, the theological study of the problems which are current today, the study of dogmas even to their spiritual and apostolic ramifications (pp. 65-71).

Formation for intellectual work . . .

"The professor must be thoroughly convinced that, besides the course he prepares and presents to his students, he has another extremely important task to perform with each student: to direct him in his efforts and to become interested in his work, in order to make each one 'produce' to the extent of his personal capacity" (p. 74).

Whence the necessity of furnishing students with an "accessible" library (p. 75), and leisure for personal work. "To be sure, it is not a question of turning our major seminaries into universities, but many dioceses believe that methods which are far too elementary must be abandoned" (p. 77).

Judicious choice of professors . . .

"Because of the need for a special and technical preparation for teaching, (a diocese) asks whether it might not be well to have, in Rome or Paris, a 'Normal School' designed for all future professors in major seminaries, both regular and secular. Diplomas do not

give the art of teaching, and practice alone is not always
enough to acquire this difficult art" (p. 79).

Spiritual formation . . .

Several dioceses suggest a little "novitiate" of spirituality at the beginning of seminary training: "A kind
of novitiate, of perhaps a month's duration, at the beginning of the seminary training, could be decisive in
the orientation of seminarians. Two years' experience
has given us admirable results" (p. 83).

A course in spirituality. "Some years ago, in the
Roman universities, His Holiness Pius XI had created a
chair of Ascetical and Mystical Theology. Such a course
in spirituality would be a methodical course distinct from
the spiritual conferences of the superior which of necessity have to derive their inspiration from world events
or seminary life" (pp. 84-85).

A more personal piety. "In mental prayer, by giving
to each seminarian, at least on several days a week, the
freedom of choosing his own subject, under the guidance
of the director; under the same guidance, some would
even hope that the meditation could be made in his room,
in order to accustom the students to being alone for this
major exercise" (p. 87).

Apostolic formation . . .

A spirit of conquest. "The word 'conquest' must be
understood in terms of *society,* and no longer only in
terms of 'individuals.' In all ages, even during the centuries of faith, there have always been souls to be con-
quered for Christ: in this sense, there would be nothing
new for the work of our major seminaries. . . . What
is new for them is the fact that, founded in the middle
of the 17th century, in a Christian society, they have to
act in this 20th century in a society which is no longer
Christian, and that they have to form future priests for
the reconquest of these de-Christianized masses" (p. 91).

Practical formation. "It is inadmissible to allow
young men to enter a profession in which public speaking plays such an important role without their being

thoroughly practiced in the art of public speaking"
(p. 97).

3. *A framework of life*

"This actually is the whole problem of our diocesan
organization. The inquiry has revealed the ills and causes
of the deficiencies from which our clergy suffers. They
can be reduced to three main ones:

1. A 'materialization' of the ministry through the
multiplicity of administrative tasks or material functions;

2. A baneful and sterile isolation;

3. The inadequacy or even the absence of a framework of life, as a support.

"If our inquiry is to achieve effective results, it must
therefore help us to perfect our diocesan organization
so that:

1. It can free our clergy of certain tasks and turn it
over to its great mission of evangelization;

2. It can put an end to isolation and assure the clergy
of a collective life;

3. It can supply our priests with a scheme of life
that will support them in their spiritual, intellectual,
apostolic work" (p. 113).

Liberation from certain tasks . . .

"It seems to me that if the clergy were able to free
itself, principally in activities, from all those material
tasks that could be performed by laymen, it would be
saving a great deal of time which could be devoted to
prayer and souls" (p. 114).

"Finally, there are ministries which impair the health
of priests . . . late Masses, 'trinating' in far-off stations
for a small number of parishioners. The relaxations
granted by Rome in the discipline of the Eucharistic
fast have already facilitated this pastoral service" (p.
119).

Organization of a diocesan community . . .

"Many priests never come to see their bishop. The bishop must therefore go to them, either by himself or through his Vicar General. At Dijon, I persuaded a Vicar General, now Bishop of Moulins, to spend two whole days a week visiting priests in their rectories, forewarning them, naturally. When he had made the rounds, he started over again. The results have been extremely encouraging" (p. 121).

"A large number of responses express the desire that the deans actually play the role intrusted to them by Canon Law. . . . Accordingly, considerable importance of the choice of deans is indicated. They should be designated, not for advancement or by way of distributing honorific titles, but for their solid qualities of zeal, interior life and judgment" (pp. 122-124).

"Finally, the questionnaire asked the dioceses for their opinions on the organization of a stable state — a common life properly so-called — in which several volunteer priests would meet under a single rule in order to place in common their spiritual lives, their apostolate, even their material goods. Here, the overall response indicates a great reserve. Generally, the institution is approved *in theory;* its definite advantages for the protection of the priest are acknowledged — a defense against isolation, the supports and resources he can find therein for his spiritual and intellectual life, the material and moral comfort at the close of a tiring day. . . . But many point out the difficulties in the way of a practical application of the formula" (pp. 133-134).

Toward a solution . . .

"A method already in use in certain dioceses consists in 'Study Days' for young priests, those, for example, from the last ten seminary ordination classes. . . ." (p. 139).

"What is to be done? Return to the idea that has already sparked certain projects called 'third year' or better, *'sacerdotal month,'* and require that young priests, those, for example, who have been ordained for two years, return and spend a month in their seminary. . . . " (p. 140).

"Several dioceses have expressed the wish that after some experience in the ministry — ten years or so — each priest might be given the benefit of a real renewal" (p. 143).

"Retreats: The newest suggestions are the following: 1. that the number of retreatants be limited — fifty at the most; 2. that the retreats be specialized: young priests, professors, deans . . ." (p. 146).

"Intellectual life. To the *Ecclesiastical Conferences* one must join, as a great means of training and of spiritual life, the *Study Sessions* in which priests, under the guidance of specialized instructors, are brought up to date on the great intellectual, social, apologetic, theological problems . . ." (p. 150).

III. RESOLUTIONS OF THE ASSEMBLY OF FRENCH CARDINALS AND ARCHBISHOPS

SPIRIT.

FIRST RESOLUTION: The Assembly expresses the following desire:

1. That during "Days for priestly vocations," in conferences in secondary schools and before youth groups, the *vocation of the diocesan clergy* be spotlighted, with its grandeur, its requirements, its proper characteristics, particularly its irreplaceable pastoral mission of taking charge of the evangelization of souls at all stages of their lives, which insures that this ministry shall be stable and lasting.

2. That in the major seminaries, the treatise *"De Ordine"* cease being left to the personal study of seminarians during vacations, and be the object of a very thorough doctrinal instruction, centering around the priesthood of Christ in its twofold office, each part inseparable from the other: office of contemplation and prayer as the mediator of men with God; office of apos-

tolate and witness, as God's mediator with men; then the priesthood of the bishop, his spiritual paternity, his mission of sanctification; finally, the priesthood of the priest, connected with that of the bishop, and the sacrament of Holy Orders, studied in its relationship to the life of the Church, the Mystical Body of Christ.

3. That preachers of priests' retreats take their inspiration for instructions from the *spirituality of the diocesan clergy*, the spirituality of the Church forming souls to live the life of the Church intensely, in her teachings, her liturgy, in filial and loving docility to the Supreme Pontiff; an apostolic spirituality animating the souls of pastors, of apostles completely given to Jesus Christ for the work of redemption, finding their sanctification in and through the performance of their pastoral ministry.

THE FORMATION.

A. *Intellectual formation*

SECOND RESOLUTION: Regarding the teaching of theology as a living science.

The Assembly expresses the wish that *dogmatic theology* be taught as a living science:

a) As a *science,* therefore, it should be studied for itself, in its proper object, with the whole scientific apparatus, both positive and scholastic, which supports it, with all the effort of erudition, reflection and assimilation, which it demands. In this way, the dangers of a vulgarization that would entail a lowering of the level of theological studies and a too-utilitarian adaptation to the exigencies of the times, would be avoided.

b) As a *living science,* not as an abstract science or an arid and desiccating speculation, because it is in itself the science of life *par excellence,* the divine life, and because it is oriented toward the highest expression of life: union with God, whence priestly action must be derived.

To this end:

1. That the professor not content himself with using, as proofs, quotations from Scripture and Tradition, taken out of context, but lead his students to a *direct and personal contact with the sources* of revelation; that he connect his theses to Holy Scripture not only in order to establish them but also to cause them to be born of the word of God which renders them alive and imperative; that he make the Fathers of the Church known, with their temperaments, their influence, the particular witness which they gave to this or that dogma, through their lives or through their teachings.

2. That the professor present the divine message as it is in reality: an ensemble of truths, rich with life and light; that he strongly stress *the reality of these riches;* that he not only bestow knowledge of but esteem and admiration for all these revealed truths, thanks to the warmth of his own convictions and his fervent familiarity with the dogmatic truths; that he generate in his disciples an ardent enthusiasm for the message they will be called upon to communicate.

3. That the professor, in his teachings, try to develop *what is certain and essential* for the life of souls, being careful not to expatiate at too great length on controversial questions or subtle and accessory research.

That, while knowing how to bring out the dogmatic development, he can avoid expositions which are too completely historical and retrospective, and, while it is necessary to study the heresies of past centuries which help in the understanding of the formulation of the dogma, he will show the analogy and the mutual interrelationships between them and modern forms of error.

4. That the teaching of theology open itself more to the *human problems which are posed today* in the life of the world: work, property, leisure, family, profession, civic affairs, war and peace, according to the orientation given by the Supreme Pontiffs in their great encyclicals.

5. That the professor lead his students to discover the present needs of souls and show them the applica-

tions of dogma to their own spiritual and apostolic lives.

For *moral theology,* the Assembly expresses the wish that its teaching be clearly positive and doctrinal, psychological and human, as well as supernatural.

a) *Positive:* by stimulating souls in the practice of the virtues and the search for perfection, rather than indicating the limits of sin;

b) *doctrinal:* by being above all a solid presentation of the principles that will form the conscience and the judgment, and not a simple collection of cases of conscience, often borrowed from another era; it should use the acquisitions of psychological science and often point out the relationship of the human and the supernatural.

THIRD RESOLUTION: For a doctrinal formation concerning modern problems.

In order to give future priests doctrinal knowledge which will enable them to carry out in the future their teaching mission in the midst of all the modern errors on the nature of the State and on social problems, the Assembly expresses the desire that two courses be introduced where they do not as yet exist:

1. *A course in public Church law,* as it is taught in the Roman universities, teaching the doctrine regarding the nature of the Church, the juridically perfect society; regarding the relations of Church and State; regarding the rights and essential liberties of the Church.

2. *A complete course on the pontifical encyclicals* and the teachings of the Supreme Pontiffs concerning the great problems of human and social life.

FOURTH RESOLUTION: concerning the practical formation for intellectual work.

The Assembly expresses the desire:

1. That the professor make an effort to awaken in his students *the taste for intellectual work,* on the one hand, by ceaselessly combatting their too-natural attraction for external activities, a sufficiency of spirit because they

do not know the problems, the mentality of collegians who work only toward an exam; on the other hand, by showing them the need for a complete theological and human culture if they wish to be capable of carrying out a fruitful pastoral ministry.

2. That the professor then teach his students to work by giving them *a method*, by directing and requiring the preparation of a card index, a filing cabinet for notes, for papers; that, to this end, a few orientation courses in personal work habits be given each year to new students entering the major seminary.

3. That the professor demand of each student a *personal effort* adapted to his capacities; that he require of each person in the course a personal effort at reflection, not contenting himself with dictating notes or having lessons recited by heart.

4. That each one's efforts be stimulated by the organizing of a *group task* under the authority of the teachers; for example, in the form of teams exploring further some questions indicated by the professor.

5. That the professor, finally, check the personal work by periodic revisions, by serious examinations with accompanying sanctions, written assignments and a personal report on the instruction received.

The Assembly hopes that the *library of major seminaries* will be given the very special attention of seminary superiors; that it be composed of necessary books, kept constantly up to date; that the students have a workroom at their disposal where they may consult books, dictionaries and magazines at certain hours under the guidance of a professor in charge of the library.

FIFTH RESOLUTION: Concerning the selection of professors.

The Assembly attaches the greatest importance to the judicious selection of major seminary professors.

In addition to the general qualities which together inspire confidence in the students (justice, sincerity,

kindness, devotion, selflessness), the professor should
be impressive in the strictly pedagogical area by his
scientific competence, his conviction in the way he
teaches, and his ability to awaken minds, by his concern for helping students, directing their intellectual
training, enjoying personal contacts with them, and
finally, by his firmness in excluding students who are too
obviously deficient on the intellectual level.

On the question of the contacts which major seminary
professors should have with activities and action, the
Assembly believes that, regardless of the methods
adopted, it is desirable that they be inspired by the two
following rules:

1. That the *duties of state of the director of the
major seminary* take precedence over all other ministries: for these duties are too important not to require
that one give his full time to them.

2. In order to fulfill the duty of forming future
priests better, *it is useful for the professor to be familiar
with the ministry.*

— either through having been personally acquainted
with it before being named to the major seminary;

— or through contacts he may have with the men
of action;

— or through the exercise of the ministry in which
the professor is especially competent: conferences for
priests, courses in religious instruction, retreat days for
movements, or, during vacations, through preaching
and hearing confessions;

— or, finally, and above all, by continuing to keep in
close touch with his former students now in the ministry,
thereby bringing the latter inestimable support and also
receiving from them a whole wealth or renewal of pastoral experience.

Finally, the Assembly draws the attention of major
seminary professors to the necessity of forming a very
united, homogeneous corps possessing a team spirit,
and a sense of the common good.

B. *Spiritual formation*

SIXTH RESOLUTION: By reason of the importance to be attached to spiritual formation of seminarians, either for their own inner life, or for their future apostolic ministry, especially that of directing souls, the Assembly expresses the desire that wherever the reverend bishops deem it useful, there be instituted:

1. A kind of *novitiate of spirituality* lasting from one month (as certain dioceses have already done successfully) to three months (according to the wish expressed by others), a novitiate designed to take the young seminarian from the moment of his arrival in the major seminary and plunge him right into the spiritual life, presenting him at the very outset with his ideal of sanctity, teaching him the science of mental prayer, of intimacy with our Lord discovered in a personal experience, in an atmosphere of piety, of fervor, and without any worry about studies.

2. *A course in spirituality* (ascetical and mystical theology) extending over several years in the major seminary, presenting the principal elements of this science of Christian perfection, teaching these future priests to be familiar with the great masters of the spiritual life.

3. A very complete *practical instruction* in the two main staples of the priest's spiritual life, which are his Mass and his Breviary: the Breviary to be studied, starting with the subdeaconate year, in all its parts (psalms and lessons), the Mass to be studied during the year of priestly ordination itself not only with regard to the rubrics of the Missal but in each of its rites and each of the words of the liturgy.

As for the traditional exercises of piety in our major seminaries, the Assembly desires that, in order that they might produce all their fruits, they *leave more room for personal prayer* (initiative and responsibility in the choice of mental prayer subjects, examinations of conscience, under the director's guidance), and that they be oriented in a more communitarian sense (praying as members of the Mystical Body, and with others).

C. *Apostolic formation*

SEVENTH RESOLUTION: The major seminaries must today form a clergy of Catholic Action, animated with the apostolic spirit of conquest.

1. In order to develop or awaken this spirit, the Assembly expresses the wish that in addition to a doctrinal and theoretical course in social problems, seminarians be furnished *frank, realistic, solid* information on the extent and the depth of the evil of dechristianization, by means of specific inquires pertaining not merely to all France as a whole, but to certain areas of the diocese, to the conditions in the various professions, to the mentality of different milieux, and to the special social problems which arise there. Then, the professor is to have the students reflect on these data, make them aware of the responsibilities which await them, discover the responses made by Christian doctrine, in order to awaken in them the conviction and the desire to work at the great task of rechristianization. Finally, to fortify this conviction and this desire, the professor is to set forth the great motives for hope contained in the beautiful results of movements of Catholic Action or inspiration.

2. The Assembly believes that a very effective means of forming seminarians in the apostolic spirit is to have them live, in the major seminary, as apostles one to the other, each feeling himself responsible for the soul of his brethren and one with them in the proper operation of the whole. It is incumbent upon the corps of professors to create *this apostolic climate* by making the clerics live under the law of charity, so that the seminary is a real family, a unique and real community where, instead of turning into oneself in a desiccating selfishness, each will be ready to give himself to the various services or efforts of the team, to collaborate actively in the campaigns organized for the collective practice of a virtue or the observance of a point of the rule; finally, in a

general way, to live his seminarian's life as the "member of a body." Thus, a "community" spirit will be formed and the sense of working together will be acquired, and these will directly prepare the future priests for an apostolate which is collective and community-organized.

3. The Assembly strongly desires that along with the pastoral courses, a *practical training in the essential tasks of the ministry* be given by the major seminary, particularly:

a) For *preaching:* through numerous exercises in elocution, through practical conferences by preachers or diocesan missionaries, by composing a certain number of sermon outlines or complete sermons, by frequent questioning during the course.

b) For *catechizing:* not only by a presentation of methods of catechetical pedagogy, but by practice in teaching the catechism under the guidance and supervision of a priest with experience in a parish, as required by Roman regulations.

c) For the *direction of souls:* to prepare priests to be true directors of conscience, not only for children, but also for adolescents and adults.

The Assembly submits to the reverend bishops a plan for a school parish near the seminary in which this training would be given methodically under the enlightened direction of priests in the ministry.

4. Concerning the *technical preparation for activities*, the Assembly believes:

a) That it is best to reserve it for the final year in seminary, in order to avoid giving seminarians any occasion to evade their present duties of state;

b) That it is well to remind the students often that technical procedures which vary with the times, must never make them lose sight of the essential, which is the apostolic spirit;

c) That this technical preparation for activities, whether outside the major seminary (youth groups, summer camps), or on the inside (study circles), is only of value if it is directed and supervised by a competent priest.

As to the summer camps and the youth groups, the Assembly interprets the desires of the reverend bishops on the following points:

1. The director should really be an educator not only of the children but also of the seminarians;

2. The seminarians should have the time and freedom to perform all their exercises of piety;

3. They should not be subjected to excessive physical fatigue likely to harm their health and their studies.

WAY OF LIFE.

A. *Freedom from certain tasks*

EIGHTH RESOLUTION: Taking into account, on the one hand, the hierarchy of functions and needs and, on the other, the lack in the number of clergy, the Assembly believes that the organization of the parish ministry must be adapted to the times by freeing priests of certain tasks in order to let them attend to their urgent mission of evangelization.

1. For *material tasks* (movies, plays, bookkeeping and administrative duties) there should be an increasing demand for the collaboration of competent, devoted and reliable laymen, as certain dioceses have begun to do.

2. For *parish services* good in themselves which, however, take up the time of the priests, especially in cities (notably funerals and marriages) : there should be prudent progress toward a simplification of the external trappings of the ceremonies. . . .

The Assembly submits to the reverend bishops the desire expressed by some to see the Church in France take advantage of the present difficulties to move toward the elimination or at least a modification of the system of "classes."*

* (T.N.: The reference here is to the French system of various "classes" for weddings and funerals, with greater or less solemnity depending on the price paid.)

3. *Excessively tiring ministries,* which ruin the priests' health. Late Masses should gradually be eliminated, and the custom of morning weddings should be extended more and more.

B. *Organization of a real diocesan community*

NINTH RESOLUTION: Concerning the regular liaison between the bishop and his priests through the dean.

The Assembly expresses the wish that *the dean* be truly, as required by Canon Law, the "travelling vicar" of the bishop; that besides the functions of a juridical and administrative nature conferred on him by the Code, the dean also be concerned about the priests of the deanery and about the Catholic Action in his area.

TENTH RESOLUTION: Relationships of priests among themselves. The Assembly expresses the wish that, wherever the reverend bishops deem it possible and useful, there be established in each deanery, a *placing in common* of the spiritual, intellectual and apostolic activity of the priests, thus forming the "deanery community" in periodic study meetings, spiritual recollections, and the organizing of common action throughout the deanery.

The Assembly also encourages the establishment of community life properly so called, with volunteer priests subject to the same rule, in certain areas designated by the bishop.

C. *A way of life that will support the clergy in its ministry*

ELEVENTH RESOLUTION: For the first years of the ministry.

1. Convinced that there is a serious problem regarding the incorporation and formation of young priests in the first years of the ministry, the Assembly expresses the wish that a *second formation,* continuing that of the seminary, be assured them in the field: first by the pastor himself, then in study sessions especially organized for them, by serious examinations, finally, by a director of conscience.

The Assembly hopes that the reverend pastors will come to a greater understanding of the heavy responsibility they assume when they are intrusted with watching over a young curate, and the duty incumbent upon them of giving him, with completely paternal authority, a gradual and methodical introduction to the ministry.

2. *Study sessions for young priests* should be organized at regular intervals (for example, every three months), which could even become mandatory, in order to make them rethink their theology in a living manner adapted to the needs of their ministry.

3. A real importance should be attached *to the examinations of young priests;* these exams should not be merely oral, but each one should be required to compose a personal memorandum pertaining to one of the themes of the examination.

4. Young priests, at the moment they are ordained to the priesthood, should be forcefully reminded of the need for having a *director of conscience.* Priests of experience and proven discretion should understand the importance of this ministry of priestly charity.

The Assembly believes that seminary directors are particularly qualified to carry this out and expresses the wish that they will continue to follow their former students, at least during the first years of their ministry.

TWELFTH RESOLUTION: After ten years of ministry.

Interpreting the desire expressed by several dioceses, that priests who might welcome a renewal after a certain amount of experience in the ministry (for instance, about ten years) could obtain it, the Assembly strongly encourages the *institution of the "sacerdotal month,"* commonly called "the third year," as certain dioceses have already done.

THIRTEENTH RESOLUTION: For the spiritual life: retreats.

The inquiry having revealed that the dioceses were unanimous in recognizing that *the pastoral retreat,* whose usefulness is obvious, should be organized under conditions that would furnish priests with the opportunity of a real retreat, the Assembly echoes these desires, and indicates the conditions: that a time of personal reflection after each instruction be given to the retreatants, that silence be more rigorously preserved, that administrative matters be postponed until the last day, that outsiders not be permitted to conduct their business in the neighborhood of the corridors.

The Assembly immediately stresses the benefits to be expected from a *specialized retreat*, either by age groups (perhaps young priests), or by ministry (curates, professors, deans), as well as from a retreat where the number of participants is limited.

The Assembly hopes that, independently of the pastoral retreat, priests will have every facility available for doing what His Holiness Pius XI asked in the encyclical "Mens Nostra," i.e., to make *a more extended retreat* in great silence (eight or ten days). It transmits to the reverend bishops the desire expressed by certain dioceses of seeing this retreat become mandatory at regular intervals (every five or ten years).

FOURTEENTH RESOLUTION: For the intellectual life.

The Assembly, along with the entire Episcopate, is concerned about the intellectual quality of the French clergy and about the need for helping the latter, at grips with all the problems of life and the cares of action, to maintain and develop its intellectual life. For this reason, it strongly encourages *study sessions organized for priests of the ministry*, in order to supply them with complete information on the great questions which are presently being posed. — (Excerpt from: *The diocesan clergy face to face with its mission of evangelization*, pp. 151-164.)